£1·50

THE
DAYLILY

THE
DAYLILY

A Guide for Gardeners

JOHN P. PEAT AND TED L. PETIT

TIMBER PRESS

PORTLAND · CAMBRIDGE

Published in 2004 by

Timber Press, Inc.

The Haseltine Building

133 S.W. Second Avenue, Suite 450

Portland, Oregon 97204-3527, U.S.A.

Timber Press

2 Station Road

Swavesey

Cambridge CB4 5QJ, U.K.

www.timberpress.com

Cover and Interior Design: Karen Schober

Printed in China

Library of Congress Cataloging-in-Publication Data

Peat, John P.

The daylily : a guide for gardeners / John P. Peat and Ted L. Petit.

    p. cm.

Includes bibliographical references and index.

ISBN 0-88192-666-3 (hardback)

1. Daylilies. I. Petit, Ted L. II. Title.

SB413.D3P43 2004

635.9'34324--dc22

                    2004001333

A catalog record for this book is also available from the British Library.

To our families and fellow daylily
enthusiasts, who have supported us and share
our love of the daylily

Contents

Preface and Acknowledgments

The book *Hemerocallis: The Daylily* by R. W. Munson Jr. has been one of the primary sources of information on daylilies since it was published in 1989. That book has now gone out of print. Timber Press approached us about writing this book to fill the void created by the loss of Munson's book. While no volume can ever fully replace that original work, we agreed to undertake this task in hopes of continuing to provide gardeners and daylily lovers with a current source of information on this wonderful plant. Thus, we have attempted to follow the general outline, framework, content, and size of the Munson book, updating and adding to it as appropriate. We would like to thank Betty Hudson for her permission to use and update part of the Munson book on the history of the daylily.

Not being experts on every aspect of daylilies, we invited some of the top daylily authorities to contribute chapters in their areas of expertise. We also included chapters on Australia, Canada, and Europe in an effort to show how daylilies are having an ever increasing influence on gardeners in countries other than the United States, though the overwhelming amount of hybridizing and growing of daylilies is still going on here. We would like to thank all the chapter authors for their contributions. We would also like to thank those hybridizers and photographers who provided slides for inclusion in this book.

One challenge in writing this book was to choose a limited number of cultivars to represent the many types and faces of daylilies. With more than 50,000 registered daylilies to choose from, we had a difficult task indeed. Since the intent of this book is to focus on the modern daylily, we limited our selections to those that were introduced since 1992. Due to intense efforts of hybridizers around the world the modern daylily is transforming quickly, with many new features adding to its beauty every year. Increased ruffling, gold edging, and petal width; alterations in size, shape, color, and three-dimensional substance; additions of fancy edging; and more have made the most recent daylily introductions unmistakably different from those of even a decade ago. We have tried to portray these various aspects of the modern daylily to give readers a view of this very rapidly changing flower.

Through all this change the daylily remains a most versatile and maintenance-free perennial, growing from one climatic extreme to another with few pests and maintenance requirements. These characteristics make it important to both backyard gardeners and daylily enthusiasts; therefore, this book includes chapters on daylily cultivation, hardiness, and diseases and its place in the garden.

It is often repeated in daylily clubs and societies that gardeners "come for the flower, but stay for the people."

This has never been truer than today. The number of daylily clubs, societies, meetings, and events is exploding. Chapter 16 includes more specific information on these events as well as ways for readers to contact daylily organizations in their local areas.

As the daylily flower has changed with accelerating speed, it has become increasingly exotic and coveted with a fervor virtually unparalleled in horticulture. We would like to thank those friends and loved ones who have encouraged us to persevere through these exciting but often precarious times.

CHAPTER 1

Introduction

During the more than 28 years in combination that we have been involved with daylilies we have watched daylilies, daylily people, and the surrounding world change dramatically. And yet, this time period represents only the most recent history of our beloved plant.

The daylily plant itself once grew wild in the Orient and only slowly made its way across Asia to Europe and eventually to North America. Because of its natural beauty and rugged nature, inevitably someone began to collect the species plants and hybridize them to create new, more evolved daylilies. Although the earliest collecting and hybridizing attempts were in Europe, the popularity of the daylily was greatest in the United States, led by Arlow Stout beginning in the 1920s.

The early years of hybridizing were slow, as relatively few people were attracted to the flower. Gradually the daylily changed from the yellow and rusty flowers of the species to clearer colors with a greater variety in form. By the 1950s the popularity of the daylily had begun to increase markedly as more individuals began to hybridize and the flower petals became wider, more ruffled, and generally more pleasing to the eye. By the 1960s and '70s, daylilies were being treated with colchicine, a chemical used to convert them to tetraploid plants, which contain twice the genetic code of the original plants (see Chapter 3 for a more detailed explanation of tetraploidy). This increased genetic material produced plants that were bigger and more vigorous, with larger flowers that have greater substance and stronger colors. Two strongly divided camps arose, diploid versus tetraploid supporters. Most recently, tetraploid daylilies have emerged from that divided era as the most favored type.

Considering that the hybrid daylily is still less than 100 years old, the future presents little doubt that daylilies will increase their impact in private and public gardens, especially with the ever increasing concern for the environment. Daylilies are among the most carefree perennials, requiring little attention. Home gardeners are searching for low-maintenance plants, and government agencies are beginning to dictate the use of plants that require no chemical sprays and minimal watering. Daylilies are perfect plants for this type of garden and public landscaping. With appropriate selection, daylilies typically require no sprays and can survive flood and drought. Daylilies also thrive over a very large climatic range, from southern Florida to northern Canada in North America. This dramatic versatility is not common in horticulture. Since very few other plants can span the extreme range of climates that daylilies can, Chapter 6, "Landscaping with Daylilies," suggests an extraordinary number of companion plants, those for colder and those for warmer climates.

The ease of hybridizing daylilies is a major attraction for many daylily enthusiasts. Any backyard gardener can hybridize daylilies, creating new plants that have characteristics more pleasing to their personal tastes. Most other popular perennials are difficult to grow from seed, or take many years to bloom from seed. For example, orchids require a laboratory for germination and five years to bloom, while camellias take five to seven years to bloom. Daylilies, however, are easy to produce from seed, and the seeds can be coaxed into blooming the following year in many places, or anywhere in a modest greenhouse. The result has been a new generation of change in daylilies every year. Such fast generational turnover means daylilies are changing rapidly and dramatically. The latest introductions bear little resemblance to the flowers of the original species or even those of just 10 years ago, and the next decade will likely show the greatest explosion yet in the production of modern daylilies.

The increased hybridization and rapid alteration of the daylily plant and flower have come at a price. Diseases and pests are taking a greater toll on this typically robust plant, and the flower itself is beginning to show problems. Hybridizers must be vigilant about breeding with plants that are resistant to crown rot and daylily rust, plants that thrive across a wide climatic range, and flowers that open well and are not overly susceptible to insects. In this ever growing and quickening race for the most beautiful flower, eternally remembering the importance of the entire daylily plant is a crucial but often difficult task.

This increasingly exotic flower has also brought complications of a more human nature, as all coveted things elicit the unfortunate aspects of humanity. Critical new plants have been stolen by thieves who dig from gardens by torchlight after carefully marking their spoils earlier in the day. As can happen with organizations, in-fighting occurs, clubs split, and egos pursue their own agendas and personal vendettas. Insecure, frustrated hybridizers, consumed with envy, sabotage and attack their more successful colleagues in public forums. The world of daylilies has become a Hollywood drama, making the activities of orchid thieves look like tamer stuff. But many daylily enthusiasts thrive on adventure and tingle with excitement at the possibility of becoming the creator of the next greatly coveted daylily and having their moment in the spotlight. It is such excitement that has generated such beauty, and there are few legacies greater than leaving the world a more beautiful place.

Despite these potential horticultural and human pitfalls, the modern daylily still holds one of the greatest hopes for gardeners passionate for new forms of beauty. The daylily remains a strong, tough plant, and a most versatile and reliable perennial. We are always amazed at how many gardeners do not immediately know what a daylily is, even though they grow wild across most of North America. Still fewer gardeners have any idea of the beauty of modern daylilies. They are changing so dramatically that today's hybrids are almost unrecognizable as daylilies to most gardeners. These sensational beauties are too new to have found their way into local garden centers and are not yet grown in most backyard gardens. We often say that a "steamroller" of new and beautiful daylilies is coming up behind most gardeners. These incredible new creations will soon find their way into garden centers and commercial landscapes everywhere. Combined with their rugged, indestructible nature, daylilies are poised to become the most popular perennial of the future.

CHAPTER 2

The Daylily Species

by Linda Sue Barnes

The genus *Hemerocallis* was officially described by Linnaeus in 1753 in his book *Species Plantarum*. However, written records of the daylily go back as far as Confucius who died in 479 BCE. Presumably daylilies have been used for food and medicine by the Chinese for more than 2,500 years, yet the taxonomy of the species within the genus is still a source of confusion. Even the number of species is unclear. Several things are responsible for this confusion. Some species descriptions came from cultivated plants whose origins were unknown or from herbarium specimens that are very different in appearance from the living plant. Some descriptions came from single specimens, meaning the morphological diversity of the species was not taken into consideration. A single species can show a good bit of variety as to height, length and width of leaves, color and size of flower, and time of bloom. In addition, collecting living material to use in taxonomic studies has been difficult. Much of China, Korea, and Japan was off-limits to Western scientists for much of the twentieth century, and areas where populations of daylilies had been documented were stripped of native vegetation as early as 1969 when Hu went to Korea and Japan to collect daylilies. Adding to the difficulty of forming an accurate taxonomy is the natural ability among most *Hemerocallis* species to cross naturally, yielding fertile hybrids.

Only since the last decade or so of the twentieth century have scientists begun to look at the genus *Hemerocallis* at a genetic or biochemical level. Kang and Chung looked at enzyme systems in five species of *Hemerocallis* native to Korea. They analyzed samples from 1,410 plants in 30 populations to assess genetic diversity within single species and genetic relationships among the five species. Noguchi, Tasaka, and Iwabuchi examined chloroplast DNA variety to study differentiation within one species in Japan. Tompkins used a DNA fingerprinting technique (AFLP) to determine genetic relationships among 15 species or varieties of *Hemerocallis*. Much more work along these lines is needed, plus field studies to gain information about morphological diversity and ecological distribution of species, in order to determine the true relationships among the species of *Hemerocallis*.

In an interesting correlation, Erhardt's dichotomous key based on morphological features, Guzinski's grouping based on primary pigmentation, and Tompkins's work based on DNA analysis all indicate very similar groupings among the species. Guzinski's work finds that the primary pigment in *Hemerocallis coreana* Nakai (1932) and *H. multiflora* Stout (1929) is zeaxanthin, placing them in the group with *H. dumortieri* Morren (1834) and *H. middendorffii* Trautvetter and Meyer (1856). Erhardt, on the other hand, aligns *H. coreana* more closely with the *H. citrina* Baroni (1897) group. He also places *H. multiflora* in a smaller group with *H. micrantha* Nakai (1943) and *H. plicata* Stapf (1923). At the time of his study Tompkins did not have *H. coreana* available to him and he was unable to extract usable DNA from *H. multiflora*, so he did not include these two species in his data. His work indicates that *H. thunbergii* Barr emend. J. G. Baker (1890) is closely related to *H. lilioasphodelus* Linnaeus emend. Hylander (1753) and *H. citrina* is closely related to *H. minor* Miller (1768); these four species are all in the citrina group according to Erhardt, and the last three have the same major pigment, violaxanthin. Tompkins's data shows *H. dumortieri*, *H. middendorffii*, and *H. hakuunensis* Nakai (1943) to be closely linked, and Guzinski identifies zeaxanthin as their major pigment; these three also are together in the *H. middendorffii* group according to Erhardt. Tompkins's work, however, also indicates that the distinction between the citrina group and the middendorffii group is not clear; overlaps between the group members suggest that the two groups should be merged.

Since no single reference includes all the commonly described species of daylilies, I have chosen to follow the groups suggested by Erhardt, with a few modifications, adding newer species where their descriptions seem to fit.

Fulva Group

The members of this group are distinguished from all other daylilies by the presence of water-soluble pigments, anthocyanins, in the epidermis. Zeaxanthin, a carotenoid, is the major pigment in the chromoplasts. Viewing the carotenoid through the anthocyanins in the epidermal layer results in the fulvous, or brownish yellow, coloration of these species.

Hemerocallis aurantiaca Baker (1890) may be the one species generally included in the fulva group that does not have this pigmentation. Baker described the species from plants growing at Kew Gardens without knowing their origin. Stout, in several publications from 1929 to 1942, indicated that all the plants considered to be *H. aurantiaca* in America and Europe had come from one clone that was probably a hybrid. Coe, in 1958, also indicated that it might not be a true species but a horticultural form. In 1969 Hu found a plant that she identified as *H. aurantiaca* growing in Japan at the edge of a field mixed with plants of African, North American, and South American origin. The local farmers said they did not know where it had come from.

Whatever the origin, the plant has diurnal, pale fulvous flowers. It is semi-evergreen and was used in early hybridizing because it produced evergreen offspring. Another plus, according to Sprenger, is that it has a very long bloom season—from April to November in Naples, Italy—making it the longest blooming species. Every plant I have obtained under the label *Hemerocallis aurantiaca* has turned out to be a variety of *H. fulva* Linnaeus (1762).

A plant sold as *Hemerocallis aurantiaca* 'Major' Baker (1890) is even less likely to be a true species or variety. It is more commonly available than *H. aurantiaca* and has larger flowers that are uniformly orange with no trace of the fulvous pigments. Stout reported that it does not thrive or bloom freely in New York and farther north.

Hemerocallis aurantiaca 'Major'. Photo by Curtis and Linda Sue Barnes

Hemerocallis fulva, the tawny daylily, is probably the oldest daylily in cultivation outside the Orient. The clone *H. fulva* 'Europa' (Stout, 1929), also known as the ditchbank or outhouse daylily, is distinctly fulvous in coloration with an arching, reddish orange eye. 'Europa' has an obvious network of dark veins and an orange throat. It is strongly rhizomatous and will quickly spread beyond its anticipated boundary in a flowerbed. The roots are often enlarged and fleshy. Coarse foliage makes a mound about 36 in. (91 cm) high. The scapes are strong, branched, and easily support the 20 or more flowers. Bloom is midseason and very rarely leads to a seed pod. Several clones of *H. fulva*, including the Europa daylily, are now known to be triploid ($3n = 33$); they have three sets of the 11 chromosomes. This leads to problems during meiosis so that selfed seedlings are virtually impossible to obtain. These clones will rarely set pods with viable seeds when pollinated with other daylilies. One exception is *H.* 'Super Tawny' (Keener, 2000) from the cross *H. fulva* 'Europa' × *H.* 'Bess Ross'.

The only doubles among the species of *Hemerocallis* are selections of *H. fulva*. Stout described them as para-doubles, which have at least some functional stamens or petaloids with anthers attached. Flowers can have a gradation of petaloidy, from stamens that are normal in appearance, to those that are petal like in appearance but with a complete anther attached, to highly reduced petaloids with no evidence of an anther. The pistil is absent, aborted, or malformed. The selections that fit this category are *H. fulva* 'Kwanso' Kaempfer (1712) and *H. fulva* 'Kwanso Variegata' Thunberg (1784), which originated from Japan, and *H. fulva* 'Flore Pleno' Sienicka (1929), which originated from China. All these are triploid, and their bloom season begins toward the end of the bloom of *H. fulva* 'Europa'. Some major differences between 'Flore Pleno' and 'Kwanso' are that the former has more well-formed petals and fewer stamens, whether aborted or well formed. 'Flore Pleno' often gives the appearance of a hose-in-hose double, but 'Kwanso' often has petals and petaloids that are twisted and curled. In addition to having what to my eye is a

Hemerocallis fulva 'Flore Pleno'. Photo by Curtis and Linda Sue Barnes

more pleasing form, 'Flore Pleno' is shorter and less invasive than 'Kwanso'. 'Kwanso Variegata' may have variegation extending all the way up the scape and into the flower. Unfortunately this variegation is not stable and clumps must be rogued to remove completely green fans or the variegated ones will be overgrown. An interesting note is that Tompkins's DNA study indicates that 'Flore Pleno' and *H. fulva* var. *rosea* Stout (1930) may be more closely related than the two double forms.

Hemerocallis fulva var. rosea, which is native to Kiangsi Province, China, has flowers that are rosy red. Steward sent plants to Stout at the New York Botanical Garden and to Nesmith at the Royal Botanic Gardens, Kew. Three clones were marketed—*H. fulva* var. *rosea* 'Rosalind' (A. B. Stout, 1938), which has a distinct red eye; 'Pastelrose' (L. E. Plouf, 1942), which has no eye; and 'Mrs. Nesmith Clone', which also lacks an eye. These forms are fertile and were much used by early hybridizers. 'Rosalind' was even treated with colchicine by Traub and became one of the first tetraploid daylilies. 'Rosalind' and 'Pastelrose' are still fairly common in commerce.

Several other varieties of *Hemerocallis fulva* are known and still available in commerce. *Hemerocallis fulva* var. *longituba* Maximowicz (1885) has orange-yellow flowers that are only slightly fulvous, if at all, and which have very long perianth tubes. The clones in my garden grew from seed collected from the top of Mt. Chiri, South Korea, by Tony Avent of Plant Delights Nursery. The plants were growing above the tree line with *Hosta* species at 4,800 feet (1460 m) (personal communication with Tony Avent). Kang and Chung do not list this variety as native to Korea. Plants matching the description have been collected in China and Japan. *Hemerocallis fulva* var. *maculata* Baroni (1897) is very robust with scapes about 48 in. (122 cm) tall; the scapes branch two to four times and have up to 12 flowers on pedicels less than 0.5 in. (1.25 cm) long. The flowers are about 6 in. (15.2 cm) in diameter with recurved seg-

Hemerocallis fulva var. *cypriani*. Photo by Curtis and Linda Sue Barnes

ments that are less fulvous than *H. fulva* 'Europa', and the flower has a distinct purple-red eye. The plants are triploid and flowers are self-sterile although they produce some viable pollen. *Hemerocallis fulva* var. *cypriani* Muller (1906) is named for a missionary who sent plants from Hupeh Province, China, to Sprenger. The blooms are coppery red with a distinct gold midrib and gold throat. *Hemerocallis fulva* var. *littorea* Matsuoka and Hotta (1966) was found in Japanese meadows near the coast and is sometimes called the coastal daylily. Nakai sent plants to Stout from Japan, and they were at that time considered the separate species *H. littorea*. The plants had pale fulvous flowers similar to those of *H. aurantiaca*, but Stout thought they were more closely related to *H. fulva*. According to Hu, flowers range in color from dark orange-red to orange-yellow. The flowers are wide spreading with a dark brown eyezone, a pale midrib, and membranous edges on the petals. The stout scapes often bear proliferations. Roots are spindle shaped and the plant is rhizomatous. *Hemerocallis fulva* var. *sempervirens* Hotta and Matsuoka (1966) apparently arrived in the United States from seeds of plants found on a small island south of Okinawa. I am surprised this variety is not more commonly grown, for in my garden it begins to bloom very late and is often blooming when the first frost hits. The coloration is distinctly fulvous with an obvious red-brown eye. The scapes on my plants bear many flowers, but the number of flowers does not appear to match the 104 buds reported by Barr.

Several other forms of fulvous daylilies are listed in various sources as either separate species, varieties of *Hemerocallis fulva*, or varieties of *H. aurantiaca*. There seems to be no consensus about the plants, however, and I cannot distinguish the plants under these names in my garden from other varieties of *H. fulva*.

Hemerocallis hongdoensis Chung and Kang (1994) was found on Hong Island as the authors were conducting field studies on natural populations of daylilies in Korea in 1988 and 1993. After determining that it was different from any known species they named it for the island on which it was found. They described it as being closely related to *H. aurantiaca*, however it is not rhizomatous, has deciduous leaves, and the flowers are orange-yellow, lacking a reddish tinge. The roots are highly swollen compared to other species. The greenish yellow leaves are 24–40 in. (61–102 cm) long and 0.67–1.2 in. (1.7–3 cm) wide. Scapes are 24–30 in. (61–76 cm) long with two or three short branches clustered at the top and bear 5 to 17 flowers, occasionally more. The funnel-formed or trumpet-shaped flowers are 0.17–5.6 in. (0.4–14.2 cm) long with a stout perianth tube up to 1.25 in. (3.2 cm) long. To my knowledge this species is not yet growing in the United States. In Korea it flowers from mid June to July, or August in the mountainous regions. *Hemerocallis hongdoensis* is morphologically similar to *H. hakuunensis*, but enzyme studies have shown it to be distinct from other Korean species.

Hemerocallis taeanensis Kang and Chung (1997) is also in the fulva group. It differs from other species by having roots that are only slightly swollen; no rhizome; small, deciduous leaves; a slender scape that branches once with two to five flowers; and small flowers that are typically orange-yellow, rarely lemon-yellow. Bloom in Korea is from the middle of May to June, about the same time as *H. middendorffii*. It would be distinguished from that species by its single, Y-shaped branch in the inflorescence, no odor, and slightly enlarged roots. *Hemerocallis middendorffii* has buds clustered at the tip of the scape, is faintly fragrant, often exhibits extended bloom, and has slender, cylindrical roots. I have not yet seen either of these species and do not know of any specimen in the United States at this time.

Citrina Group

Members of the citrina group are nocturnal, fragrant, and mainly yellow in color. Those species that have been analyzed have violaxanthin as the major pigment.

Hemerocallis altissima Stout (1942) is the tallest species of *Hemerocallis*, growing 6–8 ft. (1.8–2.4 m) tall. The well-branched scape carries sweetly scented yellow flowers that have no band of color. The flowers are trumpet shaped with a long perianth tube. Ironically on this very tall plant the flowers are smaller than those of *H. citrina*, having a diameter of about 3 in. (7.6 cm). The perianth tube is about half the length of the segments. Buds begin opening around 4 p.m. and flowers will be closed by 8 a.m. on a hot sunny day. A trait that enhances the garden value is that they bloom late in the season, July to September in North Carolina. Coe did not think the species had much value for breeding, but recently it has become more popular for those producing very tall hybrids, and it has even been converted to a tetraploid form. One word of caution is that some sources claiming to sell *H. altissima* and some well-known botanical gardens have applied this name to a plant with diurnal blooms and a very distinct band of color on the petals.

Hemerocallis citrina has yellow, nocturnal, strongly scented flowers that bloom midseason. The flowers are 4.7–6.6 in. (12–17 cm) long with narrow segments; the petals may be slightly wavy. The sepals are green on the outside with purple tips. Scapes are 40 in. (102 cm) or more tall, stiff and well branched. Foliage is 30–43 in. (76–109 cm) tall and is dark green. Many clones have noticeable red pigment at the base of the leaves. The species is self-sterile, but it has been and is still used for breeding in hope of passing on the lemony scent and good branching. The narrow segments lend themselves well to breeding for spiders and unusual forms.

Hemerocallis citrina var. *vespertina* (Hara) Matuoka and Hotta (1966) was originally described by Hara as *H. vespertina*, but several authorities have concluded that it is not a separate species. Hu believed it to be a clone of *H. thunbergii*. The DNA fingerprinting done by Tompkins shows that this plant does not group closely with *H. citrina*. He also pointed out that since *H. citrina* is self-sterile, a variant would have to come from out crossing, and thus *H. citrina* var. *vespertina* would be a hybrid if it were related to *H. citrina* at all.

Hemerocallis coreana is a species that needs much more study. Hu indicated that all the specimens she found from Korea could be identified as either *H. lilioasphodelus* or *H. minor*. Nakai described *H. coreana* as having spreading roots, leaves 5–17 in. (12.7–43.2 cm) long, and scape 20–32 in. (50.8–81.3 cm) tall with numerous branches at the top. The yellow flowers are subsessile with a yellow-green tube 1–2 in. (2.5–5.1 cm) long. Kang and Chung consider *H. coreana* to be a form of *H. thunbergii*. Possibly, it does not even belong in the citrina group. According to Guzinski's data the major carotenoid in *H. coreana* is zeaxanthin, which would make this species more closely related to the middendorffii group. Some clones grown in the United States as *H. coreana* have flowers with color more orange than yellow, which fits with Guzinski's data, and flowers more widely open than those of *H. citrina* or *H. altissima*. One clone I received under this name is indistinguishable from *H. hakuunensis*, which is in the

Hemerocallis citrina. Photo by Curtis and Linda Sue Barnes

middendorffii group; a second is virtually identical to one of my clones of *H. thunbergii*; and a third matches the description of *H. micrantha*, which Kang and Chung consider to be a form of *H. hakuunensis*.

Hemerocallis lilioasphodelus was called *H. flava* for many years and is still found under that name in many gardens, although it is not botanically correct. This species is commonly called lemon lily and was one of the first two species of *Hemerocallis* to reach Europe. The scape reaches well above the 30-in. (76.2-cm) foliage but arches widely to form a large tuft. The lemon-yellow flowers have short stalks and a tube about 1 in. (2.5 cm) long; the diameter ranges from 3 to 4 in. (7.6 to 10.2 cm). The fragrant flowers open at night but also have extended bloom; in cool weather the blooms may last more than 48 hours. The plant is rhizomatous and has fibrous roots with spindle-shaped swellings.

Hemerocallis minor is called the grass-leaved daylily; the leaves may grow to 21 in. (53.3 cm) long but are only 0.25–0.33 in. (0.64–0.76 cm) wide. The slender scape is 18–24 in. (45.7–61 cm) tall and normally bears two to three flowers, occasionally as many as five, in early spring. The cadmium-yellow flowers are nocturnal, fragrant, and long lasting; they are bell shaped with a tube 0.75 in. (1.9 cm) long and segments 1.2 in. (3 cm) long. The perianth tube is green and the outside of the sepals is tinged brownish red. Roots are slender with fibrous lateral roots; rhizomes are lacking.

Hemerocallis pedicellata Nakai (1932) was described from specimens collected by Hara on Sakhalin Island, a territory long disputed between Russia and Japan, and has not been collected since then. Orange-red flowers are attached to the 25-in. (63.5-cm) scape by pedicels that are 1.2 in. (3 cm) long. The perianth tube is 1 in. (2.5 cm) long and segments are 3.5 in. (8.9 cm) long. I have not seen this species.

Hemerocallis thunbergii comes from northern China and Japan. The widely cultivated plant spreads by rhizomes and was frequently used by early hybridizers. Scapes are about 45 in. (114 cm) tall and well branched in the upper part. The lemon-yellow flowers are tinged with green on the outside of the sepals and have a green perianth tube. They are nocturnal, have a spread of about 3 in. (7.6 cm), and wilt in the afternoon on hot, sunny days. Bloom season is midsummer, just as *H. fulva* 'Europa' finishes its bloom. Hu classifies *H. vespertina*, now often called *H. citrina* var. *vespertina*, as *H. thunbergii*.

Hemerocallis yezoensis Hara (1937) is of Japanese origin; Hara remarked that it is closely related to *H. thunbergii*. He also noted that it is quite variable in width of the leaves and size of the flowers. Leaves can be up to 30 in. (76 cm) tall and 0.25–0.88 in. (0.64–2.2 cm) wide; they are erect, recurving only at the tip. Scapes are 17–34 in. (43–86 cm) tall with 4 to 12 flowers. The lemon-yellow, slightly fragrant flowers vary in diameter from 2.75 to 4 in. (7–10 cm). The perianth tube is about 1 in. (2.5 cm) long and usually greenish yellow.

Middendorffii Group

This group has unbranched scapes, bracts that are broad and overlapping, and flowers described as orange in most references. The color appears to me to be gold rather than a pure orange.

Hemerocallis dumortieri is among the first daylilies to bloom in the spring. Plants have two to four buds atop an unbranched scape less than 24 in. (61 cm) tall. The buds are strongly tinged reddish brown, and the open flower remains brown on the sepal reverse. The roots of the plant are distinctly enlarged. The species was much used by early hybridizers, and its influence can be seen in the brown sepal reverse of hybrids such as *H.* 'Gold Dust' (George Yeld, 1906) and 'Orangeman' (originator unknown, 1906).

Hemerocallis esculenta Koidzumi (1925) and *H. exaltata* Stout (1934) are native to Japan, but Japanese

Hemerocallis dumortieri. Photo by Curtis and Linda Sue Barnes

Hemerocallis hakuunensis. Photo by Curtis and Linda Sue Barnes

botanists disagree about both these species. The only agreement seems to be that they belong to the middendorffii group. I will not discuss these plants, therefore, due to a lack of definitive information.

Hemerocallis hakuunensis is a Korean species with robust, branched scapes up to 39 in. (99 cm) tall. The 6 to 11 flowers are orange-yellow, diurnal, and odorless. The flower is fairly large with perianth tube up to 1 in. (2.5 cm) long and narrow segments that may be 3 in. (7.6 cm) long and only 0.5–0.67 in. (1.2–1.5 cm) wide. Flowering is midseason. Some of the roots are slightly enlarged.

Hemerocallis middendorffii blooms in early spring, typically along with *H. dumortieri*. Three to five intense orange flowers arise from an unbranched scape that is about 35 in. (89 cm) tall. The flowers are 3 in. (7.6 cm) in diameter with spatulate petals and a perianth tube barely more than 0.39 in. (1 cm) long. Sepal reverses are not brown, as in *H. dumortieri*, and the plant reblooms in the fall in warmer climates. The fibrous roots are cylindrical and not wide spreading.

Nana Group

The plants in the nana group are dwarf with scapes less than 20 in. (51 cm) tall and often shorter than the leaves. Stout recorded that *Hemerocallis forrestii* Diels (1912) and *H. nana* Smith and Forrest (1916) are not winter hardy in New York City. Since all plants in this group are native to the high mountains of China, I am more inclined to accept the vague, but probably more accurate, statement by Coe that *H. nana*, and the others in this group, "probably needs some special condition not furnished in cultivation." I received plants from China in the fall of 2002 that were supposed to be *H. forrestii* and *H. nana*, but true to Stout's description only one of the three plants survived the first winter in North Carolina.

Hemerocallis darrowinia Hu (1969) was found on Sakhalin Island. Hu noted that it had many characteristics in common with the high altitude plants of China. She described the plant as only 5 in. (13 cm) high with leaves 2.5–3 in. (6.1–7.6 cm) long and less than 0.33 in. (0.76 cm) wide; outer leaves are folded and recurved. It blooms in mid August in Japan and has flowers about 2.4 in. (6.1 cm) long, segments 1.7 in. (4.3 cm) wide, and perianth tubes 0.75 in. (1.9 cm) long. I have not yet found a source for this plant.

Hemerocallis forrestii has foliage about 12 in. (30 cm) long and a branched scape of the same length or slightly longer. Each scape bears 5 to 10 flowers with pedicels that are about 1 in. (2.5 cm) long. The species has two forms, one with red-orange flowers and one with pure orange flowers. Segments of the flowers are more than 1 in. (2.5 cm) wide, and the perianth tube can be almost 1 in. (2.5 cm) long. Roots are fleshy.

Hemerocallis nana has flat leaves about 15 in. (38 cm) long. The scape typically bears one reddish orange flower just above the foliage. The flower opens to 3 in. (7.6 cm) in diameter, has narrow segments giving it a spidery appearance, and has brown sepal reverses. Roots are narrow with a club-shaped or spindle-shaped swelling at the ends.

Multiflora Group

Plants in this group have scapes with multiple branches, small flowers with short perianth tubes, and short pedicels.

Hemerocallis micrantha was described from one herbarium specimen and was considered by Matsuoka and Hotta to be a form of *H. hakuunensis*. Chung and Kang confirmed this during their extensive study of daylilies in Korea.

Hemerocallis multiflora is called the many flowered daylily because some clones have as many as 100 cadmium-yellow flowers with fairly wide-spreading segments, although 20–30 blooms is more common on plants that I have seen. The perianth tube is tinged green and the sepal reverses are slightly brown. The scape is about 40 in. (102 cm) tall and branches repeatedly from the middle. The roots are fleshy and the plant has no rhizomes. Leaves are approximately 30 in. (76 cm) long but the foliage arches so that it is about 20 in.

(51 cm) high. This species does not have a lot of garden value because the scapes are very slender and do not support the weight of the flowers well, even though the flowers are only about 3 in. (7.6 cm) in diameter. Early breeders used it extensively for its late bloom season, which is also long because of the large number of flowers. It is a parent of *H.* 'Bijou' (A. B. Stout, 1932).

Hemerocallis multiflora. Photo by Curtis and Linda Sue Barnes

Hemerocallis plicata was described as different from *H. nana* by having folded leaves and more buds per scape. The irregularly branched scape can reach 21 in. (53 cm) tall and have up to 11 flowers. Trumpet-shaped flowers are orange-yellow with a 0.6-in. (1.5-cm) perianth tube and segments that are 2.8 in. (7 cm) long. Pedicels are 0.75 in. (1.9 cm) long or less. Erhardt indicates that the folded leaves can disappear if the plants are growing in rich soil.

Many questions remain about the species of *Hemerocallis* and the relationships among them. To fully answer these questions, taxonomists need to examine as many populations as possible and coordinate data from ecological, morphological, and biochemical studies.

CHAPTER 3

Hybridizers and the Changing Daylily

with R. William Munson

The breeding of daylilies is a relatively new development that has emerged over the past 95 years with little activity prior to the turn of the twentieth century. Daylilies were introduced into Europe by explorers traveling from the Orient to Europe by land and by sea; oversea routes generally came via Lisbon, Portugal. People accepted and admired these plants but showed little interest in "improving" them through hybridization. The first known breeding programs were established in the mid 1850s by George Yeld and Amos Perry in England. Though breeding started slowly, now early in the twenty-first century it has reached a fever pitch with literally hundreds of people making crosses and registering cultivars with the American Hemerocallis Society (AHS). Estimates state that between 300,000 and 500,000 new daylily seedlings are grown annually in the United States alone.

We cannot capture the significant contribution that a host of amateur, "backyard" hybridizers have made on the development of daylilies. Between 1945 and 1957, when the first daylily checklist of named cultivars was compiled, more than 250 people were breeding, introducing, or selling daylilies. Today, that number has more than quadrupled. Because so many have been involved, assessing a particular individual's impact or judging the plants created is impossible, as is following any heritage that could be traced to the species or early hybrids. (Daylily cultivar names have no species epithet but begin with the genus name *Hemerocallis*, which we have dropped throughout this book to avoid repetition.) We will not attempt to list all breeders or breeders' programs but will identify or describe specifically those breeding programs that we know firsthand, or those which we believe have had a major impact on the daylilies we know today. But we do acknowledge the significant contribution made by all who have worked with daylilies from the beginning. Since interest in daylilies has increased exponentially, we would certainly be unwise to assert that any one breeder has made the greatest progress or the greatest contribution, but over the years certain breeders and their programs have risen to the forefront and therefore warrant special recognition.

We have chosen to divide the hybridizing years into three eras: "The Diploid Years," "The Early Tetraploid Years," and "The Present and Future Years" (for an explanation of ploidy, see the section on tetraploids). These periods have no specific relationship to special events or historical landmarks, but they do relate to time periods associated with certain breeders, their programs, and the impact they have had on subsequent breeders.

The Diploid Years

The foremost breeder and collector of daylilies in the United States during the early years was Arlow Burdette Stout. His love affair with daylilies began in the 1920s while he was director of the New York Botanical Garden. He registered his first cultivar 'Mikado' in 1929. The Farr Nursery Company of Weiser Park, Womelsdorf, Pennsylvania, was the first to offer it for sale. Other cultivars followed, including 'Dauntless' in 1935, a buff-cream-yellow, which won the Stout Silver Medal in 1954. He also received Awards of Merit for the cream-lemon 'Patricia' (1935), the rose and yellow bicolor 'Caballero' (1941), and the dark red 'Dominion' (1941).

Stout was not only a collector, grower, breeder, and scientist, but also the author of the first and perhaps still the most definitive work on the daylily species—*Daylilies: The Wild Species and Garden Clones, Both Old and New, of the Genus Hemerocallis*, first published in 1934. The work has been reprinted and remains the standard by which others are measured. It has withstood the test of time, and although taxonomic questions are now emerging, extensive collecting, growing, and evaluating must go forward before any significant modifications are warranted. His approach was experimental and included all forms of daylilies, species and hybrids, but with a special interest directed to red coloration, late flowering cultivars, and *H. altissima*, a species from China with great potential for breeding tall cultivars suitable for the garden. His interest in very late cultivars that prolonged the season was exemplified by his 'Autumn Prince' (1941). His work on collecting and disseminating as well as hybridizing provided the foundation for future breeding programs, especially in the United States.

Two English plantsmen began work with daylilies late in the nineteenth century. They were George Yeld and Amos Perry and each left a marked impression on the development of daylilies. Because of problems with distribution, however, their plants never had the impact they should have had in North America. Though these two English breeding programs emerged many years before the renaissance of daylilies across the Atlantic, work in the US in the early 1940s and '50s was soon to eclipse their early and masterful beginning. George Yeld, a schoolmaster, lived from 1845 to 1953 in Enfield, North London. He was the founder of Perry's Hardy Plant Farm and a breeder of many hardy plants, including more than 300 daylilies.

As the work of Yeld and Stout became better known and their plants disseminated, interest in daylilies began to grow and expand. Several distinctive breeding programs emerged that greatly influenced daylilies and their transformation from a generally utilitarian landscape plant to one of unique and uncommon beauty. Leaders in this transformation were Ralph W. Wheeler, Bright "Ophelia" Taylor, and Elizabeth "Betty" Nesmith.

Wheeler worked in Winter Park, Florida, in a low-lying, sandy, marshlike area. He began hybridizing in the late 1930s and by the '40s had produced a series of very special, unique cultivars. Wheeler directed himself to the new, different, and unique, particularly in terms of form. He had an incredibly discerning eye, and was one of the few breeders who practiced the art of mixing pollen, which he spread with a sable brush. The scientist in all of us objects to not knowing the parentage of a cultivar and what specific parental influences could be showing in a cultivar, but still, the achievements of this man immediately set standards that dictated our perception of daylilies and what they could be. Some of his achievements were 'Narajana' (1948), a rich orange that won the Stout Silver Medal in 1956, as well as several cultivars that won Awards of Merit, including 'Asia' (1948), a gold, pink, and beige blend; 'Cellini' (1949), a flat, round lemon-yellow; 'Raven' (1951), a black-red; and 'Show Girl' (1951), a round lavender.

Florida produced another breeder of major significance in the early 1940s. Ophelia Taylor was a gardener and grower of daylilies who grew a particular seedling from a cross she believed to be *Hemerocallis aurantiaca* 'Major' × (*H. fulva* var. *rosea* × F2): 'Prima Donna' (1946). This cultivar became the foundation for her most significant work. Though the parentage may not be entirely accurate, it appears very plausible based upon the common characteristics of *H. aurantiaca* 'Major', *H. fulva* var. *rosea*, and their various offspring.

'Prima Donna' rose in the ranks of the daylily world to win many awards. It was also an easy and productive parent, producing lush, large, wide, full pastels in hues not previously seen in daylilies. The pastel, multi-blended daylily had arrived. 'Prima Donna' left its mark not only in a visual way but as an evergreen daylily with a tendency to be somewhat tender in the coldest locations. Its progeny possessed the same tendency, but beauty can strike us blind to such "libelous traits." The beauty the future was to hold was foreshadowed in her 'Sugar Cane' (1949), a honey-cream pastel of very broad, voluptuous form.

No account of breeders in the early years would be complete without mention of the work of Betty Nesmith, known as Miss Betty. Her breeding program and her Fairmount Gardens were synonymous with quality. She was most interested in color and experimented extensively with pinks, reds, and purples. Her 'Sweetbriar' (1938) heralded the beginning of pink coloration in daylilies. Twelve years later she introduced to commerce 'Pink Prelude' (1949), a true milestone in style and pink color. Compared to today's cultivars it is muddy and poorly formed, but it was a trendsetter.

In 1942 Nesmith introduced 'Potentate', a violet-plum which, along with Wheeler's 'Amherst' (1946) and Stout's 'Theron' (1934), formed the foundation of most lavender and purple breeding programs for the next 15 years. Her 'Royal Ruby' (1942) was just as important to future red programs.

Though Taylor emphasized form and style, and Nesmith color clarity and plant refinements, these two women were remarkably similar. Each had an uncanny eye for selection and an intuitive breeding talent. Each produced major advancements in daylilies at a time when only primitive material was available, just a step or two from the species. Few records are available regarding the heritage of their hybrids; neither viewed record keeping as terribly important. Although both kept some records, neither saw much need for them.

During the late 1940s and early '50s three extremely important breeders with diverse, small, but significant programs emerged: Hooper P. Connell of Baton Rouge, Louisiana; Mary Lester of Atlanta, Georgia; and Carl S. Milliken of Arcadia, California. Connell produced 'Mentone' (1956), a pale old-rose self that won an Award of Merit in 1964. Lester's light rose 'Maid Marian' (1950), large rose-pink 'Picture' (1952), and apricot self 'Garden Sprite' (1957) all won Awards of Merit. Two of Milliken's orange-yellow introductions won Stout Silver Medals: 'Ruffled Pinafore' (1948) in 1957, and 'High Noon' (1949) in 1958.

The period from 1950 to 1975 produced some extremely exciting advances in daylilies. The fact that more than 15,000 cultivars were registered with the AHS attests to the fevered pitch that breeding had reached. More than 450 people were breeding, naming, or selling daylilies during this period. In light of this overwhelming number, any overview of the period is perhaps doomed before it is started. However, looking to the giants of the period, we can sketch a sound impression of the work accomplished. We must recognize that cultivars that never became "stellar stars" still ultimately served the cause of improving daylilies and played a vital part in their history. Record keeping continued to be poor during this period, except in a few isolated instances. Many of the foremost breeders began their work earlier but did not hit their stride or have considerable impact until this period.

Ezra Kraus was a professor of botany and breeder of daylilies and chrysanthemums. His record keeping was exemplary and his program very complex and expansive. He grew many seedlings from a single cross to study the subtle variations and any dramatic mutations that might occur. He used many numbered seedlings repeatedly in his carefully planned search for the unique and beautiful. He studied the results of the numbered seedlings he crossed as carefully as he studied for perfection, and he insisted on quality at all cost. His untimely death cut short a very impressive and productive career. He named hundreds of cultivars, but a few that set new standards in breeding daylilies were 'Chetco' (1956), a Chinese-yellow self; 'Evelyn Claar' (1950), a light red self; 'Mabel Fuller' (1950), a medium orange-red self; 'Ringlets' (1950), an orange-yellow self; and 'Ruth Lehman' (1951), a patterned, light orange-red, all of which won Awards of Merit. His 'Multnomah' (1954), an apricot blend overlaid with pink, won the Stout Medal in 1963.

David F. Hall, a breeder of irises, turned his attention to the task of improving daylilies. He was a lawyer living in Wilmette, Illinois, and could be described as an amateur, backyard breeder, but his work was anything but amateurish. His love for the clear bright colors of irises inspired him to try to create daylilies in similar colors. He established two major line-breeding programs, one in pink and one in red, that forever changed the face of modern daylilies and how we would look at them. He was the first to truly unlock the colors pink and rose in daylilies.

The Gilbert H. Wild Nursery Company of Sarcoxie, Missouri, bought the rights to the Hall cultivars in 1950, but Hall continued to build upon these early lines and orchestrated their continued development until 1975 by traveling to Sarcoxie each year during the bloom season. Some of his premier achievements were the shell-pink self 'Coral Mist' (1955), the rose-pink self 'Magic Dawn' (1956), the salmon-peach to shell-pink 'Pink Orchid' (1956), and the dark red self 'War Eagle' (1957), all of which won Awards of Merit. His 'May Hall' (1957), a pink blend, won the Stout Medal in 1969.

Elmer A. Claar was a Chicago businessman active in construction and management of real estate and hotel projects who carried on his modest hybridizing program at his home in Northfield, Illinois. He grew a limited number of seedlings but achieved most spectacular success by creating the broadest, most creped and ruffled yellows and most brilliant, rich, broad-petaled reds of any breeder of this period. The parentage of 'Alan' (1953), his first major red breakthrough, is regrettably unknown. Some of his foremost creations were his reds—'Sail On' (1964) and 'Red Siren' (1964)—and yellows—'Lexington' (1959), 'President Rice' (1953), and 'President Marcue' (1956). His reds affected more breeding programs and influenced more breeders than any red cultivars from the earlier history of daylilies.

W. B. MacMillan of Abbeville, Louisiana, began hybridizing daylilies in the early 1950s and emerged as the breeder who had the greatest impact on this period. In the 1960s, Mr. Mac, as he was known, became discontented with his early work and planned to start afresh. He planned to begin with a new cultivar that he had bloomed and registered in 1962, 'President Giles'. He bought two other cultivars that same year: 'Satin Glass' (Orville Fay, 1960) and 'Dream Mist' (R. William Munson, 1958), which together with 'President Giles', 'Dorcas' (Edna Spalding, 1958), and Kraus's 'Chetco' became the bricks and mortar of his new program. He crossed these five in every conceivable combination.

That same year, he also decided to bring his seedlings to bloom in 9–12 months, rather than 24–36 months as was generally done. His superior climatic location of Abbeville, Louisiana, rich Delta soil, and horticultural expertise allowed him to achieve this goal. He produced three generations of seedlings in three years, while elsewhere three generations took six to nine years. His comprehensive program featured cultivars with low scapes, evergreen foliage, and broad, full, round, flat, and ruffled flowers. His greatest successes were in cream-pinks, pastels, and yellows.

His typical round, ruffled form came to be called "The MacMillan" and remained the form of comparison until the 1980s. A generous man, quietly proud and genuinely modest, he affected daylilies in so many ways that he almost eclipses all who came before him. It is remarkable, and regrettable, that his record keeping was minimal. He developed his own line and stayed well within it for many, many years. He was not studying options or permutations—why cultivar A did such and such and cultivar B did not. He was out to create beauty and leave his mark on the daylily. Years after his death his standards of quality and beauty remained unchallenged. Some of his special cultivars were 'Ethel Baker' (1968), a deep rose-pink; 'Hope Diamond' (1968), a near white self; and 'Robert Way Schlumpf' (1968), a lavender self, all of which received Awards of Merit. His 'Moment of Truth' (1971), a near white self, and 'Sabie' (1974), a golden yellow self, both won the Stout Medal.

Edna Spalding of Iowa, Louisiana, was an early breeder of daylilies who made formidable contributions. She did not hybridize daylilies, for as she once said to Bill Munson, "I merely crossed them for my own pleasure." Daylilies shared space in the vegetable garden of this housekeeper, gardener, and flower arranger. She had the strong, silent, and self-assured appearance of an early pioneer woman with her cloth bonnet. Since she made few if any records of her cultivars, we have had to rely on first-hand knowledge from

her friends. Being friends with Betty Nesmith, Spalding grew several of her early pinks, including 'Pink Prelude' and 'Mme. Recamier' (1948), and several early lavenders, including 'Potentate' and 'Su-Lin' (1941). These cultivars were very likely those that ultimately led to Spalding's 'Luxury Lace' (1959), 'Lavender Flight' (1963), and 'Blue Jay' (1961).

Pink and purple were Spalding's specialty, and just as she built upon the early Nesmith introductions, so MacMillan and others built upon hers. She probably grew no more than 400–500 seedlings a year, but those she selected were first-rate, for she had a magnificent eye for quality and beauty as well as a great intuitive breeding sense. Her standards were the highest. She always carried a large kitchen knife as she walked the garden, and if a new seedling displeased her or did not meet her exacting standards, out it would go, cut below the crown, never more to plague her with its shortcomings. Her impact on daylily breeding appeared not only in her cultivars but also in the standard of quality of the day.

Cultivars from Spalding that were unique and considerably ahead of their time include 'Dorcas', a salmon-coral-pink, and 'Grecian Gift' (1960), a salmon-pink self, both of which won Awards of Merit. Her 'Lavender Flight', a deep lavender self, and 'Luxury Lace', a pale lilac-lavender-pink self both won the Stout Medal.

Frank and Peggy Childs of Jenkinsburg, Georgia, a couple devoted to daylilies, started with a small program that grew and expanded to include work in singles and doubles, both diploids and tetraploids, and every color available in daylilies. Their work was comprehensive and spanned a period of more than 30 years. They rarely grew more than 5,000 seedlings a year. Their first major breakthrough occurred with, 'Pink Dream' (1951), a clear pastel pink of great holding qualities and pristine beauty, a color that was as pink as any daylily had been up to that time. As a husband and wife team, they were exemplary; as a breeding team they complemented each other's efforts. Frank emphasized pinks and yellows and Peggy worked in lavenders and purples, but each creation was "theirs."

Several major milestones came from the Childs garden. All Award of Merit winners, 'Frank Fabulous' (1962) was a melon-pink blend, 'Nobility' (1957) a light yellow self, 'Pink Dream' a clear pink self, 'Pink Reflection' (1959) a pink and cream-pink bitone, 'Showman' (1963) a rich apricot and peach blend that fades to pink in the sun, and 'Top Honors' (1976) a cream-yellow. If 'Catherine Woodberry' (1967), a clear, pristine, pale pinkish lavender with whitish green throat, had been their only creation, their place in the history of daylilies would be more than secure. This plant has markedly influenced many breeding programs, most notably those of Virginia Peck, Steve Moldovan, and Bill Munson, who converted it from diploid to tetraploid.

Early Tetraploids

Early work on tetraploid daylilies began in the 1940s, but major hybridizing work did not begin before the late 60s, when inevitably a conflict between tetraploid and diploid breeders emerged and continued for another 20 years. The oustanding qualities of tetraploids, however—rich color, new patterns and distinctive eyes and edges, heavier texture, sun resistance, increased resistance to disease and insects, added vigor and stamina—assured them of their rightful place in the world of daylilies.

In the mid-to-late 1950s increasing genetic knowledge led to a growing interest in the ploidy of daylilies and the possibility of converting diploids to tetraploids. All plants and animals have a basic complement of chromosomes, small bodies within the cell nucleus that carry the genes. This basic complement is known as the haploid number of chromosomes. The gametes, or sex cells, of each sex carry the haploid number of chromosomes typical for a particular species. When two gametes, male and female, unite to form the zygote, the latter acquires the diploid number, twice the haploid number, of chromosomes. Most

flowering plants are diploids; that is, they have two sets of chromosomes, one from each parent in each somatic cell, or cell that makes up the body of the plant. "Polyploid" is the word used to describe plants with three or more sets of chromosomes. Diploids have two sets, triploids have three sets, tetraploids have four sets, pentaploids have five sets, and so on. The number of sets of chromosomes may be increased either by natural or artificial means. Tetraploids can arise accidentally in the vegetative cells due to sudden cold or heat or as the result of the union of unreduced gametes in the case of sexual reproduction. They also can be induced artificially, either chemically, through the use of colchicine, or physically by radiation.

Spontaneous chromosome doubling occurs with some frequency in nature among both cultivated and wild species. Sources tend to agree that an estimated 50 percent of flowering plant and fern species are polyploid in some form. With the exception of a few triploids, polyploid daylilies resulting from natural processes have not been reported. In 1932 Stout described the results of a general survey of chromosome numbers in daylilies. The somatic number of 22 chromosomes, or two sets, is basic for all species of daylilies, with the exception of several clones which were found to have 33 chromosomes, making them triploids. Gametes in diploid daylilies have 11 chromosomes, or one set. Gametes in triploids have an even number of sets, two for example, and consequently triploids are sterile.

In 1937 the antimeotic effect of colchicine, an alkaloid isolated from the autumn crocus (*Colchicum autumnale*) was discovered. The effect of colchicine is to inhibit synthesis of tubulin, the substance that makes up the spindle fibers that pull the duplicate sets of chromosomes apart during cell division. This discovery gave rise to extensive attempts to induce polyploidy artificially, in both ornamental and agricultural plants, using colchicine as the agent for increasing chromosome numbers. In the course of cell division in plants treated with colchicine, similar, or homologous, chromosomes fail to separate, so a double set enters one daughter cell.

The years 1945–65 saw much experimentation with techniques to convert diploid daylilies into tetraploids. Approaches varied from treating the daylily crown—by cutting off the foliage and scooping out a hollow in the flesh of the crown to expose the growing tip and saturate it with colchicine—to injecting colchicine into the crown with a hypodermic needle, to soaking newly germinated seeds in colchicine and then washing them in a bath of clear water. The strength of the colchicine varied with each method as did the exposure time. Success was not guaranteed and identification of tetraploid material after treating and flowering was difficult. A further frustration arose when in many cases colchicine treatment led to the production of a chimera, a mosaic plant with both tetraploid and diploid tissue, rather than a complete tetraploid.

With the tedious and often frustrating work and effort required to convert plants, few hybridizers openly embraced the concept or altered their own breeding programs. But conversion was only half the problem, for induced tetraploids lacked the fertility common at the diploid level. Seed production was not easy at best. Tetraploid daylilies were understandably of interest to only a handful of botanists and amateur breeders. Three of the earliest scientists and plantsmen to experiment with tetraploids were Hamilton Traub, Quinn Buck, and Robert Schreiner. Each reported successful flowering of a tetraploid daylily in 1949, 1948, and 1947 respectively.

Hamilton Traub began to breed tetraploid daylilies in 1949 while working in the laboratory of the US Department of Agriculture in Beltsville, Maryland. There he developed the Beltsville series of tetraploids. He introduced the induced 'Tetra Starzynski' (1949), 'Tetra Apricot' (1951), 'Tetra Peach' (1951), and numerous others in the years following, all distributed through the US Department of Agriculture. They were primitive and quite ordinary in comparison to the diploids of the day.

Though the work of Traub, Buck, and Schreiner began the movement, the tetraploid effort did not begin to take hold or have much effect until Orville Fay and Bob Griesbach in the Chicago area, Virginia Peck in Tennessee, and Toru Arisumi in Washington, D.C., developed their approaches and techniques to plant conversion. During the 1960s James Marsh, Brother Charles Reckamp, Bill and Ida Munson, Frank and Peggy Childs, Steve Moldovan, Willard Barrere, Edgar Brown, Lucille Warner, and Nate Rudolph also began their work. From 1960 to 1965 only 17 induced tetraploids were registered, but by 1968, 66 additional seedling tetraploids, or cultivars resulting from tetraploid parents, were registered. Now in the early twenty-first century virtually all the major breeders are working with tetraploids.

Why tetraploids? Breeders generally agree that tetraploids have a number of advantages over diploids. Tetraploid flowers are normally larger, the colors brighter and more intense, the scapes stronger and sturdier. Tetraploid plants possess heavier substance and greater vegetative vigor. These characteristics are, in most cases, clearly visible when comparing a diploid cultivar with its tetraploid version. Another major advantage lies in the greater breeding potential of tetraploids, which derives from the increased number of chromosomes controlling plant characteristics. A double set of chromosomes means that each gene locus is represented four times in the genetic material instead of the normal two times. This in turn means that characters controlled by multiple genes, each contributing a small effect, may be more intense in tetraploids.

Daylilies have 11 different kinds of chromosomes. Each kind has a place, or locus, for genes that control specific characters. A diploid has two alleles, or forms, such as dominant or recessive, of each gene. A tetraploid has four alleles, the same or different.

In diploids the individual chromosomes pass at random into the gametes, pollen or egg, so each daughter cell inherits one of each of the 11 kinds; this process is called "independent assortment." Valid reasons indicate that the four homologous chromosomes in each of a tetraploid's sets of 11 may not always be randomly assorted, but each tetraploid is a different case. Tetraploid genetics becomes very complex not only because twice as many chromosomes and gene loci are involved, but also because distribution of chromosomes into the gametes may differ in pattern from one tetraploid to another.

Major criticism of tetraploid hybrids in the early years centered on their coarseness, their lack of finesse, ruffling, and distinction, and their lack of variety. Further, many of the early tetraploids were subject to cracking, or blasting, scapes in the presence of an overabundance of water, extreme temperature changes, or heavy fertilization. Regardless of the breeders' perspective, these allegations were entirely correct, but time and a group of dedicated hybridizers have minimized these limitations.

Virginia Peck of Murfreesboro, Tennessee, a major early tetraploid daylily breeder, began to work with tetraploids in the late 1950s and early '60s. Assisted by her husband, Richard Connelly Peck, they made a formidable team. Her early work revolved around converting diploid material into tetraploid to expand the very limited tetraploid gene pool. Her work in converting the Claar reds alone—such as 'Sail On' and 'Red Siren'—entitles her to a significant place in daylily history. She was a scholar and professor of English literature at Middle Tennessee State College, Murfreesboro, during this period—her literary bent shows in the names of some of her earliest cultivars. A quiet, self-possessed, and unassuming woman, she was sure of her program and of what she wanted to achieve. Her major focus in her later years was on black and white daylilies, although she continued to work with reds, yellows, pinks, and purples. She received Awards of Merit for 'Bonnie John Steton' (1969), a light yellow self; 'Douglas Dale' (1969), a red blend; 'Golden Prize' (1969), a gold self; 'Heather Green' (1969), a pink blend; and 'Jock Randall' (1971), a rose self.

A truly significant breeder of tetraploids was James Marsh of Chicago. Marsh had a major impact on both diploids and tetraploids, beginning in the 1950s and continuing until his untimely death in 1978. As were most significant breeders of daylilies, Marsh was an amateur. His garden was small by any standard, but his work has withstood the test of time. He was a painter with an artist's eye, a quiet, unassuming man, pleased with his work but modest and unpretentious. In the early 1960s his 'Prairie Maid' (1963), a pale ruffled pink with a large rose eye, was taking the AHS by storm.

Marsh's early work was with diploids—he used the prefix "Prairie" for all his diploid cultivars. His interest was in pinks, lavenders, reds, and eyed varieties, though he did breed minimally in other color classes. Some of his most significant diploid cultivars were 'Prairie Blue Eyes' (1970), a lavender with near blue eyezone, and 'Prairie Chief' (1963), a red self, both of which won an Award of Merit.

When he reached a major plateau with diploids his interest shifted to tetraploids, an interest intensified by living in the same area as Orville Fay, Robert Griesbach, and Brother Charles Reckamp. His tetraploid program was so successful that in time it eclipsed all he had previously done. His interest in lavender and purple was all consuming. Early on, he made a cross of 'Prairie Thistle' (1963) × 'Lavender Flight' and treated the newly germinated seeds in an effort to convert the best of his lavender diploid line to tetraploid. A seedling of extraordinary lavender-purple color bloomed. It was not a true tetraploid, but a chimera. In 1967 Marsh crossed this major milestone with every tetraploid in his garden. Regrettably, the chimera reverted to diploid or somehow was lost, but Marsh was able to collect several hundred seeds from seedling tetraploids ranging in color from cream-melon to salmon and rose. These were the beginnings of his lavender and purple lines. He had turned a major page in daylily history, and though he would do many fine reds and a few yellows, he will be remembered for his lavenders and purples. As with his diploids, Marsh chose one prefix for all his tetraploid cultivars, and the Chicago series was born. His 'Chicago Knobby' (1974), a purple bitone with a deeper center, and 'Chicago Candy Cane' (1975), a pink and cream with a creamy green throat, both won an Award of Merit.

Another truly great breeder of this period was Orville W. Fay of Northbrook, Illinois. His work spanned 20 years and was exemplified by 'Frances Fay' (1957), a soft pastel melon-cream-yellow diploid that grows easily, multiplies well, and won both the Stout Silver Medal and the Lenington All-American Award. 'Frances Fay' continues to remain on nearly all AHS popularity polls each year. In 1957 and '58 he bloomed two diploid cultivars that dramatically changed the breeding direction of daylilies. Both registered in 1960, 'Superfine', a large rose-pink-melon self that won an Award of Merit, and 'Satin Glass', a large cream-melon pastel that won the Stout Medal, were new plateaus in size, finish, finesse, and breeding ability. Another of his significant diploid cultivars was 'Louise Russel' (Fay and Russel, 1959), a deep baby-ribbon-pink self. An amateur daylily breeder, his profession was that of a chemist in a candy factory. He was a meticulous record keeper and his results clearly show the benefit of such records. His work was very limited in scope for he stayed in very narrow, well-defined lines.

During the 1950s, Fay and Robert A. Griesbach embarked on a program to produce tetraploid daylilies. They introduced a technique of soaking the newly germinated seeds in a colchicine solution before washing and planting them. A high percentage of the survivors were tetraploid. Fay and Griesbach introduced a group of these induced tetraploids, all with the prefix "Crestwood." The most significant of these was 'Crestwood

Ann' (1961), a cream-melon-pink self. Together with another of their tetraploids, 'Kathleen Elsie Randall' (1965), a creamy melon with orchid midribs, it won an Award of Merit.

Mission Gardens and Brother Charles Reckamp were synonymous with quality daylilies. By the mid 1960s, Reckamp had already made a name for himself with diploids; however, he was soon to eclipse that work with his astounding advances in tetraploids. Reckamp was a quiet, unassuming man, consumed with a desire to improve daylilies that spanned more than 30 years. His efforts were directed exclusively to pastels, ranging from near cream-white to ivory rouged pink, and yellows, golds, apricots, and oranges. His trademark, large pastels with heavily ruffled petals edged in gold, emerged early.

By 1967, realizing the extent of Reckamp's work with tetraploids, the daylily world finally understood the significance tetraploids would have. As far as one could see at Mission Gardens were row after row of magnificent seedlings in a large array of pastel creams, yellows, and golds. Stiff and erect scapes of varying heights held broad, full flowers with thick, heavy, waxlike substance. 'Holy Grail' (1968), a cream-yellow blend, first bloomed in 1967 and it left a mark on history. Measured by the standards of nearly 40 years later, it pales, but for its day it was perfection, a milestone of the highest quality. A new plateau had been reached.

Prior to 'Holy Grail', Reckamp had produced 'Envoy' (1966), 'Bountiful Harvest' (1967), and 'Changing Times' (1966). All were pastel hallmarks in that incredibly small, primitive arena of early tetraploids. 'Little Rainbow' (1963), a polychrome of melon, pink, cream, yellow, and orchid, won an Award of Merit and the Annie T. Giles Award, and his 'King Alfred' (1975), a light yellow-gold double won the Ida Munson Award.

Steve Moldovan became involved with daylilies and irises as a young man and pursued a degree in ornamental horticulture. He founded Moldovan Gardens, located in Avon, Ohio, stressing quality plants and distinctive beauty. As a protégé of Orville Fay, his early work was with diploids, but he changed direction in 1961 and tetraploids became his primary concern. In 1962 he embarked on a major program to convert diploid daylilies to tetraploids using the method of treating newly germinated seedlings with colchicine. He treated thousands upon thousands of seedlings, and the resulting early conversions were the basis for most of his subsequent work.

The Moldovan program has always been diverse, unique, and imaginative. He quickly broke with tradition by crossing many new and unique cultivars from the South, especially Florida and Louisiana, with the strongly dormant cultivars of the North, particularly those of Fay. By crossing evergreens with dormants he was also attempting to increase the adaptability of various cultivars by making them either semi-evergreen or semi-dormant, thus broadening their geographical range. New, unique, and clear colors were also major goals. Purples were a passion. His early cultivar 'Buried Treasure' (1962), an ivory-yellow with white midribs, won an Award of Merit.

R. William "Bill" Munson Jr. began growing and hybridizing daylilies in 1947. He worked with his mother, Ida Munson, and together with his sister, Betty Hudson, started Wimberlyway Gardens in Gainesville, Florida. To start his first line he used cultivars from his three mentors, Ralph Wheeler, Ophelia Taylor, and David Hall. His first cross was 'Prima Donna' (Ophelia Taylor, 1946) × 'Mission Bells' (David Hall, 1945). He then selected several seedlings to cross with 'Show Girl' (Ralph Wheeler, 1949), and a line of voluptuous pastel diploids followed. The line was taken to the sixth generation before Munson became intoxicated with tetraploids in 1960 and decided to abandon it. His significant diploid cultivars were 'Dream Mist' (1958), a very full, round cream-pink-rose, and 'Jimmy Kilpatrick' (1964), a rose-pink blend, both of which won an Award of Merit.

In 1960, Munson developed a consuming drive to breed the best possible tetraploids. He obtained all the tetraploid cultivars available at that time and simultaneously embarked upon converting significant diploids by all possible methods. His first induced cultivar bloomed in 1962, a tetraploid blending the lines of Orville Fay and Edna Spalding. He crossed this plant with 'Crestwood Ann' to produce 'Oriana' (1966), which in turn produced 'Kings Cloak' (1969). Along with an induced tetraploid from 'Satin Glass' and his own 'Sleeping Beauty' (1959), these plants became part of an elaborate foundation that he was still building on 20 years later.

In the 1960s one had to search endlessly to find new tetraploid material, for the gene pool was meager and the need for more exoteric material became more obvious with each passing year. Using a number of converted diploids as well as the best of the new tetraploids, Munson carved out his tetraploid program. His 'Kings Cloak', a wine-rose blend with a mauve-wine eyezone, and 'Yasmin' (1969), an ivory-cream-flesh blend, won Awards of Merit. Later, he continued to work in many colors, but he developed a particularly fine line of pastels, which included 'Fred Ham' (1982), 'Kate Carpenter' (1980), and 'Betty Warren Woods' (1987), all of which received Awards of Merit. He had a passion for lavenders and purples, and some of his finest cultivars include 'Benchmark' (1980) 'Court Magician' (1987), 'Malaysian Monarch' (1986) and 'Respighi' (1986), also Award of Merit winners.

Present and Future Years

At no time in history have more people been involved or more work been directed toward the improvement of daylilies than now in the early years of the twenty-first century. The current list of breeders is virtually endless. Almost exclusively tetraploid daylilies are being bred by the top hybridizers, and what little diploid breeding continues is primarily for the purpose of ultimately converting the results to tetraploids. Some hybridizers who led the way in breeding tetraploids continue today, primarily Steve Moldovan, who is known for his work on clear pinks and purples.

One of today's great daylily breeding teams is Patrick and Grace Stamile. They began hybridizing in Long Island, New York, where their program produced a large number of beautiful flowers with a high percentage of dormants and very winter hardy plants. The Stamiles were school teachers, and their meticulous habits transferred well to their hybridizing efforts. Later, the Stamiles moved their Floyd Cove Nursery to central Florida, where they continue to hybridize.

Pat hybridizes medium to large tetraploid flowers. His program is varied, but he has focused on several major lines. His Candy series involves medium-sized, eyed flowers. 'Raspberry Candy' (1989) and 'Wineberry Candy' (1990) won Awards of Merit, and 'Strawberry Candy' (1989) and 'Custard Candy' (1989) both went on to win the Stout Medal. Others of his eyed daylilies, such as 'Druid's Chant' (1993), 'Creative Edge' (1993), 'Joe Marinello' (1989), 'El Desperado' (1991), and 'Tigerling' (1989), received Awards of Merit. Pat also developed a line of near white daylilies, which includes Award of Merit winners 'Arctic Snow' (1985) and 'Admiral's Braid' (1993) and Stout Medal winner 'Wedding Band' (1987). His plants of 'New Direction' (2000), 'Key Lime Ice' (1998) and 'Knights in White Satin' (1998) remain among the finest near whites available. Pat also works heavily with pinks and has received Awards of Merit for his 'Seminole Wind' (1993), 'Chance Encounter' (1994), and 'Splendid Touch' (1994), all superb, wide-petaled pinks. More recently, Pat has developed a line of tetraploid spiders, many of which go back to his 'Ruby Spider' (1991), which won an Award of Merit and the Lambert/Webster Unusual Forms Award.

Grace Stamile works with small-flowered daylilies. She hybridizes with mostly diploids but has also started working with tetraploids—her tetraploid introductions carry the prefix "Broadway." Her plants are known for their excellent overall plant characteristics, carrying multiple blooms on perfectly proportioned scapes. Many of her small-flowered introductions have patterned or near blue eyes, and her 'Baby Blues' (1990) won the Donn Fischer Memorial Award. She has also developed a line of miniature doubles, which are often referred to as "popcorn doubles," such as 'Cute As a Button' (1999), a cream self, and 'You Angel You' (1993), a cream with red eye. Grace's work is further discussed in the section on small and miniature daylilies in Chapter 4.

Another of the important breeding teams today is Jeff and Elizabeth Salter of Rollingwood Gardens in Eustis, Florida. Jeff is trained as a lawyer, and Elizabeth is the niece of Bill Munson. She grew up surrounded by daylily hybridizers at Wimberlyway Gardens. The Salters have one of the largest hybridizing programs, with a great variety of daylilies.

Jeff Salter focuses exclusively on large-flowered tetraploids, primarily single, full-formed flowers in a range of colors. While Jeff pushes the envelope on very wide-petaled flowers with gold edges, among his most important concerns is clear, vivid colors on daylilies with excellent overall plant habits. His line of pinks and pastels includes 'My Darling Clementine' (1988), 'Something Wonderful' (1991), 'Elizabeth Salter' (1990), and 'Chris Salter' (1993), all of which won Awards of Merit. His 'Ed Brown' (1994) was a plant ahead of its time and remains one of the most important pinks used by breeders. His boldly eyed and edged flowers have been some of his most highly acclaimed, with 'Cindy's Eye' (1994), 'Mask of Time' (1993), 'Moonlit Masquerade' (1992), and 'Daring Dilemma' (1992) all receiving Awards of Merit. 'Canadian Border Patrol' (1995), 'Pirate's Patch' (1991), and 'Sabine Baur' (1997) won the Don Stevens Award.

Elizabeth Salter's small-flowered hybridizing program has produced some of the finest patterned eyes in daylilies, as well as the bluest eyes. She has received

Awards of Merit for her small-flowered, eyed cultivars such as 'Jason Salter' (1987), 'Mary Ethel Anderson' (1995), and 'Dark Avenger' (1997). Her 'Dragons Eye' (1992) also received the Annie T. Giles Award, as did 'Witches Wink' (1999). She also received the Donn Fischer Memorial Award for many of her small, eyed, and patterned cultivars, including 'Dragon's Orb' (1986), 'Morrie Otte' (1996), 'Bibbity Bobbity Boo' (1992) and 'Patchwork Puzzle' (1990). The eyes in her 'In the Navy' (1993) and 'Crystal Blue Persuasion' (1996) are generally considered to be the closest to true blue coloration currently available in daylilies.

Ted Petit, a coauthor of this book and a professor of brain research at the University of Toronto, also maintains a large, diversified breeding program at Le Petit Jardin in McIntosh, Florida. Petit breeds large-flowered, single and double daylilies in a wide range of colors with a goal of producing plants that will survive in both his Florida and Canadian gardens.

Early on, Petit decided to focus on wide-petaled, very ruffled flowers with heavy gold edges. His pastels include 'Dripping with Gold' (1998), 'Bill Munson' (1998), 'Coral and Gold' (2000), 'Kings and Vagabonds' (1994), and 'Ferengi Gold' (1994), which won an Award of Merit. His purples and lavenders have all been edged in gold and include 'Light Years Away' (1996), 'Forbidden Desires' (1995), 'John Peat' (2001), and 'Leaving Me Breathless' (2003). He has maintained one of the foremost lines in near black daylilies with gold edges, including 'Edge of Eden' (1994), 'Bohemia After Dark' (2000), 'Quest for Eden' (2001), 'Burning Embers' (1996), and 'Baby Jane Hudson' (2003). Petit's program of tetraploid doubles is among the largest and includes the significant 'Memories of Paris' (1995), 'Gladys Campbell' (1994), 'Company of Swans' (2003), and 'Susan Pritchard Petit' (2001). His bold-eyed flowers include 'Pirate's Ransom' (1999), 'Mardi Gras Ball' (1996), 'Meet Joe Black' (2002), and 'Lady Betty Fretz' (2002), and

among his most important reds are 'Drowning in Desire' (1996) and 'Jack of Hearts' (2000).

The other author of this book, John Peat of Toronto, has been making an important impact on breeding daylilies, with a particular love for eyed and edged daylilies. As a Canadian, his hybridizing program and important cultivars are discussed in greater detail in Chapter 14.

A retired physician, Robert Carr also maintains a broad program in large-flowered tetraploids. Some of his more significant pastel flowers are 'America's Most Wanted' (1997), 'Quality of Mercy' (1994), and 'Sherry Lane Carr' (1993), which won an Award of Merit. His reds and black-reds have been important cultivars, such as 'Passion District' (1997), 'Pagan Ritual' (1999), and 'Altered State' (1997).

Working in Texas, Jack Carpenter breeds large-flowered diploids and tetraploids in a variety of colors. His 'Josephine Marina' (1987), 'Ruffled Perfection' (1989), 'Dena Marie' (1992), and 'Catherine Neal' (1981) have all won Awards of Merit. 'Lavender Blue Baby' (1996) has been a particularly important cultivar for blue-eyed daylilies.

Larry Grace of Graceland Gardens carries on a small but critical breeding program in Dothan, Alabama. He has focused primarily on pastel daylilies with excellent substance, clarity of color, and large size. His most important contributions have been 'Clothed in Glory' (1996), a lavender with a heavy gold edge, 'Felecia Grace' (2000), an extremely ruffled gold, 'J. T. Davis' (1999), a cream-pink with a gold edge, and 'Mrs. John Cooper' (2000), a lavender with a blue eye. Grace recently sold his collection of cultivars bred prior to 2003 to Frank Smith, orchid breeder and daylily collector from Apopka, Florida, who has continued breeding large-flowered tetraploids.

John Kinnebrew of Scottsmoor, Florida, has produced a number of cutting-edge, large, gold-edged flowers, along with a few small-flowered cultivars. His

'Spacecoast Starburst' (1998), 'Darla Anita' (1999), and 'Jerry Nettles' (2003) have proven to be critical breeding plants. 'Midnight Magic' (1979) won both an Award of Merit and the Lenington All-American Award.

John Benz has been breeding plants, especially dormants, that can survive the winters and perform well in Ohio. Benz has maintained a varied program, but among his more important contributions are his reds, such as 'Radar Love' (1993), and his pinks, such as 'Glittering Elegance' (1996), 'One Step Beyond' (1995), and 'Janet Benz' (2000). Another important breeder of plants for cold climates is Karol Emmerich of Edina, Minnesota, quickly emerging among the newest hybridizers. She has a diverse program and is just beginning to introduce cultivars such as 'Eyes on the Prize' (2002), a boldly eyed and edged flower.

A number of breeders have specialized in breeding spiders, spider variants, and unusual forms. Bob Schwarz of Long Island, New York, has been focusing on unusual forms, such as 'Twisted Sister' (1999) and 'Laughing Giraffe' (1997). Jamie Gossard in Ohio is working mostly with edged spiders and unusual forms, such as 'Heavenly Beginnings' (2001) and 'Radiation Biohazard' (2000). Ludlow "Luddy" Lambertson has been breeding for unusual forms and blue-eyed daylilies, such as 'Jenny Butterfield' (1998) and 'Raptor Rap' (2001). John J. "Jack" Temple has been breeding diploid spiders, producing 'De Colores' (1992), 'Shirley Temple Curls' (1996), and 'Wildest Dreams' (1993).

The double daylily also has its followers, including Jan and Enman Joiner of Savanna, Georgia. Some of the Joiners' most important contributions include 'Frances Joiner' (1988), 'Peggy Bass' (1993), and 'Peggy Jeffcoat' (1995), all large-flowered, pastel doubles. David Kirchhoff of Sanford, Florida, has also focused on diploid and tetraploid doubles, such as 'Betty Woods' (1980) and 'Layers of Gold' (1990), as well as single reds such as 'Dragon King' (1992) and golds such as 'Bill Norris' (1993).

A number of hybridizers are breeding primarily for eyes and patterns. Lee Pickles of Chattanooga, Tennessee, has produced a number of important eyed and edged daylilies, such as 'Pardon Me Boy' (1995). He has also focused on particular colors, such as his red 'Awesome Bob' (2001). Mort Morss of Sanford, Florida, has also worked with eyes and edges, as well as patterned eyes. Morss has produced a long list of excellent flowers and has received Awards of Merit for his patterned flowers 'Paper Butterfly' (1983), 'Witch Stitchery' (1986), and the incomparable 'Fortune's Dearest' (1994), a dark purple with a white shark's-tooth edge. Dan Trimmer of Enterprise, Florida, has converted numerous diploid plants to tetraploid, incorporating them into his program of eyed and edged cultivars. His important introductions include 'Dan Mahony' (1999), 'Cherry Valentine' (1999), and 'Jane Trimmer' (2000), all having bold eyes and edges. George Doorakian of Bedford, Massachusetts, working with patterned daylilies, has contributed important flowers with huge intensely green throats, such as 'Malachite Prism' (1999). Jeff Corbett, a fairly new hybridizer, is working in California, breeding flowers that perform well in the arid climate and open well following cool desert nights, such as 'For Your Eyes Only' (2000) and 'Shelter Cove' (2002).

CHAPTER 4

Different Types of Daylilies

Daylilies can be categorized in many ways, such as by color, presence or absence of an eye or watermark, size, doubling, petal form, and so on. The most popular style for most collectors tends to be the round, full-formed, single daylily. Several other major types, however, are widely recognized within the daylily community and are significant among the primary awards in the Awards and Honors System of the American Hemerocallis Society (AHS). These other important daylily groups include the doubles, polytepals, small and miniatures, and spiders and unusual forms.

Double Daylilies

Double daylilies are quite different from single blooms and have their own group of passionate followers. The appeal of double daylilies is not a surprise, since gardeners are naturally attracted to the double blooms of many other perennials, such as roses and camellias.

Today's large, voluptuous double daylilies come from years of hard work by hybridizers. Double daylilies are found among selected wild plants, such as

Hemerocallis fulva 'Kwanso' and *H. fulva* 'Flore Pleno', but these plants are triploids and therefore sterile. Thus, hybridizers were unable to use them for breeding and instead had to start from scratch.

In the 1960s and '70s, breeders relied on single daylilies that sometimes had double tissue. Then, by diligently crossing with these flowers and selecting offspring that showed increasing amounts of double tissue, double daylilies began to emerge. These early doubles were narrow-petaled flowers, lacking any ruffling, and often only semi-double. As hybridizers worked on improving the doubles, petals widened and ruffles began to appear, giving them a more finished look. After generations of double breeding, the blooms became more consistently and fully double. Betty Brown was an important breeder in these early days, winning two Ida Munson Awards for her diploid doubles: 'Double Razzle Dazzle' (1974), a red self, and 'Double Cutie' (1972), a yellow-green self.

When the tetraploid revolution began in the 1960s and '70s, hybridizers had to begin again. Betty Hudson, the sister of Bill Munson, took on the arduous task of beginning a double tetraploid program by selecting tetraploid plants that showed a tendency to double. Other hybridizers, such as Patrick Stamile, did some breeding of double tetraploid daylilies during that era, but Hudson's program was among the largest. These tetraploid doubles had heavier substance and clearer, brighter colors than the diploids. Some of Hudson's early introductions, such as the cherry-red 'Wayne Johnson' (1984) and the diamond-dusted cream-pink 'Renaissance Queen' (1985), were critical breaks in tetraploid doubles. They were not only consistently double, but they were modern in appearance and, most important of all, fertile, usable tetraploids. Hudson went on to create a number of other beautiful doubles, including the extremely popular 'Fires of Fuji' (1990), a red double with wide orange-red edges.

As tetraploid doubles began to emerge, many other hybridizers, such as David Talbott, Clarence Crochet, and Pauline Henry, continued to work with their double diploid lines. Others, such as David Kirchhoff and Enman Joiner, worked with diploids and slowly converted their programs to tetraploids. Still others, such as Ted Petit and John Peat, simply began with tetraploids.

Though the look of a double can be quite different from one cultivar to another, and even from one flower to another on the same plant, double flowers come in only two basic forms. One type of double results from the addition of petaloids, or stamens that have extra tissue on the sides. Petaloids, which stick out of the center of the flowers, are different from petals, since they are really modified stamens. This type of double is generally referred to as a "peony double." The other type of double has more true petals on the flower. These petals generally lie flat, like the extra petals of roses and camellias. This type of double daylily is referred to as "hose-in-hose." These types of doubles, which can both appear on the same plant, are easy to tell apart by close examination, keeping in mind that they are modified single daylilies.

The daylily flower is made up of four layers, or whorls, of different flower parts. Starting from the base of the flower are (1) a layer of sepals, (2) a layer of petals, (3) a layer of stamens, and (4) the pistil. The ideal way to form a double flower of any genus would be by adding extra tiers of petals to layer two. Double daylilies with extra true petals, the hose-in-hose type, are relatively rare. Most daylily doubles are formed by modifying the stamens in layer three.

Some peony doubles add tissue to only one side of the stamen, creating petaloids that are easy to recognize as modified stamens. Flowers that add tissue to both sides of the stamen have petaloids that more closely resemble true petals, although the anther, or pollen sac, can generally be found on the petaloid. Sometimes, however, the anther becomes rudimentary or nonexistent, so that the petaloid does look like a perfectly normal petal. Most peony doubles have some petaloids and few or no normal stamens. Since a petaloid is formed from stamen tissue, and daylily flowers have only six stamens, six is the maximum number of petaloids that the double-flowered daylily can have. If a flower has fewer than six petaloids, the remainder will appear as normal stamens and the flower will appear semi-double. Unlike the production of petaloids, the addition of extra true petals does not appear to have any limit. Theoretically, many layers of petals could be stacked one on top of the other. Potentially a double daylily could have the number of petals of a rose or camellia. And since hose-in-hose doubles have added extra true petals and have retained their stamens, all six stamens can also be present.

After many years of hard work, double daylilies have taken on a more sophisticated, modern look. The colors have become clearer and brighter, with clear pinks such as 'Gladys Campbell' (Ted Petit, 1994), 'Memories of Paris' (Ted Petit, 1995), and 'Peggy Jeffcoat' (Jan Joiner, 1995), as well as white, such as 'Company of Swans' (Ted Petit, 1994). The form has become much more formal, including the very formal hose-in-hose appearance, characterized by flowers such as 'Formal Appearance' (Ted Petit, 2000), 'Leader of the Pack' (John Peat, 1999), 'Trials of Life' (John Peat, 2001), 'Separate Reality' (Ted Petit, 2002), and 'Frances Joiner' (Enman R. Joiner, 1998). Further, the features of the modern single daylily have appeared in the double tetraploids. An important feature of the modern singles is the heavily crimped, ruffled, gold edges that are now seen in doubles such as 'Golden Mansions' (Ted Petit, 2001) and 'Susan Pritchard Petit' (Ted Petit, 2001). The shark's tooth edges have also appeared, for example in 'Dark Wonder' (Patrick Stamile, 2000) and 'Outrageous Fortune' (Patrick Stamile, 2001). Double flowers now also contain bright eyezones and picotees, such as 'Shadows Within' (Ted Petit, 1999) and 'Candyman Can' (Ted Petit, 2002). Extremely small "popcorn" doubles have also appeared, such as 'Little by Little' (Grace Stamile, 1998) and 'Piglet and Roo' (John Peat, 1998).

The double daylily has finally come into its own, with a degree of sophistication and refinement to rival the singles. Now that we have come this far, the future potential for double daylilies seems endless.

Polytepal Daylilies

Polytepal daylilies are among the newest and least common types of daylilies. The typical single daylily has three sepals and three petals. The sepals and petals together are known as tepals. Polytepals are flowers that contain more than the typical number of tepals. Most people would more easily understand a reference to the flowers as "poly-petaled." When most of us look at polytepal flowers, we see that they have more than the typical three petals.

As mentioned in the section on doubles, the daylily flower is composed of four layers, or whorls: the sepals, petals, stamens, and pistil. Normally, each of the layers is associated with a characteristic number. For example, typical daylilies have three sepals and three petals. Also, two stamens are typically associated with each petal, for

a total of six stamens. Each flower has only one pistil, but close inspection shows that it is also divided into three parts. The typical daylily is a three-part affair, with layers of flower parts formed in groups of three. The most common polytepal flower changes all this by altering the basic number from three to four: four sepals, four petals, eight stamens, four chambers of the pistil, and if pollinated, four seed chambers in the seed pod, rather than the typical three.

Polytepal flowers are not limited to four petals and associated flower parts. Four-petaled polytepal daylilies are most common, but several hybrids often produce five-petaled flowers. Naturally, this is associated with five sepals, 10 stamens, and so on. Although we are not aware of any daylilies at this time having more than five segments, we know of nothing to stop this number from increasing further.

Polytepal daylilies are sometimes confused with double daylilies since both contain more than the normal number of petals. Rather than adding layers as doubles do, polytepals change the number of segments within a layer.

Polytepals with four petals tend to look square, which has less of an aesthetic appeal for many people. Also, most lack much of the refinement of other modern hybrids, but this flower type is just in its infancy. Polytepals have only recently become a flower form that daylily enthusiasts recognize and hybridize. Their potential is just now beginning to be explored. Though few hybridizers are working with them, some of the major advancements are being made by Bill Reinke—'Fuscia Four' (1995) and 'Give Me Eight' (1993)—and Bobby Baxter—'Got No Goat' (2000) and 'Resistance Is Futile' (2000).

The future of polytepal daylilies is very exciting. One major goal of some hybridizers is to breed the round and full-looking five-petaled, or more, daylilies. Hibiscus blooms, for example, have five petals, which give the flower a full, round form that most gardeners find appealing. One major hybridizing effort to make daylilies more beautiful has been increasing the petal width to produce a more round flower form; five petals instantly imparts an even rounder form to the flower. With additional petals, features such as fancy edges become even more obvious and dramatic. At this time we can only imagine other possibilities for polytepal daylilies, such as polytepal spiders and polytepal doubles. This is a very new and exciting area of daylily hybridizing with a great deal of potential.

Small and Miniature Daylilies
by Pam Erikson

Miniature and small-flowered daylilies have long been a passion of mine, in both collecting other breeders' work and in striving to create new varieties of my own. Many gardeners seem to be looking for low-maintenance, small-space gardening ideas for balconies, patios, and small home gardens. My own grandmother, who is approaching 93 years old, has a balcony full of miniature daylilies that give her months of enjoyment each year, with very little labor involved. When visitors see her collection of these colorful miniatures, they marvel at how completely different they are from the tall, elegant varieties that they are used to seeing, and how easily some of these little treasures would fit into their perennial borders or small gardens.

Within the AHS award system lie two awards for miniature and small-flowered cultivars: the Annie T. Giles Award for small flowers measuring between 3 and 4.5 in. (7.6–11.4 cm) in diameter, and the Donn Fischer Memorial Award for miniature flowers measuring under 3 in. (7.6 cm) in diameter. Each year, registered AHS judges vote for the most meritorious cultivars in their particular region from a ballot compiled of nominated cultivars submitted by their breeders. All candidate cultivars must have been registered at least three years prior to the ballot. The results of such judging give a good overview of which plants will do well in each re-

gion. It makes perfect sense that some varieties grown in Florida may not perform as they do in Washington State and vice versa.

Starting from the small-flowered species *Hemerocallis minor*, *H. citrina*, and *H. middendorffii*, hybridizing has taken these little beauties to new heights and popularity. Early breeders had very few plants to work with, but they led the way to later hybridizers' successes. Though few of the early introductions can be found today, their importance in the evolution of the modern miniature and small-flowered varieties are never to be forgotten. In 1963, Lucille Warner introduced 'Bitsy', a miniature yellow rebloomer that is still listed on popularity polls and that was a pioneer for small-flowered breeding. Cultivars such as 'Bertie Ferris' (Ury G. Winniford, 1969), 'Little Grapette' (Dalton Durio, 1980), and 'Puddin' (Robert M. Kennedy, 1972) made most of the popularity polls of the 1960s and '70s, but the introduction of 'Stella De Oro' by Walter Jablonski in 1975 got the world's attention. This ruffled, golden, reblooming miniature was a milestone in hybridizing. 'Stella De Oro' is still one of the most well-known and respected miniatures in the daylily world, reblooming in most areas well into the fall months. Subsequent breeding with 'Stella De Oro' produced 'Happy Returns' (Darrel A. Apps, 1986), a lemon-yellow variety just a bit taller but with equal blooming capacity, and 'Mini Stella' (Walter Jablonski, 1983), an even smaller miniature of butter-yellow with tiny 1.5-in. (3.8 cm) blooms on 10-in. (25 cm) scapes. Every garden certainly can find room for this one!

While 'Stella De Oro' continued to be a big favorite, people wanted more colors. Pauline Henry of Siloam Springs, Arkansas, filled this niche and became a leader in miniature and small-flowered breeding. Her Siloam series of daylilies are prevalent in most gardens, and her plants are still being used in modern breeding lines. Henry won the Annie T. Giles Award an amazing six times, and the Donn Fischer Memorial Award five times. Her 'Siloam Virginia Henson' (1979) was converted to a tetraploid and is an ancestor to many of the names on the present-day popularity lists. Henry dedicated her life to the creation of beautiful flowers, which is apparent when you see blooms on 'Siloam Grace Stamile' (1984), a vibrant cranberry that catches your eye from across a garden; 'Siloam Bye Lo' (1980), a soft pink with red eye that clumps up so quickly gardeners have lots to share with friends; and 'Siloam Ury Winniford' (1980) an ivory cream with stunning purple eye which continues to be a big favorite for me in my own breeding lines.

Another well-known name in small and miniature breeding is Elizabeth Anne Hudson. She is the niece of renowned tetraploid breeder Bill Munson and grew up surrounded by daylilies in a family of hybridizers. Famed in her own right, she won the Annie T. Giles Award for 'Enchanter's Spell' (1982), went on to marry Jeff Salter, and then proceeded to introduce cultivars under the name Elizabeth Anne Salter. Her small-flowered varieties are among the cornerstones of modern daylilies, including 'Dragons Eye' (1992), which also won the Annie T. Giles Award, and three particular favorites 'Jason Salter' (1987), 'Patchwork Puzzle' (1990), and 'Morrie Otte' (1996), all winners of the Donn Fischer Memorial Award. Salter has won the Donn Fischer Memorial Award eight times and the Annie T. Giles Award three times. Her work in the field of hybridizing is ongoing, and with introductions like 'In the Navy' (1993), a breakthrough in blue eyes, and 'Vivid Vision' (2001), a spectacular cream with a kaleidoscope purple eye, she clearly has many award-winning days ahead of her.

Another of my idols in miniature breeding is Grace Stamile. Hybridizing in Florida alongside her husband, Patrick, who concentrates on larger flowers and spiders, Stamile has excelled in miniatures. A large container of her 'Cosmopolitan' (1989), best described as hot cherry-coral-red, is forever drawing comment from visitors. Stamile won the Donn Fischer Memorial Award for her 'Baby Blues' (1990), an incredibly intricate pale lavender miniature with a washed blue-gray eye. Her recent strides resulted in the Broadway series of tetraploid miniatures, a collection of work that will undoubtedly be sought after for years to come. Solid little plants, high bud counts, short scapes on proportionally balanced plants, and fabulous colors will ensure that these minis are the forerunners of the next generation of miniature daylilies. Her line of miniature doubles has also captured the hearts of daylily collectors everywhere.

Being classed as a "northern" breeder, I envy the ability of the southern hybridizers to see blooms in under a year from seed. The climate here in British Columbia means that seedlings will bloom after three years, or perhaps two, if the plant is extremely vigorous. Dormants grow with ease, but my personal aim has been to incorporate the wonderful colors and patterns of hybridizers like Grace Stamile and Elizabeth Salter, and pass those along to hardy dormants.

As each year goes by, we see many changes in the miniature and small-flowered varieties—eye patterns that cover almost the whole petal, doubles that look like tiny carnations, picotee edges that appear to stand up above the flower. With so many hybridizers having done such wonderful work, the future is bright with new possibilities. As award time comes around each year, the winners are surely going to be more and more difficult to choose.

Spiders and Unusual Formed Daylilies
by Sharon Fitzpatrick

Spiders and unusual formed daylily flowers have been a source of controversy ever since big round flowers hit the world of daylilies, and the AHS award process has followed that lead. For most daylily enthusiasts, spidery daylilies elicit either love at first sight or an expression of distaste. For a long time spiders were looked upon as outcasts, and when it came time for the AHS to formulate rules for the spider award, the committee was not dedicated to definite criteria possibly because they felt that no one would register a daylily as a spider if it could be avoided. Little did they know that in the not-so-distant future, spidery daylilies would come into prominence.

The AHS Harris Olson Spider Award came into being in 1989, and the Lambert/Webster Unusual Forms Award followed in 2000. The Lambert/Webster Award was created because many of the big, unusual forms did not qualify as spiders or variants, and their hybridizers tried to place them as spiders in order to be eligible for the award. But to really understand the turmoil, we must understand its history.

The original "spider lady" Rosemary Whitacre believed that this thin form of daylily is a direct descendant of *H. fulva* var. *rosea*, as spidery daylilies first began to show up in hybridizer's gardens six to eight years after *H. fulva* var. *rosea* was introduced to the United States from the Orient. The word "spider" was first printed in the 1952 edition of the Gilbert H. Wild and Son catalog to describe the shoestring-like form of 'Kindly Light' (LeMoine J. Bechtold, 1950). Many daylilies in the 1940s and '50s were spidery.

During the big round tetraploid revolution of the late 1960s and '70s, the desire for thin-petaled daylilies went out of vogue. Most daylily connoisseurs did not consider this type of flower to be of any value for future development. Spiders had become the ugly stepchild of an old-fashioned, weak-scaped diploid and were banished to the compost pile.

Throughout the tetraploid revolution, Whitacre and Lois Burns shared their love of this unusual, graceful type of flower with two AHS round-robin groups who were also devoted to growing, breeding, and evaluating diploid spidery daylilies. During this era, their common interest had a major part in keeping the exotic types of daylilies from becoming extinct. Producing new spiders became a challenge, as they were not diploid but irregular polyploids, triploids or spontaneous tetraploids. These exotics had so many crazy, mixed-up chromosomes plus an extra long pistil that a hybridizer had to find the right two parents before a proper genetic mix would produce a viable seedpod. In 1982, the *Daylily Journal* published an article by Whitacre entitled "Can You Mistake a Spider?" which was followed by a second article, "What Is a Spider?" By the time Lois Burns's article "Choice and Available" appeared in "The Spider Web" section of the 1987 spring/summer *Daylily Journal*, spidery daylilies were back in favor.

Harris Olson was a life member of the AHS and possibly one of the greatest ambassadors for daylilies in the history of the society. Olson promoted his favorite flower by using cast-off daylily seedlings from area hybridizers to single-handedly plant and maintain a huge daylily garden at the Congregational Church of Birmingham, Michigan. Olson was well known for sharing plants and growing tips with garden visitors. During an AHS national convention held in Detroit, a thin-petaled, cream seedling growing in a clump at the church garden was the hit of the convention. Afterward, a division of this seedling went to the Texas garden of Nell Crandall and was later registered as 'Spiral Charmer' (Margaret Dickson and Nell Crandall, 1985). To further promote spiders, Olson donated $2,000 for a new award to be added to the AHS Awards and Honors ballot in 1988.

The AHS Board of Directors was to determine exactly what traits constitute a spider daylily. They left it to the AHS Registration Committee to develop guidelines as to what would make a daylily eligible for the award. Thus began one of the most turbulent decision-making processes in AHS history. At this time the general consensus was that thin flower petals meant a spider. Upon seeing the first list of spider cultivars, Rosemary Whitacre and her band of record-keeping measurers picked up the sword as to what traits constitute a spider. After many a "bloody battle," the AHS established a preliminary ruling that included a list of registered cultivars that would be eligible for this new award. Whitacre fought long and hard, but several names still on the list were spider imposters.

In 1989, official AHS spider rules stated that segments of spider daylilies are narrower than other daylilies and should be longer than wide. Length-to-width petal ratio could be as high as 5:1, but most spiders will have a ratio of 4:1. In some rare cases, the ratio could be 3.5:1. The length of a segment divided by its width is the flower ratio. To obtain length-to-width ratio, petals and sepals would be measured as the flower stands in the garden. Length would be determined by measuring the segment from the base of the flower to the tip of the flower. Width was a single measurement taken at the widest part of the petal without flattening the flower segment. Spider flowers should have an open form. To qualify for being a classic spider, petals should not overlap petals, and sepals should only overlap at the base. Responsibility of classifying new spider introductions was left up to the hybridizers. Winner of the 1989 Harris Olson Spider Award was the classic spider 'Kindly Light' (LeMoine J. Bechtold, 1950), followed by 'Lady Fingers' (Virginia L. Peck, 1967) in 1990, 'Cat's Cradle' (Ben R. Hager, 1985) in 1991, and 'Red Ribbons' (George E. Lenington, 1964) in 1992.

With a new AHS award up for grabs and official spider rules rather vague, hybridizers began registering as spiders any exotic-looking cultivars that were measured with a "rubber ruler." One prominent hybridizer went so far as to lobby that the measurement for a spider should be determined by the diameter of bloom divided by narrowest point of the petal. By 1991, the great spider debate was still going strong. Spidery daylilies were in demand. Any plant with the term spider or spidery in catalog descriptions would sell out quickly. Growers who were purchasing spiders for use in hybridizing began to moan about the integrity of the system. To smooth ruffled feathers, the AHS Awards and Honors Committee began to redesign the official

spider rules. In the fall of 1991, the AHS Board of Directors tossed out the old spider criteria and approved a new ruling stating that to be classified and registered as a classic spider, a daylily should have a petal length-to-width ratio of 5.0:1 or more. As this ruling would only qualify a handful of cultivars nominated for the Harris Olson Spider Award, the board had to come up with another name for all those beautiful, baroque spider "wannabes." They coined "spider variant" to distinguish a variant from a true spider. A spider variant should have a petal length-to-width ratio of 4.0:1 and up to but not including 5.0:1. This new rule also stated that after 1991 a cultivar must be registered with these ratios to be eligible for the Harris Olson Spider and Spider Variant Award.

In 1993 'Trahlyta' (Frank Childs, 1982), a wondrous, purple-eyed exotic won the Harris Olson Spider Award. Spider lovers revolted because they knew 'Trahlyta' did not fall into either spider or variant measurements. The AHS Awards and Honors Chair bit the bullet by removing 'Trahlyta' from the official list and granting the award to runner-up 'Mountain Top Experience' (John J. Temple, 1988). Since 1993 Temple's 'Lois Burns' (1986), 'Green Widow' (1980), and 'De Colores' (1992) have also won the coveted award.

Voting for the Harris Olson Spider Award has become an AHS Garden Judge's nightmare. Hard dormant, northern-bred spiders would turn into grass and disappear when grown in the heat of the South. With cooler temperatures, southern-bred spiders would "fatten-up," or grow wider petals. Of the past fourteen winners of the Harris Olson Spider Award at least five are considered by spider experts not to fit the proper definition. Once again the AHS is planning to revamp the rules governing the award.

Adding to the age of spider confusion, two hybridizers from North Carolina, John Lambert and Richard Webster were producing flamboyant daylily forms different from any other daylily on the market. Webster was the first to produce tetraploid oddities that were created with a gene pool he obtained from converted diploid spidery daylilies. Lambert was coming up with diploid flowers whose petals and sepals spooned, twisted, or curled. Both men were nonconformists who hybridized simply for their own enjoyment. Having waiting lists of spider devotees who wanted their latest unusual-looking cultivars was a bonus.

Hybridizers also began to convert some of the lovely true spiders to tetraploids. Those first tetraploid spiders were usually no longer spiders, even though they had the open form and longer-than-wide petals. The new flowers were huge, so they attracted interest from people who had never been interested in spiders. They were also not very fertile, but people persisted in hybridizing with them, eventually producing spiders of greater fertility. Today's tetraploids are much closer to the strict definition of a spider, but the measurements seem much different in the North than in the South. Another difference with the tetraploid spiders was the loss of the graceful movement in the wind—the tetraploid scapes were too thick to allow the dancing that gives spiders some of their beauty.

As more and more "near spiders" began to appear on the official list, rumbling from spider enthusiasts grew louder. The AHS Awards Chair, in an effort to ward off another spider war that seemed to be looming on the horizon, began to look for a way to reward hybridizers for their open form daylilies that did not meet spider or spider variant measurements. A committee headed by exotic form daylily hybridizer Bob Schwarz of New York went to work on defining criteria for unusual form daylilies and clearing names of unusual form cultivars off the official AHS spider and spider variant list. A new AHS award was established—the Lambert/Webster Unusual Forms Award. The Unusual Form Class is based exclusively on flower form. The flower petals and sepals, or both, must have distinctive shape or combination of the following shapes:

- Crispate—floral segments have pinching, twisting, or quilling. 'Asterisk' (John R. Lambert Jr., 1985), 'Fire Arrow' (R. L. Webster, 1985), and 'Karen Burgoyne' (Betty Harwood, 1998) are examples of crispate.
- Cascade—narrow cascading or curling floral segments. 'Orchid Corsage' (Stanley E. Saxton, 1975) and 'North Wind Dancer' (Gary Schaben, 2001) are considered cascade.
- Spatulate—Floral segments that are markedly wider at the end. 'Cerulean Star' (John R. Lambert Jr., 1982) is an example of spatulate form.

No cultivar whose measurement meets the definition of a spider or spider variant, or is on the official AHS Spider and Spider Variant List, or has won the Harris Olson Spider Award is eligible for The Lambert/Webster Unusual Forms Award. To be eligible for this award a cultivar must have been registered with the AHS for a minimum of five years and must be listed in the annually published AHS Guidelines for Daylilies of Unusual Form. The AHS Board of Directors accepted Schwarz's proposal for the Lambert/Webster Unusual Forms Award in the summer of 1999, with the award to be placed on the ballot in 2000. At this time the board has also approved a one-year time period in which hybridizers and their heirs could reclassify their registered cultivars as unusual form, spider, or spider variant.

The confusion and conflict over classifying these daylilies are likely not yet over. The wars over spiders, variants, and unusual formed daylilies will continue as long as plants grow differently in the South than they do in the North, and for as long as people seek to find a place to fit a favorite cultivar so it wins an award. In the eyes of some, the spidery daylily has always been a black widow, and they wish that every spider would become a brown recluse.

CHAPTER 5

A Selection of Daylilies for the Garden

More than 50,000 daylilies are registered, with 1,650 new daylilies introduced into commerce each year. It is impossible to include every daylily, or even every worthy daylily, in this chapter. This selection of daylilies are those that we feel are among the most important daylilies available today. These cultivars were chosen based on our own personal observations in the many gardens that we visit each year, along with continuous discussions with other daylily growers and hybridizers. We have endeavored to select modern daylilies that grow and perform well over a wide climatic range, that have had a significant impact on breeding programs, and that have won American Hemerocallis Society (AHS) awards for superior performance as well as remaining on AHS popularity polls.

Some of these daylilies are too new yet to have worked their way through the awards system. Many will likely win awards in the future and are, therefore, recommended to all who would like to grow cutting-edge, modern hybrids in their gardens to enjoy, hybridize, and share with their friends and neighbors.

White

'Admiral's Braid' (Patrick Stamile, 1993). Semi-evergreen. Scape 21 in. (53.3 cm); flower 5.5 in. (12.7 cm). Midseason. A white and pale pink bicolor with a gold edge above a green throat. Tetraploid. 'Wedding Band' × ('Pink Scintillation' × Seedling). Honorable Mention 1996. Award of Merit 1999.

'Anniversary Gold' (Ted Petit, 1994). Evergreen. Scape 19 in. (48.3 cm); flower 5.5 in. (12.7 cm). Midseason. An ivory-cream-pink self with a gold edge and a green throat. Tetraploid. 'Wedding Band' × 'Ida's Magic'.

'Canadian Snow Angel' (John Peat, 2001). Dormant. Scape 25 in. (63.5 cm); flower 7 in. (17.8 cm). Midseason. A very large cream-white with heavily ruffled, crimped edges of light gold and a yellow eyezone above a dark green throat. Tetraploid. 'Dripping with Gold' × 'Winter in Eden'.

'Company of Swans' (Ted Petit, 1994). Evergreen.

Scape 19 in. (48.3 cm); flower 5.5 in. (12.7 cm). Midseason. A light cream to ivory-white double with a green throat. The consistently double flowers are typically the hose-in-hose form. Tetraploid. 'Mykonos' × 'Champagne Chilling'.

'Company of Swans'. Photo by Ted Petit

'Cortina' (Patrick Stamile, 2001). Evergreen. Scape 23 in. (58.4 cm); flower 6 in. (15.2 cm). Early midseason. A smooth heavy white, glistening with overtones of green and pale yellow, carrying a distinct gold edge with green highlights. Tetraploid. 'Victorian Lace' × 'Key Lime Ice'.

'Cortina'. Photo by Patrick Stamile

'Cute As a Button' (Grace Stamile, 1999). Semi-evergreen. Scape 15 in. (38 cm); flower 1.75 in. (4.4 cm). Early midseason. A very small cream double with a cream throat. Diploid. 'Little Wild Flower' × ('Bubbly' × 'You Angel You').

'Diamonds and Pearls' (Jeff Salter, 1994). Semi-evergreen. Scape 24 in. (61.0 cm); flower 5.5 in. (12.7 cm). Early midseason. A large, wide-petaled, cream self with a heavily ruffled gold edge above a green throat. Tetraploid. Parents unknown. Honorable Mention 2000.

'Diamonds and Pearls'. Photo by Jeff Salter

'Diamonds in the Sky' (John Peat, 2000). Semi-evergreen. Scape 25 in. (63.5 cm); flower 5.5 in. (12.7 cm). Midseason. A heavily diamond-dusted, near pure white with a deep lime-green throat. Tetraploid. 'White Crinoline' × 'Winter in Eden'.

'Dripping with Gold' (Ted Petit, 1998). Semi-evergreen. Scape 25 in. (63.5 cm); flower 5.5 in. (12.7 cm).

Midseason. A large ivory flower with a cream-pink blush, green throat, and heavy gold ruffling. The petals drip with heavy clumps of gold. Tetraploid. ('Wedding Band' × 'Wrapped in Gold') × 'Deanna's Gift'.

'Dripping with Gold'. Photo by Ted Petit

'Glacier Bay' (Patrick Stamile, 1995). Evergreen. Scape 28 in. (71.1 cm); flower 5.5 in. (12.7 cm). Midseason. A large cream-white self with a braided, bright gold edge above an olive-green throat. Tetraploid. 'Arctic Ruffles' × 'Admiral's Braid'. Honorable Mention 1999.

'Glacier Bay'. Photo by Patrick Stamile

'Great White' (Patrick Stamile, 1996). Evergreen. Scape 28 in. (71.1 cm); flower 6.25 in. (15.2 cm). Early midseason. A large, wide, full and flat near white with edges deeply ruffled and surrounded in gold. Tetraploid. 'Glacier Bay' × 'Whisper White'.

'Green Mystique' (Patrick Stamile, 2002). Evergreen. Scape 27 in. (68.6 cm); flower 5.75 in. (12.7 cm). Early midseason. A pastel cream with hints of pink. The heavily ruffled, golden edges glow with a green tint accenting the green throat. Tetraploid. 'Platinum and Gold' × ('Great White' × 'Key Lime Ice').

'Key Lime Ice' (Patrick Stamile, 1998). Evergreen. Scape 21 in. (53.3 cm); flower 6 in. (15.2 cm). Early midseason. A large ivory-cream blend with a heavily braided, gold edge and a grass-green throat. Tetraploid. 'Mal' × 'Great White'.

'Key Lime Ice'. Photo by Patrick Stamile

'Knights in White Satin' (Patrick Stamile, 1998). Semi-evergreen. Scape 32 in. (81.3 cm); flower 6.5 in. (15.2 cm). Midseason. A very large cream-white self with deep, heavy gold ruffling above a green throat. Tetraploid. 'Druid's Chant' × 'Big Blue'. Honorable Mention 2002.

'Mal' (Patrick Stamile, 1998). Evergreen. Scape 30 in. (76.2 cm); flower 7.25 in. (18.4 cm). Midseason. A large cream-white blend with a green throat and a ruffled, wire gold edge. Tetraploid. ('White Zone' × ('White Hot' × Seedling)) × ('Papillon' × Seedling).

'Knights in White Satin'. Photo by Patrick Stamile

'Michael Miller' (Patrick Stamile, 2000). Evergreen. Scape 30 in. (76.2 cm); flower 6 in. (15.2 cm). Early midseason. A large, wide-petaled, white flower with a ruffled and looped gold edge above a contrasting green throat. Tetraploid. 'Great White' × 'Platinum and Gold'.

'Michael Miller'. Photo by Patrick Stamile

'New Direction' (Patrick Stamile, 2000). Evergreen. Scape 26 in. (66.0 cm); flower 6 in. (15.2 cm). Very late.

A large, heavily ruffled white with a deep pie-crust, gold edge above a dark green throat. Tetraploid. 'Big Snow' × 'Nordic Mist'.

'New Direction'. Photo by Patrick Stamile

'Nordic Mist' (Patrick Stamile, 1998). Dormant. Scape 26 in. (66.0 cm); flower 6.5 in. (15.2 cm). Midseason. A cream-white, tightly ruffled flower edged in gold with very wide petals. Tetraploid. 'Glacier Bay' × ('Rhythm and Blues' × 'Seminole Wind').

'Peggy Jeffcoat' (Jan Joiner, 1995). Dormant. Scape 18 in. (45.7 cm); flower 6.5 in. (15.2 cm). Late midseason. A soft cream-white, lightly ruffled, hose-in-hose double with a light green throat. Diploid. 'Jean Swann' × 'Rebecca Marie'. Honorable Mention 1998. Award of Merit 2001. Ida Munson Award 2001.

'Presumed Innocent' (Robert Carr, 1998). Evergreen. Scape 28 in. (71.1 cm); flower 5.5 in. (12.7 cm). Early midseason. An ivory-cream flower with a heavily ruffled gold edge above a green throat. Tetraploid. 'Quality of Mercy' × 'America's Most Wanted'.

'White Crinoline' (Patrick Stamile, 1992). Dormant. Scape 21 in. (53.3 cm); Flower 6 in. (15.2 cm). Early midseason. A wide-petaled, near white, creped self with a green throat. Tetraploid. 'Ptarmigan' × 'Tet. Gentle Shepherd'.

'Winter Palace' (Ted Petit, 1998). Semi-evergreen. Scape 23 in. (58.4 cm); flower 5.5 in. (12.7 cm). Midseason. An ivory-cream flower with a pale pink blush, a green throat, and a heavy gold edge. Tetraploid. 'Untamed Glory' × 'Admiral's Braid'.

'Winter Palace'. Photo by Ted Petit

Yellow

'Bas Relief' (Patrick Stamile, 1999). Evergreen. Scape 26 in. (66.0 cm); flower 7 in. (17.8 cm). Early. A gold to yellow blend with a green throat. The petals have a deep carving in the throat area. Tetraploid. 'Apricot Jade' × ('Olympic Showcase' × 'Betty Warren Woods').

'Bas Relief'. Photo by Patrick Stamile

'Betty Warren Woods' (R. William Munson, 1987). Evergreen. Scape 24 in. (61.0 cm); flower 4.5 in. (11.4 cm). Early midseason. A very ruffled, cream-yellow self with a green throat. Tetraploid. ('Capella Light' × 'India House') × 'Ruffled Dude'. Honorable Mention 1997. Award of Merit 2000.

'Circle of Life' (Ted Petit, 1996). Semi-evergreen. Scape 23 in. (58.4 cm); flower 5 in. (12.7 cm). Midseason. A bright gold, large, round flower with excellent substance, a green throat, and nice ruffles. Tetraploid. 'Betty Warren Woods' × 'Pharaoh's Gold'.

'Deflector Dish' (John Peat, 2001). Semi-evergreen. Scape 24 in. (61.0 cm); flower 5.5 in. (12.7 cm). Midseason. A very round, ruffled, creamy gold flower with a deep green throat and a darker gold edge. Tetraploid. 'Capella Nova' × 'Diamonds in the Sky'.

'Deflector Dish'. Photo by John Peat

'Empire Returns' (Jeff Salter, 2001). Semi-evergreen. Scape 28 in. (71.1 cm); flower 6 in. (15.2 cm). Midseason. A bright golden yellow flower with very deep, three-dimensional sculpting in the throat area and heavy substance. Tetraploid. 'Empire Strikes Back' × 'Childhood Treasure'.

'Ferengi Gold'. Photo by Ted Petit

'Ferengi Gold' (Ted Petit, 1994). Dormant. Scape 19 in. (48.3 cm); flower 5.5 in. (12.7 cm). Early midseason. A flesh-pink-yellow polychrome with a yellow eyezone above a green throat. Very ruffled. A heavy rebloomer. Tetraploid. 'Betty Warren Woods' × ('Emerald Dawn' × 'Betty Warren Woods'). Honorable Mention 1998. Award of Merit 2002.

'Forsyth Navajo' (Wyatt LeFever, 1999). Semi-evergreen. Scape 28 in. (71.1 cm); flower 7.5 in. (19.1 cm). Early midseason. A very large, heavily ruffled ivory self with faint peach overtones above a green throat. Tetraploid. 'Something Wonderful' × 'Tet. Siloam Ralph Henry'.

'Forsyth Navajo'. Photo by Wyatt LeFever

'J. T. Davis' (Larry Grace, 1999). Evergreen. Scape 24 in. (61.0 cm); flower 5 in. (12.7 cm). Midseason. A light yellow-and-pink blush blend with very ruffled gold edges and a green throat. Tetraploid. 'Surprises Inside' × Seedling.

'J. T. Davis'. Photo by Larry Grace

'Joy and Laughter' (David Kirchhoff, 1995). Evergreen. Scape 28 in. (71.1 cm); flower 6 in. (15.2 cm). Early. A ruffled, golden yellow self with a gold to green throat. Tetraploid. 'Kathleen Salter' × 'Bill Norris'. Honorable Mention 2000.

'Lace Cookies' (Matthew Kaskel, 1998). Evergreen. Scape 30 in. (76.2 cm); flower 5 in. (12.7 cm). Early. A cream to yellow, golden melon self with wide, very ruffled petals and a green throat. Tetraploid. Parents unknown. Honorable Mention 2002.

'Larry Grace' (Jeff Salter, 1994). Semi-evergreen. Scape 24 in. (61.0 cm); flower 6 in. (15.2 cm). Early midseason. A wide-petaled, yellow self with a very ruffled, crimped, gold edge above a green throat. Tetraploid.

'Ben Adams' × ('Untamed Glory' × 'Kathleen Salter'). Honorable Mention 2000.

'Lime Peel' (Patrick Stamile, 2002). Evergreen. Scape 38 in. (96.5 cm); flower 9.5 in. (22.9 cm). Midseason. A beautiful, narrow-petaled, waxy, green to yellow blend with a large, extended green throat. Spatulate Unusual Form 3.0:1 Tetraploid. 'His Highness' × 'Tet. Spider Miracle'.

'Power of Silence'. Photo by Ted Petit

'Macho Macho Man'. Photo by Jeff Salter

'Macho Macho Man' (Jeff Salter, 1998). Semi-evergreen. Scape 26 in. (66.0 cm); flower 7 in. (17.8 cm). Early midseason. A wide-petaled, ruffled cream with a gold edge above a green throat. Parents unknown.

'Moonlight Becomes You' (Robert Carr, 1997). Evergreen. Scape 28 in. (71.1 cm); flower 6 in. (15.2 cm). Early midseason. A pale cream-yellow bloom with a ruffled gold edge above a green throat. Tetraploid. Seedling × ('Sherry Lane Carr' × Seedling).

'Power of Silence' (Ted Petit, 2003). Semi-evergreen. Scape 25 in. (63.5 cm); flower 6 in. (15.2 cm). Midseason. Large, heavily ruffled, yellow flowers with very ruffled gold edges. Tetraploid. 'Karl Petersen' × 'Joint Venture'.

'Puccini' (Patrick Stamile, 1999). Evergreen. Scape 30 in. (76.2 cm); flower 7 in. (17.8 cm). Midseason. A cream-yellow blended double with fluted ruffling above a green throat. Tetraploid. 'Clovette Adams' × 'John Kinnebrew'.

'Shelter Cove' (Jeff Corbett, 2002) Evergreen. Scape 30 in. (76.2 cm) scape; flower 5 in. (12.7 cm). Early mid-

'Shelter Cove'. Photo by Jeff Corbett

season. A deeply sculpted, heavily ruffled, wide-petaled, cream-yellow blend with a green throat and a gold edge. Parents unknown.

'Spacecoast Scrambled' (John Kinnebrew, 2000). Semi-evergreen. Scape 20 in. (50.8 cm); flower 6 in. (15.2 cm). Early midseason. A light yellow-cream with a round, flat form and extremely ruffled, fluffy, gold edges.

Tetraploid. 'Something Wonderful' × ('Glory Days' × 'My Darling Clementine').

'Stone Ponies' (Ted Petit, 1995). Semi-evergreen. Scape 24 in. (61.0 cm); flower 4.5 in. (11.4 cm). Midseason. A golden yellow self with the substance of hard plastic above a deep green throat. Tetraploid. 'Betty Warren Woods' × ('Emerald Dawn' × 'Betty Warren Woods').

'Titan It Up Jack' (John Peat, 2002). Semi-evergreen. Scape 25 in. (63.5 cm); flower 6.75 in. (15.2 cm). Midseason. A heavily ruffled, deep golden yellow flower with full substance and a super green heart. Tetraploid. 'Ferengi Gold' × ('Karl Petersen' × 'Joint Venture').

Gold to Orange

'America's Most Wanted' (Robert Carr, 1997). Evergreen. Scape 27 in. (68.6 cm); flower 6 in. (15.2 cm). Early. A large, ruffled, golden cream-yellow to melon self with a green throat. Tetraploid. 'Sherry Lane Carr' × Seedling. Honorable Mention 2000.

'Bernice Pappas' (Ted Petit, 1999). Semi-evergreen. Scape 22 in. (55.9 cm); flower 5.5 in. (12.7 cm). Late midseason. A large, bright golden orange-sherbet with very wide, round petals. The petals are extremely ruffled, with the wide ruffles extending into the green throat. Edges are crunchy, pinched golden orange. Tetraploid. 'Stone Ponies' × 'Joint Venture'.

'Byron' (Patrick Stamile, 2000). Evergreen. Scape 26 in. (66.0 cm); flower 5.25 in. (12.7 cm). Midseason. An orange-mango blended double with an olive green throat. Blooms vary from hose-in-hose doubling to peony style. Tetraploid. 'Clovette Adams' × 'Denali'.

'Caramel Crunch' (Robert Carr, 2000). Evergreen. Scape 30 in. (76.2 cm); flower 5 in. (12.7 cm). Early. A waxy golden flower with a caramel-colored picotee

'Bernice Pappas'. Photo by Ted Petit

above a dark green throat. Tetraploid. 'Moonlight Becomes You' × 'Thunder and Lightning'.

'Chateau De Ville' (Ted Petit, 2001). Semi-evergreen. Scape 20 in. (50.8 cm); flower 6.5 in. (15.2 cm). Midseason. A coral to salmon-peach flower, wonderfully formed and ruffled, carrying a knobby, ruffled gold edge. It has wide sepals and a green throat. Tetraploid. 'Ferengi Gold' × 'Splendid Touch'.

'Chateau De Ville'. Photo by Ted Petit

'Curious George' (John Peat, 2001). Semi-evergreen. Scape 30 in. (76.2 cm); flower 9 in. (22.9 cm). Early midseason. A burnt orange with slightly darker veins and slight gold edging on the petals and sepals. An extremely large flower. Tetraploid. 'Michelin House' × 'Swirling Spider'.

'Curious George'. Photo by John Peat

'Doc Branch' (Lee Pickles, 1998). Semi-evergreen. Scape 28 in. (71.1 cm); flower 5.5 in. (12.7 cm). Early midseason. A wide-petaled cream-apricot blush blend with a small green throat. Tetraploid. 'Something Wonderful' × 'Smuggler's Gold'.

'Drums of Autumn' (Ted Petit, 1999). Semi-evergreen. Scape 26 in. (66.0 cm); flower 6 in. (15.2 cm). Midseason. A large, showy tangerine to orange flower with a green throat and wide, heavily ruffled petals. Tetraploid. 'Betty Warren Woods' × 'Joint Venture'.

'Engraved Invitation' (Robert Carr, 2000). Evergreen. Scape 23 in. (58.4 cm); flower 5.75 in. (12.7 cm). Early midseason. A bright golden yellow with heavy ruffling and a beautifully sculpted throat area. Tetraploid. 'Quality of Mercy' × 'Sherry Lane Carr'.

'Gail Fox' (Ted Petit, 1996). Semi-evergreen. Scape 21 in. (53.3 cm); flower 6.5 in. (15.2 cm). Midseason. A very large tangerine to orange self with a darker orange ruffled edge above a deep green throat. Tetraploid. ('Calais' × ('Jade Lady' × 'Suva')) × (('Ida's Magic' × 'Desert Jewel') × 'Betty Warren Woods').

'Joint Venture' (Ted Petit, 1994). Evergreen. Scape 20 in. (50.8 cm); flower 6.5 in. (15.2 cm). Midseason. A large, bright solid gold, heavily ruffled, full textured flower with a deep green throat. Tetraploid. 'Betty Warren Woods' × 'Glory Days'.

'Las Vegas Gold' (Ted Petit, 1998). Semi-evergreen. Scape 20 in. (50.8 cm); flower 6 in. (15.2 cm). Early. An extremely ruffled orange-gold self with a green throat. Tetraploid. 'Betty Warren Woods' × ('Glory Days' × 'Betty Warren Woods').

'Living on the Edge' (Ted Petit, 1998). Semi-evergreen. Scape 26 in. (66.0 cm); flower 5 in. (12.7 cm). Early midseason. A melon-peach flower with a heavily ruffled and crimped gold edge above a green throat. Tetraploid. 'Ferengi Gold' × 'Admiral's Braid'.

'Magnanimous' (Ted Petit, 2002). Semi-evergreen. Scape 23 in. (58.4 cm); flower 6.5 in. (15.2 cm). Midseason. A huge, orange-melon flower with pink highlights, very wide sepals, and heavy, looping, ruffled edges above a green throat. Tetraploid. 'Gail Fox' × 'Seminole Wind'.

'Magnanimous'. Photo by Ted Petit

'New Ways to Dream' (Ted Petit, 2000). Semi-evergreen. Scape 24 in. (61.0 cm); flower 5.5 in. (12.7 cm). Midseason. A bright, clear orange with an intense crunchy orange edge and green throat. The heavily ruffled, crimped edges extend into the green throat. Tetraploid. 'Storyville Child' × 'America's Most Wanted'.

'New Ways to Dream'. Photo by Ted Petit

'October Thirty First' (Ted Petit, 1999). Semi-evergreen. Scape 21 in. (53.3 cm); flower 6.25 in. (15.2 cm). Midseason. A large, unusually colored mahogany self with ruffled edges and a black eyezone above a green throat. Tetraploid. 'Quote the Raven' × 'Ruffled Lemon Lace'.

'On Looks Alone' (Robert Carr, 2000). Semi-evergreen. Scape 25 in. (63.5 cm); flower 6 in. (15.2 cm). Midseason. A large, wide-petaled, glowing orange-coral flower with a heavily ruffled, wire gold edge. Tetraploid. Seedling × 'Ida's Magic'.

'Rags to Riches' (Robert Carr, 1997). Evergreen. Scape 28 in. (71.1 cm); flower 5.5 in. (12.7 cm). Midseason. An orange to bronze blended bitone with very heavy ruffling and a wire gold edge above an olive-green throat. Tetraploid. 'Victorian Collar' × ('Sherry Lane Carr' × Seedling). Honorable Mention 2001.

'Senegal' (Matthew Kaskel, 1994). Evergreen. Scape 24 in. (61.0 cm); flower 5.5 in. (12.7 cm). Early midseason. A wide-petaled, ruffled, pastel bronze blend with a yellow to green throat. An important breeder for doubles. Tetraploid. (('Island Empress' × 'Lemonade Supreme') × 'Ming Porcelain') × (('Most Noble' × Seedling) × 'Ever So Ruffled'). Honorable Mention 2000.

'Separate Reality' (Ted Petit, 2002). Semi-evergreen. Scape 25 in. (63.5 cm); flower 5.5 in. (12.7 cm). Midseason. A consistently double, typically hose-in-hose, peach-pink flower with a golden orange, lightly ruffled edge. Tetraploid. 'Outer Fringes' × 'John Kinnebrew'.

'Separate Reality'. Photo by Ted Petit

'Spacecoast Gold Bonanza' (John Kinnebrew, 2002). Semi-evergreen. Scape 24 in. (61.0 cm); flower 6.75 in. (15.2 cm). Early midseason. A golden, round, flat flower with wide petals and sepals. It has a terrific ruffled, golden edge and very heavy substance. Tetraploid. 'Spacecoast Krinkle' × 'Sherry Lane Carr'.

'Variegated Jackpot' (W. Stackman and Eric Denham, 2001). Dormant. Scape 20 in. (50.8 cm); flower 4 in. (10.2 cm). Midseason. A melon flower with a gold throat. The foliage is consistently variegated with green and white stripes. Tetraploid. Seedling × Seedling.

Pink to Rose

'Age of Elegance' (Jeff Salter, 2000). Semi-evergreen. Scape 29 in. (73.7 cm); flower 6 in. (15.2 cm). Midseason. A lavender-rose blend with a yellow to green throat and ruffled edges of gold. Tetraploid. 'David Kirchhoff' × Seedling.

'Age of Elegance'. Photo by Jeff Salter

'All About Eve' (David Kirchhoff, 2000). Evergreen. Scape 26 in. (66.0 cm); flower 5 in. (12.7 cm). Early

midseason. A peach-pink double with a rose halo watermark and tightly crimped ruffles. Tetraploid. Seedling × 'Tet. Siloam Double Classic'.

'All About Eve'. Photo by David Kirchhoff

'Belle Cook' (Mal Brooker, 2001). Semi-evergreen. Scape 24 in. (61.0 cm); flower 6 in. (15.2 cm). Midseason. A clear baby-ribbon-pink, round, heavily ruffled, gold-edged flower with a soft green throat. Tetraploid. 'Ed Brown' × 'Seminole Wind'.

'Beyond Words' (Ted Petit, 1996). Semi-evergreen. Scape 23 in. (58.4 cm); flower 5.5 in. (12.7 cm). Midseason. A very heavily ruffled, soft pink self with a green throat and wide, ornate gold edges. Tetraploid. 'Doma Knaresborough' × 'Serenity in Lace'.

'Bill Munson' (Ted Petit, 1998). Semi-evergreen. Scape 27 in. (68.6 cm); flower 5 in. (12.7 cm). Midseason. A clear

pink with a heavy, ruffled, gold edge and a green throat. Heavy substance and texture. Tetraploid. 'Cherry Chapeau' × (('Betty Warren Woods' × 'Emerald Dawn') × Seedling).

'Bill Munson'. Photo by Ted Petit

'Bittersweet Symphony' (Ted Petit, 2001). Semi-evergreen. Scape 20 in. (50.8 cm); flower 6.5 in. (15.2 cm). Midseason. A peach to coral-pink with darker pink to lavender highlights, carrying ruffled gold edges. Tetraploid. 'Kings and Vagabonds' × 'Splendid Touch'.

'Bittersweet Symphony'. Photo by Ted Petit

'Bringer of Peace' (Ted Petit, 2002). Semi-evergreen. Scape 26 in. (66.0 cm); flower 6 in. (15.2 cm). Midseason. Clear, light ice-pink petals accented by a green throat and a wire gold edge. Tetraploid. 'Douglas Lycett Memorial' × 'Splendid Touch'.

'Candlelight and Wine' (Ted Petit, 2001). Semi-evergreen. Scape 19 in. (48.3 cm); flower 6 in. (15.2 cm). Midseason. A rose to rose-red flower surrounded by a ruffled gold edge above a large green throat. Tetraploid. ('Betty Warren Woods' × 'Shinto Etching') × ('Ida's Magic' × 'Effay Veronica').

'Carved in Stone' (Ted Petit, 2001). Semi-evergreen. Scape 20 in. (50.8 cm); flower 5.5 in. (12.7 cm). Midseason. A beautiful orchid to salmon-pink flower with

heavily ruffled gold edges. The flowers have a deep carving in the eyezone area. Tetraploid. 'Kings and Vagabonds' × 'Romeo Is Bleeding'.

'Carved in Stone'. Photo by Ted Petit

'Castle Camelot' (Steve Moldovan, 1983). Semi-evergreen. Scape 24 in. (61.0 cm); flower 3.5 in. (8.9 cm). Early. An orchid-pink, blended flower with ruffled petals and an ivory-green throat. Tetraploid. (Seedling × 'Royal Watermark') × ('Astarte' × ('Kwan Yin' × 'Catherine Woodbery')).

'Celtic Magic' (Elizabeth Anne Salter, 2002). Semi-evergreen. Scape 25 in. (63.5 cm); flower 4.25 in. (10.8 cm). Midseason. A bright, cerise-rose-pink with a bold yellow, bubbly gold edge above a yellow to green pleated throat. Tetraploid. Parents unknown.

'Celtic Magic'. Photo by Elizabeth Anne Salter

'Clean Slate' (Matthew Kaskel, 2002). Evergreen. Scape 24 in. (61.0 cm); flower 6.5 in. (15.2 cm). Midseason. A large, pale lilac to pink self with a very ruffled gold edge. Tetraploid. Seedling × 'Ida's Braid'.

'Connie Burton' (Tom Wilson, 1999). Evergreen. Scape 24 in. (61.0 cm); flower 5.5 in. (12.7 cm). Early midseason. A very wide-petaled, coral-pink blend with a pink eyezone above a green throat. Diploid. Parents unknown. Honorable Mention 2002.

'Coral and Gold'. Photo by Ted Petit

'Darla Anita' (John Kinnebrew, 1999). Evergreen. Scape 30 in. (76.2 cm) scape; flower 7 in. (17.8 cm). Early midseason. A lavender-pink blend with very heavy, ruffled gold edges and a green throat. One of the most ornately edged daylilies. Tetraploid. 'Ida's Magic' × 'Spacecoast Starburst'.

'Denali' (Patrick Stamile, 1997). Evergreen. Scape 23 in. (58.4 cm); flower 8 in. (20.3 cm). Late midseason. A very large pink blend with consistently double flowers and a green throat. Tetraploid. 'Victoria's Secret' × 'Big Blue'. Honorable Mention 2000.

'Connie Burton'. Photo by Tom Wilson

'Coral and Gold' (Ted Petit, 2000). Semi-evergreen. Scape 25 in. (63.5 cm); flower 5.5 in. (12.7 cm). Midseason. A large coral to peach or salmon flower surrounded by a heavy, wide, and ruffled gold edge. Tetraploid. 'Light Years Away' × 'Just Infatuation'.

'Dancing Shiva' (Steve Moldovan, 1974). Dormant. Scape 22 in. (55.9 cm); flower 5 in. (12.7 cm). Early. A wide-petaled, medium-pink blend with a yellow to green throat. Tetraploid. Parents unknown. Honorable Mention 1976. Award of Merit 1979.

'Denali'. Photo by Patrick Stamile

'Dreams of Heroes' (Ted Petit, 2001). Semi-evergreen. Scape 24 in. (61.0 cm); flower 7.5 in. (19.1 cm). Midseason. An extremely large, clear rose-pink with ruffled, ornate gold edges, a large watermark, and a green throat. Tetraploid. 'Juliette Matthies' × 'Seminole Wind'.

'Ed Brown' (Jeff Salter, 1994). Semi-evergreen. Scape 28 in. (71.1 cm); flower 5.5 in. (12.7 cm). Early midseason. A baby-ribbon-pink self with a ruffled gold edge above a green throat. Heavily used as a pink parent among current hybridizers. Tetraploid. 'Something Wonderful' × 'Elizabeth's Dream'. Honorable Mention 2000.

'Enchanting Esmerelda' (Jeff Salter, 2000). Semi-evergreen. Scape 26 in. (66.0 cm); flower 5.5 in. (12.7 cm). Early midseason. A bright, intense, rose flower with a

'Enchanting Esmerelda'. Photo by Jeff Salter

lighter watermark above a deep green throat. The lighter pink petal edges are lightly ruffled and surrounded by a wire gold edge. Tetraploid. 'William Austin Norris' × 'Timeless Romance'.

'Formal Appearance' (Ted Petit, 2000). Semi-evergreen. Scape 25 in. (63.5 cm); flower 5.5 in. (12.7 cm). Midseason. A clear, medium pink double with a green throat. The flower is typically a very formal hose-in-hose. Tetraploid. 'Memories of Paris' × ('Wayne Johnson' × ('Betty Warren Woods' × F2)).

'Gladys Campbell' (Ted Petit, 1994). Evergreen. Scape 19 in. (48.3 cm); flower 5.5 in. (12.7 cm). Midseason. A hot coral to peach-pink double with a lighter watermark. Very large and striking. Tetraploid. ('French Pavilion' × 'Canton Harbor') × 'Shishedo'. Honorable Mention 2000.

'Golden Mansions' (Ted Petit, 2001). Semi-evergreen. Scape 20 in. (50.8 cm); flower 6 in. (15.2 cm). Midseason. These consistently double flowers are a soft pink with a green throat and wide, softly creped, ruffled petals. Both the petals and petaloids are surrounded by heavy gold edging. Tetraploid. ('Memories of Paris' × 'Seychelle Sands') × ('Victoria's Secret' × 'Ambrosian Rhapsody').

'How Beautiful Heaven Must Be'. Photo by Jack Carpenter

'How Beautiful Heaven Must Be' (Jack Carpenter, 2002). Evergreen. Scape 26 in. (66.0 cm); flower 5.75 in. (12.7 cm). Early midseason. A very wide-petaled peach-pink with extremely ornate, heavy gold ruffling that extends deep into the throat. Tetraploid. 'Ed Brown' × 'Larry Grace'.

'Inherited Wealth' (Robert Carr, 1998). Evergreen. Scape 28 in. (71.1 cm); flower 5 in. (12.7 cm). Early. A pink blend with a heavy, ruffled gold edge and an olive-green throat. Tetraploid. 'Victorian Collar' × 'America's Most Wanted'. Honorable Mention 2001.

'It's a Girl' (John Peat, 1999). Semi-evergreen. Scape 19 in. (48.3 cm); flower 6 in. (15.2 cm). Midseason. A bright rose-pink bitone with a darker rose-pink eyezone above a green throat. Tetraploid. 'Lorikeet Springs' × 'Sultry Smile'.

'Janet Benz' (John Benz, 2000). Dormant. Scape 28 in. (71.1 cm); flower 5.5 in. (12.7 cm). Midseason. A strawberry-rose flower eyed in a darker rose with a green throat and serrated gold edge. Tetraploid. 'Radar Love' × 'Tet. Barbara Mitchell'.

'Jerry Pate Williams' (David Kirchhoff, 1999). Semi-evergreen. Scape 27 in. (68.6 cm); flower 4.75 in. (12.1 cm). Early. An intense peach double with a pink-melon overlay and a faint rose-rouge watermark above an apricot throat. Tetraploid. 'Most Happy Fellow' × (('Layers of Gold' × 'Cool Jazz') × ('Cool Jazz' × Seedling)).

'Just Infatuation' (Ted Petit, 1996). Semi-evergreen. Scape 22 in. (55.9 cm); flower 5.5 in. (12.7 cm). Midseason. A clear rose-pink with a lighter watermark and ruffled, gold-edged petals pleating into the green throat. Tetraploid. Seedling × 'Wrapped in Gold'.

'Forsyth Comanche' (Wyatt LeFever, 1998). Dormant. Scape 30 in. (76.2 cm); flower 6 in. (15.2 cm). Midseason. A flesh-pink polychrome with a gold edge and a green throat. Tetraploid. 'Something Wonderful' × 'Tet. Siloam Ralph Henry'.

'Karl Petersen' (Ted Petit, 1995). Semi-evergreen. Scape 24 in. (61.0 cm); flower 5.5 in. (12.7 cm). Midseason. An ivory to pale cream-pink, very wide petaled with a green throat and a thick, puffy substance. Tetraploid. 'Ida's Magic' × 'Wedding Band'.

'Laurel Stevenson' (Ted Petit, 1996). Semi-evergreen. Scape 21 in. (53.3 cm); flower 6.5 in. (15.2 cm). Midseason. A very large, round, voluptuous medium pink with very wide petals above a green throat. Tetraploid. ('French Pavilion' × 'Canton Harbor') × 'Shishedo'.

'Life Saver' (John Peat, 2001). Semi-evergreen. Scape 24 in. (61.0 cm); flower 7 in. (17.8 cm). Midseason. A light sherbet-cream flower with a peach blush, complemented by a heavily ruffled, gold edge accented with a light rose-pink picotee. Tetraploid. 'Gail Fox' × 'Marilyn Siwik'.

'Little by Little' (Grace Stamile, 1998). Semi-evergreen. Scape 16 in. (40.6 cm) scape; flower 2 in. (5.1 cm). Midseason. A tiny double of a coral-pink blend above a green throat. Diploid. 'Bubbly' × 'You Angel You'.

'Little by Little'. Photo by Patrick Stamile

'Linda Agin' (Tom Wilson, 1998). Evergreen. Scape 24 in. (61.0 cm); flower 6.25 in. (15.8 cm). Early midseason. A nicely ruffled cream-blushed-pink self with a lime-green throat. Diploid. Parents unknown.

'Lori Goldston' (John Kinnebrew, 1999). Evergreen. Scape 25 in. (63.5 cm); flower 6.5 in. (15.2 cm). Early midseason. A large rose-coral flower with heavily ruffled gold edges and a yellow throat. Tetraploid. 'Untamed Glory' × Seedling. Honorable Mention 2002.

'Lorikeet Springs' (John Peat, 1998). Semi-evergreen. Scape 30 in. (76.2 cm); flower 6.5 in. (15.2 cm). Midseason. A deep rose self with a lighter pink to white hairline-edge above a green throat. Tetraploid. 'Serenity in Lace' × 'Betty Warren Woods'.

'Lorikeet Springs'. Photo by John Peat

'Nano Probe' (Grace Stamile, 2002). Semi-evergreen. Scape 18 in. (45.7 cm); flower 2.5 in. (6.4 cm). Early midseason. A very small, smoky rose-mauve, carnation double displaying characteristics of both the peony and hose-in-hose styles. Diploid. ('Little Wild Flower' × 'Roswitha') × ((('Bubbly' × 'You Angel You') × 'You Angel You') × 'Cute As Can Be').

'Ne Quitte Pas' (Ted Petit, 2001). Semi-evergreen. Scape 23 in. (58.4 cm); flower 5.5 in. (12.7 cm). Midseason. A

delicate shell-pink with wonderfully formed, wide petals surrounded in ruffled, gold edges above a green throat. Tetraploid. 'Elusive Dream' × 'Ed Brown'.

'Ne Quitte Pas'. Photo by Ted Petit

'Pacific Princess' (Ted Petit, 2000). Semi-evergreen. Scape 24 in. (61.0 cm); flower 6 in. (15.2 cm). Midseason. A clear rose-pink with a large, lighter watermark. The flowers are very nicely ruffled, with fine, crimped, gold edges. Tetraploid. 'Ferengi Gold' × 'Seminole Wind'.

'Piglet and Roo' (John Peat, 1998). Semi-evergreen. Scape 18 in. (45.7 cm); flower 3 in. (7.6 cm). Midsea-

son. A small, clear baby-ribbon-pink, popcorn double with a green throat. Tetraploid. 'Memories of Paris' × (('Wayne Johnson' × 'Renaissance Queen') × 'Merlot Rouge').

'Piglet and Roo'. Photo by John Peat

'Spacecoast Cotton Candy' (John Kinnebrew, 2001). Semi-evergreen. Scape 25 in. (63.5 cm); flower 5.25 in. (12.7 cm). Early. Large, heavy, looping ruffles completely surround these peach-pink blossoms, continuing down into the green throat. Tetraploid. 'Spacecoast Sweetness' × 'Desert Dreams'.

'Spacecoast Extreme Fashion' (John Kinnebrew, 2000). Semi-evergreen. Scape 21 in. (53.3 cm); flower 5.5 in. (12.7 cm). Early. A peach-pink and melon blend with a tremendous round flower form and perfect pie-crust, gold ruffling. Tetraploid. 'Spacecoast Sweetness' × 'Spacecoast Starburst'.

'Spacecoast Starburst' (John Kinnebrew, 1998). Evergreen. Scape 25 in. (63.5 cm); flower 6 in. (15.2 cm). Early midseason. A pink-lavender blend with a yellow halo and a very heavily ruffled, gold edge above a yellow throat. Tetraploid. 'Secret Splendor' × Seedling. Honorable Mention 2002.

'Special Agenda' (Robert Carr, 2001). Evergreen. Scape 26 in. (66.0 cm); flower 5.5 in. (12.7 cm). Early. A deep fuchsia-pink with a watermark and looping ruffles edged in yellow-gold. Tetraploid. 'Ida's Magic' × Seedling.

'Susan Pritchard Petit' (Ted Petit, 2001). Semi-evergreen. Scape 20 in. (50.8 cm); flower 6 in. (15.2 cm). Midseason. A large, rich burgundy to rose-pink double with heavy substance. The petals and petaloids carry a pronounced gold edge. Tetraploid. ('Ambrosian Rhapsody' × 'Victoria's Secret') × 'John Kinnebrew'.

'Touched by Magic' (Jeff Salter, 2000). Semi-evergreen. Scape 26 in. (66.0 cm); flower 5 in. (12.7 cm). Midseason. A coral-peach and rose blend with a heavy, gold edge and round, flat form. Tetraploid. 'Ida's Magic' × 'Wisest of Wizards'.

'Twisted Sister' (Bob Schwarz, 1999). Dormant. Scape 30 in. (76.2 cm); flower 8 in. (20.3 cm). Early. A pale rose, narrow-petaled flower with a huge green throat and sepals that not only spoon but twist and curl. Tetraploid. ('Mariska' × 'Heavenly Crown') × 'Tuxedo Junction'.

'Vanilla Sky' (Ted Petit, 2002). Semi-evergreen. Scape 23 in. (58.4 cm); flower 6 in. (15.2 cm). Midseason. A soft pink with darker pink and gold highlights and tightly crimped, gold edges on consistently double blossoms. Tetraploid. 'Golden Mansions' × 'Senegal'.

'Victorian Lace' (Patrick Stamile, 1999). Evergreen. Scape 30 in. (76.2 cm); flower 6.75 in. (15.2 cm). Early midseason. A porcelain ice-pink with a gold, braided edge and a green throat. Tetraploid. ('White Zone' × 'Alpine Snow') × 'Nordic Mist'.

'Susan Pritchard Petit'. Photo by Ted Petit

'Victorian Lace'. Photo by Patrick Stamile

'Victorian Poet' (Jeff Salter, 2002). Semi-evergreen. Scape 28 in. (71.1 cm); flower 5.5 in. (12.7 cm). Mid-season. A pale ivory-lilac-pink flower with a lighter halo, blending to ivory, yellow, and pink, surrounding a small green throat. Tetraploid. Parents unknown.

'Virginia Little Henson' (David Kirchhoff, 2002). Evergreen. Scape 26 in. (66.0 cm); flower 5 in. (12.7 cm). Early. A peach, coral, and rose with gold edges that show tentacles, hooks, knobs, and teeth. Tetraploid. 'Seminole Magic' × 'Sunset Boulevard'.

'Way Cool' (Ludlow Lambertson, 1998). Evergreen. Scape 32 in. (81.3 cm); flower 6.5 in. (15.2 cm). Mid-season. A light pink flower with a ruffled, gold edge above a green throat. Tetraploid. Seedling × (Seedling × 'Secret Splendor').

'Wonder of Innocence' (Ted Petit, 2000). Semi-evergreen. Scape 24 in. (61.0 cm); flower 5 in. (12.7 cm). Midseason. A soft, pastel pink with diamond dusting and a lighter watermark above green throat. The wide petals are nicely ruffled with a crimped, gold edge. Tetraploid. ('Karl Petersen' × ('Wedding Band' × 'Ida's Magic')) × 'Just Infatuation'.

Red

'Altered State' (Robert Carr, 1997). Evergreen. Scape 28 in. (71.1 cm); flower 5.5 in. (12.7 cm). Early midseason. A patterned cherry-red with a darker cherry-red eye, a pink-red edge, and a yellow to green throat. Tetraploid. 'Whooperee' × 'Purely Exotic'.

'Amber Storm' (Ted Petit, 1996). Semi-evergreen. Scape 22 in. (55.9 cm); flower 5.5 in. (12.7 cm). Midseason. A rose to orange-red blended double with lighter edges above a green throat. Tetraploid. ('Highland Lord' × 'Ida's Magic') × 'Fires of Fuji'.

'Amber Storm'. Photo by Ted Petit

'Awesome Bob' (Lee Pickles, 2001). Dormant. Scape 28 in. (71.1 cm); flower 5.25 in. (12.7 cm). Midseason. A cranberry-red bloom with a heavily ruffled, gold edge above a yellow-green throat. Tetraploid. 'Ida's Magic' × 'Velvet Beads'.

'Betty Ford' (David Kirchhoff, 2002). Semi-evergreen. Scape 30 in. (76.2 cm); flower 5.5 in. (12.7 cm). Extra early. A shimmering garnet to cardinal-red with a lighter watermark above a green throat. Tetraploid. ('Leonard Bernstein' × 'Crimson Wind') × ('Torrid Tango' × 'Forever Red').

'Bimini Twist' (Bob Schwarz, 1998). Dormant. Scape 28 in. (71.1 cm); flower 4 in. (10.2 cm). Late midseason. An intense red, narrow-petaled flower with an apple-green throat and sepals that bend and twist. Tetraploid. 'Cameroons' × 'Rainbow Warrior'.

'Bloodfire' (Ted Petit, 1999). Semi-evergreen. Scape 23 in. (58.4 cm); flower 5.5 in. (12.7 cm). Midseason. A wide-petaled, deep, rich, velvety blood-red with a lighter watermark above a green center. Tetraploid. 'Ten to Midnight' × Seedling.

'Carnival in Brazil' (Ted Petit, 2002). Semi-evergreen. Scape 25 in. (63.5 cm); flower 5 in. (12.7 cm). Midseason. A dark red that softens to a bronze to tomato-red as the season progresses. Nicely ruffled with a large watermark above a green throat. Tetraploid. 'Drowning in Desire' × ('Chinese Chariot' × 'Bloodfire').

'Christmas Tidings' (Patrick Stamile, 1999). Evergreen. Scape 30 in. (76.2 cm); flower 8.5 in. (21.6 cm). Early. A large red, narrow-petaled flower with a deep red eyezone above a green throat. Tetraploid. ('Swirling Spider' × 'Ruby Spider') × 'Long Stocking'.

'Cleopatra's Jewel' (Ted Petit, 2000). Semi-evergreen. Scape 30 in. (76.2 cm); flower 5.5 in. (12.7 cm). Early midseason. A bright, fire-engine-red flower with ruffled, gold, bubbly edges and a green throat. Tetraploid. ('Restless Warrior' × 'Drowning in Desire') × 'Romeo Is Bleeding'.

'Crocodile Smile' (Dan Trimmer, 1996). Semi-evergreen. Scape 36 in. (91.4 cm); flower 8 in. (20.3 cm). Early midseason. A narrow-petaled, mulberry and ivory bicolor with a yellow-green throat. The petal edges carry a toothy, ornate filigree. Tetraploid. 'Anastasia' × 'Tet. Spindazzle'.

'Crocodile Smile'. Photo by Dan Trimmer

'Drowning in Desire' (Ted Petit, 1996). Semi-evergreen. Scape 22 in. (55.9 cm); flower 5.5 in. (12.7 cm). Midseason. A rich fire-engine to blood-red with a lighter watermark, green throat, and a crimped, gold edge. Tetraploid. ('Midnight Magic' × 'Court Magician') × 'Ida's Magic'.

'Drowning in Desire'. Photo by Ted Petit

'Eclipse of the Heart' (Ted Petit, 2001). Evergreen. Scape 25 in. (63.5 cm); flower 5.5 in. (12.7 cm). Midseason. A black-red with a rose-red watermark above a green throat. The petals are nicely ruffled with a wire gold edge. Tetraploid. 'Study in Scarlet' × 'Ida's Magic'.

'Executive Decision' (Ted Petit, 2002). Semi-evergreen. Scape 23 in. (58.4 cm); flower 6 in. (15.2 cm). Midseason. A very bright fire-engine-red with a wire gold edge. The center of the flower has a small, lighter watermark surrounding a green heart. Tetraploid. ('Richard Taylor' × 'Jack of Hearts') × 'Drowning in Desire'.

'Fire Down Below' (Ted Petit, 2002). Dormant. Scape 27 in. (68.6 cm); flower 6 in. (15.2 cm). Midseason. A very large, deep, velvety blood-red with extremely wide petals. The petals have a heavy substance with beautiful ruffling. Tetraploid. 'Richard Taylor' × 'Jack of Hearts'.

'Frank Morrell' (Ted Petit, 2000). Semi-evergreen. Scape 26 in. (66.0 cm); flower 6 in. (15.2 cm). Midsea-

'Fire Down Below'. Photo by Ted Petit

son. A complex blend of bright coral-red and hints of lavender with wide, round, nicely ruffled petals carrying a slight wire gold edge. Tetraploid. ('Richard Taylor' × 'Wrapped in Gold') × ('Romeo Is Bleeding' × ('Midnight Magic' × 'Ida's Magic')).

'Happy Apache' (Dan Hansen, 2000). Semi-evergreen. Scape 24 in. (61.0 cm); flower 6.25 in. (15.2 cm). Early. Red with a wide, lighter rust-orange edge above a green throat. Tetraploid. 'Roses in Snow' × ('Calgary Stampede' × 'Untamed Glory').

'Heavenly Beginnings' (Jamie Gossard, 2001). Dormant. Scape 40 in. (101.6 cm); flower 8 in. (20.3 cm). Late midseason. A red and yellow blended, narrow-petaled bloom with huge bubbly, knobby, and toothy edges above a deep green throat. Tetraploid. 'Startle' × 'Tet. Spindazzle'.

'Helix' (Patrick Stamile, 2002). Evergreen. Scape 33 in. (83.8 cm); flower 9 in. (22.9 cm). Extra early. A Bordeaux-wine and deep beet color with a deep celery-green throat and sepals that twist and curl. Tetraploid. 'Inky Fingers' × 'Web Browser'.

'Helix'. Photo by Patrick Stamile

'Jack of Hearts' (Ted Petit, 2000). Semi-evergreen. Scape 22 in. (55.9 cm); flower 5.5 in. (12.7 cm). Midseason. An

intense, saturated, velvet-red with a lighter watermark. The petal edges are very ruffled and looped, carrying a crimped platinum to gold edge. Tetraploid. 'Restless Warrior' × 'Drowning in Desire'.

'Jack of Hearts'. Photo by Ted Petit

'Jerry Nettles' (John Kinnebrew, 2002). Evergreen. Scape 28 in. (71.1 cm); flower 6 in. (15.2 cm). Early midseason. A lavender-rose to burgundy-purple, full, flat, and trimmed with heavily ruffled, yellow-gold edges. Tetraploid. 'Spacecoast Starburst' × 'Ed Brown'.

'Jerry Nettles'. Photo by John Kinnebrew

'Lady Betty Fretz' (Ted Petit, 2002). Semi-evergreen. Scape 26 in (66.0 cm); flower 6 in. (66.0 cm). Midseason. A cream flower with a large red eyezone and picotee surrounded by a heavy gold edge. Tetraploid. 'Only Believe' × 'Mardi Gras Ball'.

'Lady Betty Fretz'. Photo by Ted Petit

'Lady of Madrid' (Ted Petit, 1998). Semi-evergreen. Scape 20 in. (50.8 cm); flower 5.5 in. (12.7 cm). Extra early. A very early blooming, extremely ruffled, red self with a green throat and very heavily branched scapes. Tetraploid. ('Lindan Toole' × ('Betty Warren Woods' × 'Elizabeth Salter')) × 'Kings and Vagabonds'.

'Laughing Giraffe' (Bob Schwarz, 1997). Dormant. Scape 36 in. (91.4 cm); flower 8 in. (20.3 cm). Midseason. A narrow-petaled, red and gold bicolor with shark's teeth surrounding the petal edges. Tetraploid. Seedling × 'Tet. Spindazzle'.

'Leader of the Pack' (John Peat, 1999). Semi-evergreen. Scape 23 in. (58.4 cm); flower 5 in. (12.7 cm). Midseason. A nine-petaled, rose-red, hose-in-hose double with a dark rose-red eyezone above a green throat. Tetraploid. 'Merlot Rouge' × ('Wayne Johnson' × 'Renaissance Queen').

'Millennium Madness' (John Benz, 2001). Dormant. Scape 24 in. (61 cm); flower 4.5 in. (11.4 cm). Midseason. A burgundy-red with a washed yellow watermark and a glistening gold, braided edge above a large green throat. Tetraploid. 'Startle' × 'Angel's Smile'.

'Outrageous Fortune' (Patrick Stamile, 2001). Evergreen. Scape 32 in. (81.3 cm); flower 6 in. (15.2 cm).

Midseason. A rose to burgundy-red, very double flower with a knobby, toothy, gold edge. Tetraploid. 'Dark Wonder' × (('Clovette Adams' × 'Lightning Strike') × 'Puccini').

'Outrageous Fortune'. Photo by Patrick Stamile

'Painting the Roses Red' (Jeff Salter, 2002). Semi-evergreen. Scape 26 in. (66.0 cm); flower 6 in. (15.2 cm). Midseason. A deep, bright cerise-rose bloom with a gold edge that has large ruffles and tiny teeth. Tetraploid. 'Ed Brown' × 'Enchanting Esmerelda'.

'Painting the Roses Red'. Photo by Jeff Salter

'Passion District' (Robert Carr, 1997). Evergreen. Scape 28 in. (71.1 cm); flower 5.75 in. (12.7 cm). Midseason. A deep ruby-red with ruffles surrounded by a wire white edge with both an eye and a watermark above a green throat. Tetraploid. 'Midnight Magic' × 'Betty Warren Woods'. Honorable Mention 2001.

'Passion in Paris' (Ted Petit, 2002). Semi-evergreen. Scape 24 in. (61.0 cm); flower 5.5 in. (12.7 cm). Early

midseason. A rich, velvety, dark red flower with very wide petals edged in wire gold, a lighter watermark, and a green throat. Tetraploid. 'Bloodfire' × 'Drowning in Desire'.

'Passion in Paris'. Photo by Ted Petit

'Potion for Passion' (Robert Carr, 1998). Evergreen. Scape 29 in. (73.7 cm); flower 5 in. (12.7 cm). Midseason. A rich crimson-red flower with heavy ruffles trimmed in a white picotee. Tetraploid. 'Betty Warren Woods' × ('Ida's Magic' × ('Harrod's' × 'Study in Scarlet')).

'Pure Indulgence' (Robert Carr, 2000). Evergreen. Scape 30 in. (76.2 cm); flower 5.5 in. (12.7 cm). Early. A rich, deep, dark red with a contrasting white picotee on its superbly ruffled edges. Tetraploid. ('Ida's Magic' × ('Harrod's' × 'Study in Scarlet')) × ('Ida's Magic' × 'Midnight Magic').

'Reason for Treason' (David Kirchhoff, 1996). Evergreen. Scape 32 in. (81.3 cm); flower 7 in. (17.8 cm). Midseason. A dark orange-red with a gold edge and a lighter watermark halo above a yellow to green throat. Tetraploid. ('White Tie Affair' × 'Enchanted Empress') × 'Perfect Pleasure'.

'Reason for Treason'. Photo by David Kirchhoff

'Red Peacemaker' (Robert Carr, 1997). Dormant. Scape 28 in. (71.1 cm); flower 4.5 in. (11.4 cm). Midseason. A velvety, dark garnet-red with looping ruffles and a distinctive white picotee edge trimmed in gold. Tetraploid. 'Midnight Magic' × 'Angel's Smile'.

'Roses in Snow' (Dan Hansen, 1999). Semi-evergreen. Scape 24 in. (61.0 cm); flower 5.25 in. (12.7 cm). Early midseason. An orange-red with wide, ivory edges above an emerald-green throat. Tetraploid. 'Calgary Stampede' × 'Untamed Glory'.

'Royal Renaissance' (Jeff Salter, 2002). Semi-evergreen. Scape 28 in. (71.1 cm); flower 5.5 in. (12.7 cm). Midseason. A large garnet-rose-red with wide, ruffled petals surrounded by a heavy, white edge. Tetraploid. Parents unknown.

'Royal Renaissance'. Photo by Jeff Salter

'Sapphire Skies' (Ted Petit, 1996). Semi-evergreen. Scape 23 in. (58.4 cm); flower 6 in. (15.2 cm). Midseason. A heavily ruffled, very bright, saturated red, an almost electric lipstick-red color. Tetraploid. ('Richard Taylor' × 'Carolyn Hendrix ') × (('Richard Taylor' × 'Dance Ballerina Dance') × 'Wrapped in Gold').

'Second Millennium' (Ted Petit, 1999). Semi-evergreen. Scape 23 in. (58.4 cm); flower 6.5 in. (15.2 cm). Midseason. A large, striking, bright red double with a very large, lighter watermark and a green throat. Tetraploid. 'Grecian Sands' × (('Royal Saracen' × 'Highland Lord') × 'Impetuous Fire').

'Shirley Valentine' (Ted Petit, 2000). Semi-evergreen. Scape 24 in. (61.0 cm); flower 5.5 in. (12.7 cm). Midseason. A dark, rich, blood-red double with a white edging on all segments. Tetraploid. 'Merlot Rouge' × ('Richard Taylor' × Seedling).

'Shirley Valentine'. Photo by Ted Petit

'Silent Heart' (John Peat, 2001). Semi-evergreen. Scape 27 in. (68.6 cm); flower 5 in. (12.7 cm). Midseason. A deep, velvety blood-red self graced by a lightly ruffled, wire white edge. Tetraploid. ('Blood Fire' × 'Drowning in Desire') × 'Chinese Chariot'.

'Spacecoast Cranberry Kid' (John Kinnebrew, 2001). Semi-evergreen. Scape 24 in. (61.0 cm); flower 6 in. (15.2 cm). Early midseason. A clear, cranberry-red with a lighter inner halo, carrying wide, ruffled, golden orange edges. Tetraploid. 'Spacecoast Cranberry Breeze' × 'Watermelon Wine'.

'Startling Creation' (Jamie Gossard, 2002). Dormant. Scape 42 in. (106.7 cm); flower 7 in. (17.8 cm). Late midseason. An orange-red bicolor with very narrow petals and heavy, knobby, shark's tooth, filigree edges. Tetraploid. 'Startle' × 'Tet. Spindazzle'.

'Still Dreaming'. Photo by John Peat

'Still Dreaming' (John Peat, 2003). Dormant. Scape 24 in. (61 cm); flower 5.25 in. (13.3 cm). Early midseason. A flesh-pink flower with an extremely large, red eyezone above a deep green throat. Tetraploid. 'Avante Garde' × 'Altered State'.

'Symphony of Fire' (John Peat, 2000). Semi-evergreen. Scape 23 in. (58.4 cm); flower 5.5 in. (12.7 cm). Midseason. A dark, rich, velvety red flower with a lighter watermark and a green throat that is accentuated by a lightly ruffled edge. Tetraploid. 'Velvet Raven' × 'Street Urchin'.

'Thin Man'. Photo by Dan Trimmer

'Thin Man' (Dan Trimmer, 2002). Evergreen. Scape 42 in. (106.7 cm); flower 12 in. (30.5 cm). Midseason. A huge, bright red, narrow-petaled flower with bold yellow midribs and yellow edges above a green throat. Tetraploid. ('Swirling Spider' × 'Red Suspenders') × 'Long Tall Sally'.

'Trials of Life' (John Peat, 2001). Semi-evergreen. Scape 20 in. (50.8 cm); flower 5.75 in. (12.7 cm). Midseason. A wide-petaled, deep cranberry-burgundy, hose-in-hose double with ruffled, wire white edges. Tetraploid. (('Wayne Johnson' × 'Betty Woods') × F2) × 'Leader of the Pack'.

'William Steen' (Ted Petit, 2003). Semi-evergreen. Scape 25 in. (63.5 cm); flower 5.5 in. (14 cm). Midseason. A velvety, blood-red flower with ruffled petal edges, surrounded by a wire gold edge. Tetraploid. 'Bloodfire' × ('Romeo Is Bleeding' × F2).

'William Steen'. Photo by Ted Petit

Lavender to Purple

'Ancient Wisdom' (Ted Petit, 2002). Semi-evergreen. Scape 24 in. (61.0 cm); flower 6 in. (15.2 cm). Midseason. A clear violet-lavender flower with a lighter watermark and a heavily ruffled, gold edge above a cool green throat. Tetraploid. ('Karla Kitamura' × 'Arabian Magic') × 'Clothed in Glory'.

'Alexa Kathryn' (John Kinnebrew, 2003). Semi-evergreen. Scape 22 in. (55.9 cm); flower 6.25 in. (15.2 cm). Early midseason. Lavender with a heavy, thick, char-

'Alexa Kathryn'. Photo by John Kinnebrew

teuse and gold edge above a yellow to green throat. Tetraploid. 'Spacecoast Cool Deal' × 'Darla Anita'.

'Banquet at Versailles' (Ted Petit, 1995). Semi-evergreen. Scape 19 in. (48.3 cm); flower 5.5 in. (12.7 cm). Midseason. A light lavender self with a cream watermark above a green throat and heavily ruffled, wide, gold edges. Tetraploid. 'Silver Sprite' × 'Ida's Magic'.

'Banquet at Versailles'. Photo by Ted Petit

'Barbara Morton' (Ted Petit, 2003). Semi-evergreen. Scape 25 in. (63.5 cm); flower 6 in. (15.2 cm). Midseason. A clear lavender to purple flower with a very heavy,

ruffled, gold edge and a small charcoal eyezone above a green throat. Tetraploid. 'Eternity's Shadow' × 'Clothed in Glory'.

'Barbara Morton'. Photo by Ted Petit

'Bella Sera' (Patrick Stamile, 2002). Evergreen. Scape 30 in. (76.2 cm); flower 6 in. (15.2 cm). Early midseason. A beautiful mauve-purple with a silver edge and lavender watermark above a green throat. Tetraploid. ('Bogalusa' × 'Seize the Night') × ('Big Sur' × 'One Step Beyond').

'Bella Sera'. Photo by Patrick Stamile

'Broadway Style' (Grace Stamile, 2000). Semi-evergreen. Scape 18 in. (45.7 cm); flower 2.8 in. (7.1 cm). Early midseason. A small, striking purple flower with a darker purple eyezone above a green throat and edges of serrated, white wire. Tetraploid. 'Broadway Jewel' × 'Broadway Pixie'.

'Clothed in Glory' (Larry Grace, 1996). Evergreen. Scape 18 in. (45.7 cm); flower 7 in. (17.8 cm). Midsea-

'Broadway Style'. Photo by Patrick Stamile

son. A lavender-mauve with a very pronounced, gold, knobby edge and a lavender halo above a large yellow to gold throat. Tetraploid. 'Collectors Choice' × 'Admiral's Braid'. Honorable Mention 2001.

'Collective Spirit' (Ted Petit, 2002). Semi-evergreen. Scape 24 in. (61.0 cm); flower 6 in. (15.2 cm). Midsea-

son. A deep, rich, royal purple with extremely wide, round, overlapping petals that carry a precise, ruffled, gold edge. Tetraploid. 'Bloodfire' × 'John Peat'.

'Collective Spirit'. Photo by Ted Petit

'Cretaceous Crunch' (Ludlow Lambertson, 2002). Semi-evergreen. Scape 28 in. (71.1 cm); flower 7 in. (17.8 cm). Early midseason. A fawn pastel petal self with lighter sepals that are accented by a large, muted purple eye and a picotee edge surrounded by large white shark's teeth. Tetraploid. Seedling × 'Crocodile Smile'.

'Dark Eyed Smile' (Ludlow Lambertson, 2000). Semi-evergreen. Scape 30 in. (76.2 cm); flower 5.5 in. (12.7 cm). Midseason. A bold red-purple with a black-purple eyezone and small white teeth surrounding the entire flower. Tetraploid. 'Fortune's Dearest' × 'Dracula'.

'Dark Wonder' (Patrick Stamile, 2000). Evergreen. Scape 27 in. (68.6 cm); flower 6 in. (15.2 cm). Midseason. A dark, rich, royal-purple double with a large silver watermark, often showing large white shark's teeth on the edges. Tetraploid. 'Plum Plume' × 'Denali'.

'Debussy' (Patrick Stamile, 1999). Evergreen. Scape 30 in. (76.2 cm); flower 6.5 in. (15.2 cm). Early midseason. A lavender self with ruffled, gold edges above a green throat. Tetraploid. 'Magic Amethyst' × 'Startle'.

'Eternity's Shadow' (Ted Petit, 1996). Evergreen. Scape 21 in. (53.3 cm); flower 6 in. (15.2 cm). Midseason. A medium purple with a darker shadow-plum eye, a second lighter purple eye, and gold, ruffled edges. Tetraploid. 'Wedding Band' × 'Secret Splendor'.

'Face of the Stars' (Ludlow Lambertson, 2001). Semi-evergreen. Scape 28 in. (71.1 cm); flower 5.5 in. (12.7

'Face of the Stars'. Photo by Ludlow Lambertson

cm). Midseason. A round red-violet with a steely red-violet eye and adorned in white teeth around the edges. Tetraploid. 'Mort's Masterpiece' × Seedling.

'Forbidden Desires' (Ted Petit, 1995). Semi-evergreen. Scape 19 in. (48.3 cm); flower 6 in. (15.2 cm). Midseason. A richly colored, dark purple flower with a green throat, lighter watermark, and prominent, ruffled, gold edge. Tetraploid. 'Louis the Sixteenth' × 'Arabian Magic'. Honorable Mention 2002.

'Forbidden Fantasy' (Jeff Salter, 2000). Semi-evergreen. Scape 29 in. (73.7 cm); flower 6 in. (15.2 cm). Late midseason. A clear, dark purple with silver to white, bubbly edges and a lighter watermark above a deep green throat. Tetraploid. Parents unknown.

'Forces of Nature' (John Peat, 2000). Semi-evergreen. Scape 22 in. (55.9 cm); flower 6 in. (15.2 cm). Midseason. A dark purple flower with bright gold, crimped, heavy, bubbly edges and a chalky watermark above a green throat. Tetraploid. ('Just Infatuation' × ('Banquet at Versailles' × 'Karla Kitamura')) × 'Clothed in Glory'.

'Forces of Nature'. Photo by John Peat

'Fortune's Dearest' (Mort Morss, 1994). Evergreen. Scape 25 in. (63.5 cm); flower 6 in. (15.2 cm). Early. A grape-purple bloom with a white, shark's tooth edge and a lighter grape-purple watermark above a chartreuse throat. Tetraploid. Parents unknown. Honorable Mention 1999. Award of Merit 2002.

'Fortune's Dearest'. Photo by David Kirchhoff

'Gilded Peacock' (Ted Petit, 2001). Semi-evergreen. Scape 19 in. (48.3 cm); flower 5.5 in. (12.7 cm). Midseason. A clear lavender with a blue-violet, patterned eye. The pattern continues as multiple picotees on the petal edges, which are surrounded by a gold edge. Tetraploid. (('Wedding Band' × 'Paper Butterfly') × 'Kyoto Garden') × (('Mardi Gras Ball' × F2) × 'Rainbow Eyes').

'Gilded Peacock'. Photo by Ted Petit

'Hollywood Lights' (Dan Trimmer, 1999). Semi-evergreen. Scape 25 in. (63.5 cm); flower 5 in. (12.7 cm). Early midseason. A dark lavender with bold, bright gold, bubbly edges above a yellow to green throat. Tetraploid. 'Ida's Magic' × 'Enchanted April'.

'Ida's Braid' (Matthew Kaskel, 1996). Evergreen. Scape 23 in. (58.4 cm); flower 5.25 in. (12.7 cm). Late midseason. A lavender self with very wide, heavily ruffled, gold edges above a yellow to green throat. Tetraploid. 'Ida's Magic' × 'Admiral's Braid'.

'Imperial Wizard' (Steve Moldovan, 1996). Semi-evergreen. Scape 30 in. (76.2 cm); flower 6.5 in. (15.2 cm). Midseason. A royal purple blend with a white border and a cream-white watermark above a creamy lemon-yellow to green throat. Tetraploid. 'Salem Witch' × 'Mephistopheles'.

'Inky Fingers' (Patrick Stamile, 2000). Evergreen. Scape 36 in. (91.4 cm); flower 8 in. (20.3 cm). Early. A beautiful, clear violet-purple with a huge, deep, Nile-green throat. Often the form is crispate or cascade. Tetraploid. ('Star of India' × 'Long Stocking') × ('Star of India' × 'Tet. Green Widow').

'Inky Fingers'. Photo by Patrick Stamile

'Jewel in a Crown' (Larry Grace, 2000). Evergreen. Scape 23 in. (58.4 cm); flower 6 in. (15.2 cm). Midseason.

A large, wide-petaled, pink-lavender blend with very ornate ruffled petals with a wide, heavy, gold edge. Tetraploid. 'Ida's Magic' × 'Clothed in Glory'.

'Jewel in a Crown'. Photo by Larry Grace

'John Peat' (Ted Petit, 2001). Semi-evergreen. Scape 22 in. (55.9 cm); flower 6 in. (15.2 cm). Midseason. A rich burgundy with an extremely heavy, gold edge and a lighter watermark above the green throat. Very high bud count and a super rebloomer. Tetraploid. ('Karla Kitamura' × 'Arabian Magic') × 'Clothed in Glory'.

'John Peat'. Photo by Ted Petit

'Karla Kitamura' (Ted Petit, 1996). Semi-evergreen. Scape 24 in. (61.0 cm); flower 5.5 in. (12.7 cm). Midseason. A lavender and cream bitone with a cream eyezone above a green throat and very wide, ruffled, gold edges. Tetraploid. 'Silver Sprite' × 'Ida's Magic'.

'Lake Effect' (Patrick Stamile, 1996). Dormant. Scape 23 in. (58.4 cm); flower 7.25 in. (18.4 cm). Midseason. A mauve-purple with a blue-gray-lavender eyezone and ruffled petal edges above a green throat. Tetraploid. 'Druid's Chant' × 'Big Blue'.

'Larger than Life' (Jeff Salter, 2000). Semi-evergreen. Scape 28 in. (71.1 cm); flower 7 in. (17.8 cm). Midseason. A very large rose-lavender flower with a huge gold edge above a deep green throat. Tetraploid. Seedling × 'David Kirchhoff'.

'Lavender Heartthrob' (Patrick Stamile, 2002). Dormant. Scape 22 in. (55.9 cm); flower 7 in. (17.8 cm). Extra early. A wide and full, clear lavender with striking, braided, ruffled, gold edges above a green throat. Tetraploid. 'Magic Amethyst' × 'Debussy'.

'Lavender Heartthrob'. Photo by Patrick Stamile

'Leaving Me Breathless' (Ted Petit, 2003). Semi-evergreen. Scape 30 in. (76.2 cm); flower 6 in. (15.2 cm). Midseason. A dark, rich purple flower with a lighter watermark and a very pronounced, wide, ruffled, gold edge. Tetraploid. 'Eternity's Shadow' × 'John Peat'.

'Leaving Me Breathless'. Photo by Ted Petit

'Lifting Me Higher' (Larry Grace, 1998). Evergreen. Scape 24 in. (61.0 cm); flower 6 in. (15.2 cm). Early midseason. A velvety burgundy-magenta-rose-purple with a wide, gold edge and a green throat. Tetraploid. Seedling × 'Clothed in Glory'. Honorable Mention 2002.

'Light Years Away' (Ted Petit, 1996). Dormant. Scape 21 in. (53.3 cm); flower 5.5 in. (12.7 cm). Midseason. A lavender to orchid self with a green throat, surrounded by a half-inch, dra-

'Light Years Away'. Photo by Ted Petit

matic, gold edge. Tetraploid. 'Eternity's Shadow' × 'Admiral's Braid'.

'Madonna Arsenault' (John Peat, 2003) Semi-evergreen. Scape 24 in. (61.0 cm); flower 7 in. (17.8 cm). Late midseason. A very large lavender-purple with gold-orange, rubbery edge above a deep green throat. The sheer size of this flower makes it stand out among

its rivals in a garden. Tetraploid. (('Just Infatuation' × 'Banquet at Versailles') × 'John Peat') × ('Eternity's Shadow' × ('Sultry Smile' × F2)).

'Madonna Arsenault'. Photo by John Peat

'Magic Lake' (Patrick Stamile, 2000). Evergreen. Scape 30 in. (76.2 cm); flower 6.5 in. (15.2 cm). Early midseason. Lavender with a washed watermark above a green throat, sporting a heavily ruffled, gold edge of hooks and knobs. Tetraploid. 'Magic Amethyst' × 'Mildred Mitchell'.

'Mort Morss' (Jeff Salter, 2002). Semi-evergreen. Scape 27 in. (68.6 cm); flower 6 in. (15.2 cm). Midseason. A dark purple bloom with a very prominent, white,

toothy edge on both sepals and petals. Tetraploid. 'Fortune's Dearest' × 'Forbidden Fantasy'.

'Mort Morss'. Photo by Jeff Salter

'Mrs. John Cooper' (Larry Grace, 2000). Evergreen. Scape 22 in. (55.9 cm); flower 5.25 in. (13.3 cm). Early midseason. A lavender self with a lavender-blue eye-zone and edge above a green throat. Tetraploid. Parents unknown.

'Nature's Showman' (Ted Petit, 1999). Semi-evergreen. Scape 26 in. (66.0 cm); flower 6.5 in. (15.2 cm). Midseason. A rich purple flower with a darker purple eye-zone and matching picotee edge surrounded by a wire silver edge with white shark's teeth. Tetraploid. 'Dripping with Gold' × 'Mardi Gras Ball'.

'Popcorn Pete' (Ted Petit, 2002). Semi-evergreen. Scape 25 in. (63.5 cm); flower 6 in. (15.2 cm). Midseason. A

dark plum-purple bloom with a lighter watermark above a green throat. The petals are surrounded by a heavy, bubbly, gold to popcorn edge. Tetraploid. ('Arabian Magic' × 'Ice Wine') × 'Clothed in Glory'.

'Popcorn Pete'. Photo by Ted Petit

'Promised Day' (John Peat, 2002). Semi-evergreen. Scape 21 in. (53.3 cm); flower 7 in. (17.8 cm). Early midseason. A deep, bright purple with a huge orange watermark above a small

'Promised Day'. Photo by John Peat

green throat. The edge is a tangerine-orange color with the substance of rubber. Tetraploid. ('Eternity's Shadow' × ('Sultry Smile' × 'Sultry Smile')) × 'Forces of Nature'.

'Raptor Rap' (Ludlow Lambertson, 2001). Semi-evergreen. Scape 28 in. (71.1 cm); flower 5.5 in. (12.7 cm). Early midseason. A narrow-petaled, purple flower with lighter purple sepals. The eye is a stippled blue-purple to violet, and the edges are surrounded in white shark's teeth. Tetraploid. 'Stippled Stars' × 'Fortune's Dearest'.

'Regal Procession' (Ted Petit, 2000). Semi-evergreen. Scape 24 in. (61.0 cm); flower 6 in. (15.2 cm). Midseason. A very large, royal purple with a large, lighter watermark and green throat. The ruffled petals carry a bubbly, gold edge. Tetraploid. 'Juliette Matthies' × 'Seminole Wind'.

'Regal Puzzle' (Ted Petit, 1999). Dormant. Scape 24 in. (61.0 cm); flower 5 in. (12.7 cm). Midseason. A dark, rich, saturated purple, consistently double flower with a lighter watermark. Tetraploid. ('Royal Saracen' × 'Highland Lord') × 'Impetuous Fire'.

'Sanctuary in the Clouds' (John Peat, 1999). Semi-evergreen. Scape 24 in. (61.0 cm); flower 5.5 in. (12.7 cm). Midseason. A lavender-mauve self with a chalky watermark and heavy, ruffled, jagged, gold edges above a green throat. Tetraploid. 'Sultry Smile' × 'Karl Petersen'.

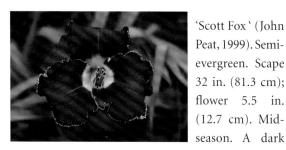

'Scott Fox ' (John Peat, 1999). Semi-evergreen. Scape 32 in. (81.3 cm); flower 5.5 in. (12.7 cm). Midseason. A dark

'Scott Fox '. Photo by John Peat

purple with a black-purple eyezone and a wire white edge carrying tiny shark's teeth above a green throat. Tetraploid. 'Didgeridoo' × 'Maltese Falcon'.

'Sea of Cortez' (Ted Petit, 2002). Semi-evergreen. Scape 23 in. (58.4 cm); flower 6 in. (15.2 cm). Midseason. A

rich, dark purple with a muted watermark, eyezone, and a heavy, ruffled, gold edge above a green throat. Tetraploid. ('Banquet at Versailles' × 'Arabian Magic') × 'Clothed in Glory'.

'Sea of Cortez'. Photo by Ted Petit

'Something to Talk About' (John Peat, 2002). Semi-evergreen. Scape 24 in. (61.0 cm); flower 6 in. (15.2 cm). Early midseason. A burgundy-purple flower with a dark purple, banded eyezone surrounding a lighter watermark above a deep lime-green throat. Tetraploid. 'Karl Petersen' × 'Mardi Gras Ball'.

'Spacecoast Sharp Tooth' (John Kinnebrew, 2002). Evergreen. Scape 22 in. (55.9 cm); flower 5.5 in. (12.7 cm). Early. A wide-petaled, rich purple with petal edges that are surrounded by bright white shark's teeth above an apple-green throat. Tetraploid. 'Spacecoast Surprise Purple' × 'Fortune's Dearest'.

'Spirit Folk' (John Peat, 2001). Semi-evergreen. Scape 27 in. (68.6 cm); flower 10 in. (25.4 cm). Early midseason. A dark purple with a deeper burgundy eyezone and wire white edges above a faint purple halo and a bright green throat. Tetraploid. (('Kyoto Garden' × 'Elusive Dream') × 'Splendid Touch') × 'Golden Epaulets'.

'Storm of the Century' (Robert Carr, 2000). Evergreen. Scape 28 in. (71.1 cm); flower 5.75 in. (12.7 cm). Early midseason. A rich, dark purple with bubbly, ruffled, gold edges above a dark green throat. Tetraploid. 'Ida's Magic' × 'Thunder and Lightning'.

'String Bikini' (Patrick Stamile, 2002). Evergreen. Scape 30 in. (76.2 cm); flower 7 in. (17.8 cm). Extra early. An orchid-lavender spider with a huge, Nile-green throat that takes up most of the flower. Ratio 5.25:1. Tetraploid. 'Waiting in the Wings' × ('Lavender Arrowhead' × 'Moving All Over').

'String Bikini'. Photo by Patrick Stamile

'Systematic Intrigue'. Photo by John Peat

'Sultry Smile' (Ted Petit, 1996). Evergreen. Scape 20 in. (50.8 cm); flower 5.5 in. (12.7 cm). Midseason. A raspberry-plum flower with a chalky eyezone and a ruffled, golden orange edge above a green throat. Tetraploid. 'Ida's Magic' × 'Cherry Chapeau'.

'Summer Solstice' (Ted Petit, 2002). Semi-evergreen. Scape 24 in. (61.0 cm); flower 6.5 in. (15.2 cm). Midseason. A clear rose-lavender flower with a small, charcoal eye. The petals are surrounded by a very heavy, bubbly, ornately ruffled, gold edge. Tetraploid. 'Clothed in Glory' × ('Arabian Magic' × 'Karla Kitamura').

'Systematic Intrigue' (John Peat, 2001). Semi-evergreen. Scape 24 in. (61.0 cm); flower 5.5 in. (12.7 cm). Midseason. An orchid-pink with lavender highlights, surrounded by ruffled and pleated gold edges that display hooks, knobs, and extra gold tissue. Tetraploid. 'Eternity's Shadow' × 'Clothed in Glory'.

'Tricou Fedora' (Ted Petit, 2001). Semi-evergreen. Scape 20 in. (50.8 cm); flower 7 in. (17.8 cm). Midsea-

son. A very large, clear lavender to lavender-pink with knobby, wire gold edges and a lighter watermark above a green throat. Tetraploid. 'Juliette Matthies' × 'Seminole Wind'.

'Tropical Trade Winds' (Ted Petit, 2001). Semi-evergreen. Scape 18 in. (45.7 cm); flower 5.5 in. (12.7 cm). Midseason. A dark, royal purple, flat flower with heavy, gold edges and a large, lighter watermark above a green heart. Tetraploid. 'Eternity's Shadow' × 'Sultry Smile'.

'Wild Child' (Jeff Salter, 2002). Semi-evergreen. Scape 24 in. (61.0 cm); flower 6 in. (15.2 cm). Midseason. A coral, unusual formed flower with a gold edge. Tetraploid. Parents unknown.

'Wild Child'. Photo by Jeff Salter

'Windward Isles' (Ted Petit, 2002). Semi-evergreen. Scape 20 in. (50.8 cm); flower 6.5 in. (15.2 cm). Midseason. A large, clear lavender-pink flower carrying a knobby, wire gold edge above a green throat. Tetraploid. 'Juliette Matthies' × 'Seminole Wind'.

Black

'Baby Jane Hudson' (Ted Petit, 2002). Semi-evergreen. Scape 26 in. (66.0 cm); flower 5.5 in. (12.7 cm). Midseason. A dark, velvety, near black-purple with a pronounced, bubbly, gold to platinum edge. Tetraploid. 'Edge of Eden' × Seedling.

'Baby Jane Hudson'. Photo by Ted Petit

'Beloved Rogue' (Robert Carr, 2001). Evergreen. Scape 26 in. (66.0 cm); flower 5 in. (12.7 cm). Early midseason. A dark black-purple bloom of heavy substance with a contrasting white picotee. Tetraploid. ('Arabian Magic' × Seedling) × 'Pure Indulgence'.

'Bohemia After Dark' (Ted Petit, 2000). Semi-evergreen. Scape 24 in. (61.0 cm); flower 5.5 in. (12.7 cm). Midseason. A very dark black-purple flower with a

'Bohemia After Dark'. Photo by Ted Petit

heavy, gold edge, lighter watermark, and green throat. Tetraploid. 'Sultry Smile' × 'Forbidden Desires'.

'Burning Embers' (Ted Petit, 1996). Semi-evergreen. Scape 23 in. (58.4 cm); flower 5.5 in. (12.7 cm). Midseason. A very dark black-red with a bubbly, platinum to gold edge above a green throat. A flower of striking contrasts. Tetraploid. ('Court Magician' × 'Desert Jewel') × 'Edge of Eden'.

'Burning Embers'. Photo by Ted Petit

'Carbon Dating' (John Benz, 2000). Dormant. Scape 28 in. (71.1 cm); flower 5 in. (12.7 cm). Midseason. A round, ruffled, black-purple flower with a green throat. Very dark, near black. Tetraploid. 'Ruffled Storm' × 'Chief Tecumseh'.

'Dakar' (Patrick Stamile, 1998). Evergreen. Scape 30 in. (76.2 cm); flower 5.25 in. (12.7 cm). Midseason. A

wide-petaled black-purple-violet blend with a green throat. Tetraploid. 'Ebony Jewel' × 'Tet. Crayola Violet'.

'Dakar'. Photo by Patrick Stamile

'Edge of Eden' (Ted Petit, 1994). Evergreen. Scape 20 in. (50.8 cm); flower 5.5 in. (12.7 cm). Midseason. A wide-petaled, black-red self with a ruffled, gold edge above a green throat. Tetraploid. 'Midnight Magic' × ('Ida's Magic' × 'Queen's Cape').

'Edge of Eden'. Photo by Ted Petit

'Pagan Ritual' (Robert Carr, 1999). Evergreen. Scape 27 in. (68.6 cm); flower 5 in. (12.7 cm). Midseason. A rich, smoky burgundy-purple flower trimmed with a golden white, bubbly edge that extends down into the green throat. Tetraploid. ((('Midnight Magic' × 'Decatur Curtain Call') × ('Midnight Magic' × 'Court Magician')) × 'Rue Madelaine') × ('Arabian Magic' × 'Wedding Band').

'Quest for Eden' (Ted Petit, 2001). Evergreen. Scape 20 in. (50.8 cm); flower 5 in. (12.7 cm). Midseason. A very dark black-purple bloom with a heavy, pronounced, ornately ruffled, gold edge above a deep green throat. Tetraploid. 'Edge of Eden' × 'Romeo Is Bleeding'.

'Quest for Eden'. Photo by Ted Petit

'Voodoo Dancer' (John Peat, 2001). Semi-evergreen. Scape 23 in. (58.4 cm); flower 5.5 in. (12.7 cm). Late midseason. A near black, purple, hose-in-hose double with a striking, dark green throat. (('Wayne Johnson' × 'Midnight Magic') × Seedling) × ('Wayne Johnson' × 'Devaughn Hodges').

Eyed and Patterned

'Adamas' (Patrick Stamile, 2002). Evergreen. Scape 23 in. (58.4 cm); flower 6 in. (15.2 cm). Midseason. Or-

chid with a plum-violet edge and eyezone above a green throat. Tetraploid. 'Creative Vision' × 'Awesome Blossom'.

'Adamas'. Photo by Patrick Stamile

'Adventures with Ra' (John Peat, 2001). Semi-evergreen. Scape 23 in. (58.4 cm); flower 5.5 in. (12.7 cm). Early

midseason. A peach-pink flower with a burgundy-purple eyezone and picotee edge above a green throat. Tetraploid. ('Clothed in Glory' × 'Pirate's Ransom') × 'Mardi Gras Ball'.

'Adventures with Ra'. Photo by John Peat

'Ageless Beauty' (Patrick Stamile, 2001). Evergreen. Scape 28 in. (71.1 cm); flower 5 in. (12.7 cm). Early. A

pink flower with a rose eyezone and a double, ruffled edge of rose and gold above a green throat. Tetraploid. ('Strawberry Fields Forever' × 'Be Thine') × 'Strawberry Lace'.

'Ageless Beauty'. Photo by Patrick Stamile

'Armed and Dangerous' (John Peat, 2001). Semi-evergreen. Scape 30 in. (76.2 cm); flower 9 in. (22.9 cm).

Midseason. A lavender-purple, unusual formed daylily with a complex, banded eyezone above a green throat. Tetraploid. 'Opal Ring' × (('Gail Fox' × F2) × 'Mardi Gras Ball').

'Armed and Dangerous'. Photo by John Peat

'Art Gallery Deco' (Ludlow Lambertson, 1998). Semi-evergreen. Scape 24 in. (61.0 cm); flower 6 in. (15.2 cm). Midseason. A medium violet with a deep blue-violet eyezone and edge braided in gold above a green throat. Tetraploid. 'Intricate Eyes' × Seedling.

'Artist at Heart' (Elizabeth Anne Salter, 2000). Evergreen. Scape 26 in. (66.0 cm); flower 3.75 in. (9.5 cm). Midseason. A pale yellow-gold with a large, smoky purple eyezone that is surrounded by a dark purple band above a green throat. Diploid. 'Mystic Mariner' × Seedling.

'Awesome Blossom' (Jeff Salter, 1996). Evergreen. Scape 24 in. (61.0 cm); flower 5 in. (12.7 cm). Early midseason. An antique-rose flower with a striking, dark raisin-plum eyezone above a yellow to green throat. Tetraploid. Parents unknown. Honorable Mention 2001.

'Baracuda Bay' (Jeff Salter, 1996). Semi-evergreen. Scape 26 in. (66.0 cm); flower 6 in. (15.2 cm). Midseason. A coral-mauve with a darker eyezone above a green throat. Petal edges are surrounded by prominent, gold shark's teeth. Tetraploid. 'Mask of Time' × 'Mort's Masterpiece'. Honorable Mention 2001.

'Bertie' (Elizabeth Anne Salter, 1998). Semi-evergreen. Scape 24 in. (61.0 cm); flower 3.5 in. (8.9 cm). Early midseason. A small yellow bloom with a washed-blue-violet eyezone edged in darker violet above a green throat. Tetraploid. 'Witches Wink' × 'Tet. Little Print'.

'Beyond Rangoon' (Lee Pickles, 1995). Semi-evergreen. Scape 26 in. (66.0 cm); flower 4.4 in. (11.2 cm). Early midseason. A true pink with a light red eyezone above a heart-shaped, yellow to green throat. Tetraploid. 'Ming Porcelain' × 'Tet. Siloam Virginia Henson'.

'Bi-colored Bite' (Ludlow Lambertson, 2002). Semi-evergreen. Scape 32 in. (81.3 cm); flower 5 in. (12.7 cm).

'Bi-colored Bite'. Photo by Ludlow Lambertson

Early midseason. A rich, stippled, diamond-dusted, deep rose, narrow-petaled flower with a deeper rose eye and shark's tooth edge. Tetraploid. 'Stippled Stars' × 'Crocodile Smile'.

'Blue Oasis' (Elizabeth Anne Salter, 2002). Evergreen. Scape 20 in. (50.8 cm); flower 3.5 in. (8.9 cm). Early midseason. A pale cream-white flower with a large, round, washed eyezone of intense blue-violet, surrounded by a darker purple band above the green throat. Diploid. 'Mystic Mariner' × 'In the Navy'.

'Blue Oasis'. Photo by Elizabeth Anne Salter

'Blueberry Baroque' (Ted Petit, 2002). Semi-evergreen. Scape 26 in. (66.0 cm); flower 6 in. (15.2 cm). Midsea-

son. A light peach flower with a dark purple eyezone and a matching dark picotee edge surrounded by a second, very bubbly, gold edge. Tetraploid. 'Cosmic Dancer' × ('Tet. Exotic Echo' × 'Tet. Elsie Spalding').

'Blueberry Baroque'. Photo by Ted Petit

'Blueberry Lemonade' (Ted Petit, 2002). Semi-evergreen. Scape 24 in. (61.0 cm); flower 5.5 in. (12.7 cm). Early midseason. A cool golden yellow flower with a large, patterned eyezone. The eyezone has layers of raspberry, violet, and charcoal. Tetraploid. 'Creative Edge' × ('Opal Ring' × 'Rhapsody in Time').

'Border Music' (Jeff Salter, 1995). Semi-evergreen. Scape 26 in. (66.0 cm); flower 6 in. (15.2 cm). Midseason. A cream flower with a striking, dark purple picotee edge and eyezone above a green throat. Tetraploid. Parents unknown.

'Both Sides Now' (David Kirchhoff, 1985). Evergreen. Scape 28 in. (71.1 cm); flower 5.75 in. (12.7 cm). Early midseason. A pastel peach-coral double with a rose eyezone. Diploid. ('Siloam Double Rose' × 'Louise Mercer') × ('Double Love' × 'Nagasaki').

'Broaden Your Horizons' (John Peat, 2002). Semi-evergreen. Scape 19 in. (48.3 cm); flower 6 in. (15.2 cm).

Early. A creamy pink flower with a bright, dark red eye above a deep green throat. The dark red, bubbly edge is

surrounded by a bubbly, gold edge, often with large shark's teeth. Tetraploid. 'Strawberry Fields Forever' × ('Pirate's Ransom' × 'Mardi Gras Ball').

'Broaden Your Horizons'. Photo by John Peat

'Broadway Doll' (Grace Stamile, 1999). Evergreen. Scape 20 in. (50.8 cm); flower 2.9 in. (7.4 cm). Early midseason. A small cream flower with a wine eye. Foliage and scape height are in proportion with the flower. Tetraploid. ((Seedling × 'Tet. Siloam Virginia Henson') × 'Atlanta Antique Satin') × 'Bibbity Bobbity Boo'.

'Calling All Angels' (Dan Trimmer, 2002). Evergreen. Scape 21 in. (53.3 cm); flower 4 in. (10.2 cm). Early midseason. A dramatic, huge, cranberry-red eyezone and edge dominate the face of this bloom, often show-

'Calling All Angels'. Photo by Dan Trimmer

ing tiny, gold shark's teeth and a wire gold edge. Tetraploid. 'Rodeo Sweetheart' × 'Sabine Baur'.

'Candyman Can' (Ted Petit, 2002). Semi-evergreen. Scape 34 in. (86.4 cm); flower 6.5 in. (15.2 cm). Midseason. A very large rose-pink double with a large, bold, red eye and picotee. The petals also carry a frilly, knobby, gold edge. Tetraploid. 'Victoria's Secret' × 'Betty Warren Woods'.

'Cardassian Border' (Ted Petit, 2000). Semi-evergreen. Scape 24 in. (61.0 cm); flower 5.5 in. (12.7 cm). Midseason. A soft cream-pink to ivory-peach double with a dark purple to burgundy eyezone. Tetraploid. 'Champagne Supernova' × 'Cotillion Maiden'.

'Carpathian Cavalier' (Elizabeth Anne Salter, 2001). Semi-evergreen. Scape 25 in. (63.5 cm); flower 3.5 in. (8.9 cm). Midseason. A small, pale ivory-peach flower with washed lavender-violet eyezone. Diploid. 'Wind Wishes' × ('Mystic Mariner' × 'Navy Blues').

'Catcher in the Eye' (John Kinnebrew, 2001). Evergreen. Scape 30 in. (76.2 cm); flower 5.25 in. (12.7 cm). Early midseason. A lavender base color with a dark purple eyezone and matching picotee edge enhanced by a patterned yellow applique throat. Tetraploid. Seedling × 'Daring Deception'.

'Celebration of Angels' (Dan Trimmer, 1999). Evergreen. Scape 25 in. (63.5 cm); flower 4.75 in. (12.1 cm). Early. A cream flower with a black-purple halo above a green throat. Tetraploid. 'Moonlit Masquerade' × 'Tet. Dragons Eye'. Honorable Mention 2002.

'Champagne and Caviar' (John Peat, 2001). Dormant. Scape 22 in. (55.9 cm); flower 6 in. (15.2 cm). Midseason. A cream-peach with a grape-purple eyezone above a green throat. The thick, rubbery purple picotee is surrounded by a gold edge. Tetraploid. ('Heady Wine' × 'Ida's Magic') × 'Mardi Gras Ball'.

'Champagne and Caviar'. Photo by John Peat

'Cherry Valentine' (Dan Trimmer, 1999). Evergreen. Scape 28 in. (71.1 cm); flower 4 in. (10.2 cm). Early. A small, wide-petaled, bright pink with a crimson-red eyezone above a green throat. Tetraploid. ('Ruby Sentinel' × 'Tet. Enchanting Blessing') × 'Tet. Dragons Eye'.

'Cherry Valentine'. Photo by Dan Trimmer

'Complicated Lifestyles' (John Peat, 1999). Semi-evergreen. Scape 22 in. (55.9 cm); flower 5.5 in. (12.7 cm).

Midseason. A lavender-pink with a rose-purple eyezone and picotee surrounded by bubbly, gold edges above a green throat. Tetraploid. ('Dripping with Gold' × ('Sylvan Delight' × 'Tet. Siloam Virginia Henson')) × 'Mardi Gras Ball'.

'Continental Holiday' (Jeff Salter, 2002). Semi-evergreen. Scape 28 in. (71.1 cm); flower 6 in. (15.2 cm). Early midseason. A pale cream with a hint of melon, a bright rose eyezone, and a heavily banded edge of rose and sparkling amber. Tetraploid. 'Lee Pickles' × ('Hillbilly Heart' × 'Barbarian Princess').

'Cotillion Maiden' (Ted Petit, 1999). Semi-evergreen. Scape 25 in. (63.5 cm); flower 5.5 in. (12.7 cm). Midseason. A pale cream with a dark purple eyezone and matching picotee above a green throat. Often double later in the season. Tetraploid. ('Tet. Siloam Virginia Henson' × 'Sylvan Delight') × 'Admiral's Braid'.

'Creme De La Creme' (Ted Petit, 2000). Semi-evergreen. Scape 24 in. (61.0 cm); flower 5.5 in. (12.7 cm). Early. Ivory-cream flowers with a pink blush and patterned eye. The very large green throat forms a large green center. Tetraploid. 'Opal Ring' × 'Rainbow Eyes'.

'Crystal Blue Persuasion' (Elizabeth Anne Salter, 1996). Evergreen. Scape 18 in. (45.7 cm); flower 2.75 in. (7.0 cm). Midseason. A small, pale lavender flower with a

slate-blue eye containing a magenta pencil-edge above a green throat. Diploid. Parents unknown. Honorable Mention 2002.

'Crystal Blue Persuasion'. Photo by Elizabeth Anne Salter

'Dan Mahony' (Dan Trimmer, 1999). Dormant. Scape 26 in. (66.0 cm); flower 4.5 in. (11.4 cm). Early midseason. A small pink flower with a striking, scarlet-red eyezone above a green throat. Tetraploid. ('Fooled Me' × 'Queensland') × 'Tet. Dragons Eye'. Honorable Mention 2002.

'Delicate Beads' (John Peat, 1999). Semi-evergreen. Scape 25 in. (63.5 cm); flower 5.5 in. (12.7 cm). Midseason. A baby-ribbon-pink with a rose-pink eyezone above a green throat. The petal edges carry gold beads. Tetraploid. 'Mardi Gras Ball' × 'Serenity in Lace'.

'Dominic Brockcain' (John Peat, 2003). Semi-evergreen. Scape 20 in. (50.8 cm); flower 5.5 in. (12.7 cm). Early midseason. A very round, heavily ruffled cream-melon with a large red eye and picotee surrounded in gold. The ruffles extend deep into the lime-green throat. Tetraploid. 'Mardi Gras Ball' × 'Tet. Siloam Virginia Henson'.

'Dominic Brockcain'. Photo by John Peat

'Elegant Candy' (Patrick Stamile, 1995). Dormant. Scape 25 in. (63.5 cm); flower 4.25 in. (10.8 cm). Early midseason. A small pink flower with a striking red eyezone above a green throat. Tetraploid. 'Lady of Fortune'

× 'Tet. Janice Brown'. Honorable Mention 1998. Annie T. Giles Award 2000. L. Ernest Plouf Award 2001.

'Erratic Behavior' (John Peat, 2002). Dormant. Scape 26 in. (66.0 cm); flower 6.5 in. (15.2 cm). Early midseason.

A light cream to pink flower with a huge chevron-shaped, candy-apple-red eyezone that extends out almost to the tips of the petals. Tetraploid. ('Kabuki Ballet' × 'Street Urchin') × 'Altered State'.

'Erratic Behavior'. Photo by John Peat

'Eskimo Kisses' (Dan Trimmer, 2002). Evergreen. Scape 26 in. (66.0 cm); flower 4 in. (10.2 cm). Midseason. A creamy, pale pink flower with a huge rose-red eyezone and matching picotee edge above a green throat. Tetraploid. ('Emperor's Dragon' × ('Tet. Elsie Spalding' × 'Raspberry Beret')) × 'Jenny Kissed Me'.

'Eskimo Kisses'. Photo by Dan Trimmer

'Expanding Universe' (Ted Petit, 1998). Semi-evergreen. Scape 26 in. (66.0 cm); flower 5.5 in. (12.7 cm). Midseason. A cream with cinnamon stippling and a green heart. The eye is formed by the stippling coming very close together. Tetraploid. ('Midnight Magic' × 'Shinto Etching') × ('Ida's Magic' × 'Wrapped in Gold').

'Eye Catching' (Patrick Stamile, 1997). Evergreen. Scape 23 in. (58.4 cm); flower 5 in. (12.7 cm). Early midseason. A large cream flower with a large purple eyezone and a wide matching picotee edge above a green throat. Tetraploid. 'Festive Art' × ('Cherry Drop' × 'Royal Braid').

'Eye of the Matrix ' (Ted Petit, 2002). Semi-evergreen. Scape 21 in. (53.3 cm); flower 6 in. (15.2 cm). Late midseason. A clear lavender flower with a large patterned

eye. The flowers have a dark picotee surrounding the eyezone and the petal edges, which are surrounded by a second bubbly, gold edge. Tetraploid. 'Didgeridoo' × 'Clothed in Glory'.

'Eye of the Matrix '. Photo by Ted Petit

'Eye on America' (Jeff Salter, 1996). Semi-evergreen. Scape 26 in. (66.0 cm); flower 5.5 in. (12.7 cm). Early midseason. A yellow-cream blend with a black-plum eyezone and picotee edge above a green throat. Tetraploid. Parents unknown. Honorable Mention 2002.

'Eye on America'. Photo by Jeff Salter

'Eyes on the Prize' (Karol Emmerich, 2002). Semi-evergreen. Scape 18 in. (45.7 cm); flower 5.5 in. (14 cm). Early midseason. A clear pink to copper-pink flower with a dark, velvety, burgundy-black eyezone and picotee surrounded by a wire white edge above an olive-green heart. Tetraploid. 'Awesome Blossom' × Seedling.

'Eyes on the Prize'. Photo by Karol Emmerich

'Eyes Wide Shut' (Jeff Salter, 2002). Semi-evergreen. Scape 26 in. (66.0 cm); flower 5 in. (12.7 cm). Early midseason. A cream near white with a dramatically con-

'Eyes Wide Shut'. Photo by Jeff Salter

trasting dark wine-purple eyezone and knobby wine-purple picotee edge. Tetraploid. Parents unknown.

'Flamingo Flight' (John Peat, 1998). Semi-evergreen. Scape 28 in. (71.1 cm); flower 5.5 in. (12.7 cm). Mid-season. A pale cream-pink with a rose-pink eyezone and picotee edge above a green throat. Tetraploid. ('Misty Memories' × ('Sylvan Delight' × 'Tet. Siloam Virginia Henson')) × 'Mardi Gras Ball'.

'For Your Eyes Only' (Jeff Corbett, 2000). Evergreen. Scape 27 in. (68.6 cm); flower 5 in. (12.7 cm). Midseason. A creamy peach with a bold raspberry eyezone and picotee edge. Overlapping petals make this a very round flower, 25 percent of which are polytepal. Tetraploid. 'Wild Mustang' × 'Dakota Destiny'.

'Forsyth Hot Lips' (Wyatt LeFever, 1988). Dormant. Scape 23 in. (58.4 cm); flower 4.5 in. (11.4 cm). Early midseason. A warm peach-pink with a red eyezone above a yellow-green throat. Diploid. 'Ambivalent Angel' × Seedling. Honorable Mention 1991.

'François Verhaert' (Patrick Stamile, 2001). Evergreen. Scape 24 in. (61.0 cm); flower 5.5 in. (12.7 cm). Early midseason. An orchid flower with a plum-violet eyezone and picotee edge above a chartreuse throat. The eye and border are very wide and almost black at times, leaving very little petal self color. Tetraploid. 'Bold Encounter' × 'Awesome Blossom'.

'Full of Spirit' (Elizabeth Anne Salter, 2002). Semi-evergreen. Scape 27 in. (68.6 cm); flower 3.75 in. (9.5 cm). Midseason. A small ivory bloom with a washed violet, patterned eyezone above a green throat. Tetraploid. 'Tet. Little Print' × Seedling.

'Gerda Brooker' (Mort Morss, 1995). Evergreen. Scape 30 in. (76.2 cm); flower 7 in. (17.8 cm). Early. A cream

'François Verhaert'. Photo by Patrick Stamile

bloom with red-violet edges and a triple eye in rings of lavender-lilac above a yellow to green throat. Tetraploid. ((Seedling × 'Opus One') × ('Paper Butterfly' × 'Fantasy Finish')) × ((Seedling × 'Opus One') × ('Paper Butterfly' × 'Fantasy Finish')). Honorable Mention 2000.

'Gift of Mischief' (Elizabeth Anne Salter, 2000). Semi-evergreen. Scape 28 in. (71.1 cm); flower 4.25 in. (10.8 cm). Midseason. A pale ivory-cream with a large, washed, very complex, lavender-slate-gray-blue, multi-banded eyezone above a deep dark green throat. Tetraploid. 'Tet. Little Print' × 'Witches Wink'.

'Hearts Abound' (John Peat, 2001). Semi-evergreen. Scape 30 in. (76.2 cm); flower 5 in. (12.7 cm). Early midseason. A cream flower base with a striking, rose-pink to muted rose-red, large eye and picotee above a deep green throat. Tetraploid. 'Mardi Gras Ball' × Seedling.

'Hello Hollywood' (Ted Petit, 2000). Semi-evergreen. Scape 25 in. (63.5 cm); flower 5.5 in. (12.7 cm). Midseason. A large cream with a darker triangular or chevron-shaped eyezone surrounding a green throat. The flowers also have a matching picotee edge, surrounded by a larger gold edge. Tetraploid. 'Elusive Dream' × 'Splendid Touch'.

'Hillbilly Heart' (Jeff Salter, 2001). Semi-evergreen. Scape 26 in. (66.0 cm); flower 5.5 in. (12.7 cm). Early midseason. A bright yellow with a large, bold red eyezone and matching picotee, ruffled edge. Tetraploid. 'Wisest of Wizards' × Seedling.

'Honky Tonk Blues' (Grace Stamile, 2002). Semi-evergreen. Scape 20 in. (50.8 cm); flower 3 in. (7.6 cm). Early midseason. A mauve self with a violet-lavender-blue, complex eye pattern above a celery-green throat. Diploid. 'Little Sensation' × ('Little Pleasure' × 'Little Fat Cat').

'Honky Tonk Blues'. Photo by Patrick Stamile

'Imperial Riddle' (John Peat, 2002). Semi-evergreen. Scape 24 in. (61.0 cm); flower 5.5 in. (12.7 cm). Early midseason. A cream, near white flower with a large, faint rose-red eyezone that bleeds out into the petals. The matching picotee edge is surrounded in gold. Tetraploid. ('Restless Warrior' × ('Romeo Is Bleeding' × 'Edge of Eden')) × ('Pirate's Ransom' × 'Didgeridoo').

'Imperial Riddle'. Photo by John Peat

'In the Navy' (Elizabeth Anne Salter, 1993). Semi-evergreen. Scape 18 in. (45.7 cm); flower 3 in. (7.6 cm). Midseason. A small lavender flower with a complex, slate-navy-blue eyezone above a green throat. One of the bluest eyed daylilies. Diploid. Parents unknown. Honorable Mention 2000.

'In the Navy'. Photo by John Peat and Ted Petit

'Jamaican Me Happy' (Dan Trimmer, 1999). Semi-evergreen. Scape 28 in. (71.1 cm); flower 5 in. (12.7 cm). Early midseason. A wide-petaled peach flower with a bold or-

'Jamaican Me Happy'. Photo by Dan Trimmer

ange eyezone and pink edges above a green throat. Tetraploid. 'Raspberry Beret' × 'Tet. Ruffled Masterpiece'.

'Jamaican Music' (Dan Trimmer, 2001). Evergreen. Scape 37 in. (94 cm); flower 5 in. (12.7 cm). Early midseason. A cream-pink flower with a huge red eye and a thick, red, ruffled, picotee edge above a green throat. Tetraploid. 'Raspberry Beret' × 'Tet. Dragons Eye'.

'Jane Trimmer' (Dan Trimmer, 2002). Evergreen. Scape 25 in. (63.5 cm); flower 5 in. (12.7 cm). Early midseason. A pale lavender bloom with a huge, bold black-purple eyezone and matching picotee edge on round, full petals. Tetraploid. 'Gillian' × 'Sabine Baur'

'Jane Trimmer'. Photo by Dan Trimmer

'Jenny Butterfield' (Ludlow Lambertson, 1998). Evergreen. Scape 26 in. (66.0 cm); flower 6 in. (15.2 cm). Early midseason. Violet with a blue eyezone and picotee and with a gold, braided edge above a green throat. Tetraploid. (Seedling × 'Ethereal Grace') × 'Admiral's Braid'.

'Julie Newmar' (Mort Morss, 2000). Evergreen. Scape 32 in. (81.3 cm); flower 7 in. (17.8 cm). Early. A pastel peach with a washed eyezone displaying a spider-web

configuration that is also displayed in a watermark on the sepals. Tetraploid. (Seedling × 'Fortune's Dearest') × 'Gerda Brooker'.

'Just a Tease' (Jeff Salter, 2002). Semi-evergreen. Scape 25 in. (63.5 cm); flower 4.75 in. (12.1 cm). Early midseason. A pale ivory-cream flower with a large lavender-rose eyezone and a wide, smokey-lavender-rose, ruffled edge. Tetraploid. 'Strawberry Lace' × 'Luck of the Draw'.

'Just One Look' (John Peat, 1999). Semi-evergreen. Scape 20 in. (50.8 cm); flower 6.5 in. (15.2 cm). Midseason. A cream-near white bloom with a large, striking, rose-red eyezone above a green throat. Tetraploid. ('Pirate's Ransom' × 'Mardi Gras Ball') × 'Strawberry Candy'.

'Key West' (Dan Trimmer, 1999). Dormant. Scape 28 in. (71.1 cm); flower 4.25 in. (10.8 cm). Early midseason. A cream self with a rose-red eye surrounded by a red halo above a green throat. Tetraploid. 'Tet. Siloam Gumdrop' × 'Tet. Dragons Eye'.

'Kissed from Afar' (Ted Petit, 2002). Semi-evergreen. Scape 26 in. (66.0 cm); flower 6.5 in. (15.2 cm). Midseason. A beautiful, huge rose-pink with a large, dark rose-red eyezone above a green throat. The gold petal edges are heavily ruffled and crimped with a narrow red picotee. Tetraploid. 'Wisest of Wizards' × 'Jenny Kissed Me'.

'Lavender Blue Baby' (Jack B. Carpenter, 1996). Dormant. Scape 28 in. (71.1 cm); flower 5.5 in. (12.7 cm). Early midseason. A lavender flower with a lavender-blue eyezone above a green throat. Diploid. Parents unknown. Honorable Mention 2001.

'Lee Pickles' (Jeff Salter, 2001). Semi-evergreen. Scape 28 in. (71.1 cm); flower 5.5 in. (12.7 cm). Early midseason. A creamy ivory with a soft, bright rose eye and a

'Lavender Blue Baby'. Photo by Jack B. Carpenter

double edge of ruffled rose and white gold. Tetraploid. 'Wisest of Wizards' × 'Strawberry Lace'.

'Licorice Candy' (Patrick Stamile, 2001). Evergreen. Scape 24 in. (61.0 cm); flower 4 in. (10.2 cm). Early. A lovely cream-white flower with a dramatic, violet-black eyezone and a violet-black picotee above a green throat. Tetraploid. 'Creative Vision' × ('Panda Bear' × ('Border Bride' × 'Tet. Eye of Newt')).

'Licorice Candy'. Photo by Patrick Stamile

'Lipstick Traces' (Matthew Kaskel, 1994). Evergreen. Scape 22 in. (55.9 cm); flower 5 in. (12.7 cm). Early midseason. A large, wide-petaled, creped yellow with a red eyezone above a yellow to green throat. Tetraploid. (('Altarmira' × Seedling) × 'Elsie Spalding') × 'Stairway to Heaven'.

'Malachite Prism' (George Doorakian, 1999). Semi-evergreen. Scape 36 in. (91.4 cm); flower 4.25 in. (10.8 cm). Midseason. A green and lavender blend with a purple chevron eyezone above a very large, dramatic, green throat. Diploid. 'Someplace Special' × Seedling.

'Malachite Prism'. Photo by George Doorakian

'Mardi Gras Ball' (Ted Petit, 1996). Semi-evergreen. Scape 23 in. (58.4 cm); flower 6 in. (15.2 cm). Midseason. A large, striking, lavender flower with green throat and a dark purple eyezone. The ornately ruffled petals carry an edge of dark purple surrounded by a second gold edge. Tetraploid. ('Tet. Siloam Virginia Henson' × 'Ida's Magic') × 'Admiral's Braid'.

'Meet Joe Black'. Photo by Ted Petit

'Meet Joe Black' (Ted Petit, 2002). Semi-evergreen. Scape 26 in. (66.0 cm); flower 5.5 in. (12.7 cm). Early midseason.

A clear peach to salmon-pink with a large, very dark, near black eye, and a wide matching picotee above a deep green throat. Tetraploid. ('Mardi Gras Ball' × Seedling) × 'Awesome Blossom'.

'Mistaken Identity' (John Peat, 2001). Semi-evergreen. Scape 20 in. (50.8 cm); flower 6 in. (15.2 cm). Early midseason. A rose-red flower with a deep, dark red eye and matching picotee. Tetraploid. 'Strawberry Candy' × ('Pirate's Ransom' × 'Mardi Gras Ball').

'Must Be Magic' (John Peat, 2002). Semi-evergreen. Scape 25 in. (63.5 cm); flower 5.5 in. (12.7 cm). Early midseason. A golden orange with a bright rose-red eyezone on both the petals and sepals and a matching picotee edge above a green throat. Tetraploid. ('Mardi Gras Ball' × 'Pirate's Ransom') × 'Moments of Intrigue'.

'Mystic Vision'. Photo by Elizabeth Anne Salter

'Must Be Magic'. Photo by John Peat

'Mystic Vision' (Elizabeth Anne Salter, 2000). Semi-evergreen. Scape 25 in. (63.5 cm); flower 3.5 in. (8.9 cm). Midseason. A cream-pink with a complex, lavender-purple eyezone above an apple-green throat. Diploid. 'Wind Wishes' × ('Mystic Mariner' × 'Navy Blues').

'Mystical Rainbow' (Patrick Stamile, 1996). Dormant. Scape 25 in. (63.5 cm); flower 5.5 in. (12.7 cm). Early midseason. Pink with a rose-raspberry-charcoal-yellow-patterned eyezone above a green throat. Tetraploid. 'Exotic Candy' × 'Rainbow Eyes'. Honorable Mention 2001.

'Only Believe' (Larry Grace, 1998). Semi-evergreen. Scape 24 in. (61.0 cm); flower 7 in. (17.8 cm). Early midseason. A large, medium cream-pink with a burgundy-red eyezone above a green throat. Tetraploid. 'Wedding Band' × 'Song Without Words'. Honorable Mention 2002.

'Opal Ring' (Matthew Kaskel, 1998). Evergreen. Scape 32 in. (81.3 cm); flower 5.25 in. (12.7 cm). Early midseason. A cream-peach with a patterned, purple and lilac eyezone above a chartreuse throat. Tetraploid. 'Etched Eyes' × Seedling.

'Organized Chaos' (Elizabeth Anne Salter, 2002). Semi-evergreen. Scape 28 in. (71.1 cm); flower 4 in. (10.2 cm). Midseason. A medium rose-plum flower with plum edges and a washed blue-violet eye surrounded by a darker pencil-edge. Diploid. Parents unknown.

'Pirate's Ransom' (Ted Petit, 1999). Semi-evergreen. Scape 27 in. (68.6 cm); flower 6 in. (15.2 cm). Midseason. A ruffled and heavily pleated lavender with a dark purple eyezone and picotee above a green throat. Tetraploid. ('Wedding Band' × 'Desert Jewel') × 'Lin Wright'.

'Queen's Coronation' (Ted Petit, 2003). Semi-evergreen. Scape 25 in. (63.5 cm); flower 5.5 in. (14 cm). Midseason. Clear pink flowers with a dramatic red eye and wide, matching red picotee. The flowers are surrounded by another wide, gold edge. Tetraploid. 'Mardi Gras Ball' × 'Only Believe'.

'Queen's Coronation'. Photo by Ted Petit

'Rainbow Candy' (Patrick Stamile, 1996). Dormant. Scape 28 in. (71.1 cm); flower 4.25 in. (10.8 cm). Early midseason. Cream with a purple, lavender, gray, and yellow patterned eyezone above a green throat. Tetraploid. 'Blueberry Candy' × 'Tet. Little Print'.

'Rapid Eye Movement' (Dan Trimmer, 2001). Evergreen. Scape 32 in. (81.3 cm); flower 6.75 in. (15.2 cm). Early midseason. A cream-yellow with a huge, dark rose-burgundy eyezone and striking picotee of the same color above a yellow to green throat. Tetraploid. 'Canadian Border Patrol' × 'Tet. Indian Sky'.

'Raspberry Beret' (Dan Trimmer, 1999). Evergreen. Scape 28 in. (71.1 cm); flower 6 in. (15.2 cm). Midseason. A gold amber with a cranberry-red eyezone and thick, ruffled, matching picotee edges above a green throat. Tetraploid. 'Fooled Me' × 'Jungle Mask'.

'Raspberry Winter' (Dan Trimmer, 1999). Dormant. Scape 28 in. (71.1 cm); flower 4 in. (10.2 cm). Early midseason. A clean, pale pink with a triangular, red-etched, complex eyezone above a dark green throat. It also carries a double edge of red and gold. Tetraploid. 'Summer Blush' × 'Tet. Dragons Eye'.

'Reyna' (John Peat, 2002). Semi-evergreen. Scape 25 in. (63.5 cm); flower 7.5 in. (19.1 cm). Early midseason. A very large, cream flower with a faint pink to violet cast and a darker violet-burgundy eyezone that bleeds toward the green throat. Tetraploid. 'Big Blue' × 'Elusive Dream'.

'Reyna'. Photo by John Peat

'Rhapsody in Time' (Jeff Salter, 1996). Semi-evergreen. Scape 28 in. (71.1 cm); flower 5 in. (12.7 cm). Early midseason. A lavender-rose with an electric blue-violet eyezone above a yellow to green throat. Tetraploid. 'Tet. Little Print' × ('Night Mist' × ('Nivia Guest' × 'Corfu')).

'Rodeo Sweetheart' (Dan Trimmer, 2000). Semi-evergreen. Scape 32 in. (81.3 cm); flower 4.75 in. (12.1 cm). Early midseason. A dark peach with a cranberry-maroon eyezone on both the petals and sepals. A double edge of cranberry-maroon and wire gold surrounds the petals. Tetraploid. 'Fooled Me' × 'Tet. Dragons Eye'.

'Sabine Baur' (Jeff Salter, 1997). Semi-evergreen. Scape 25 in. (63.5 cm); flower 6 in. (15.2 cm). Early midseason. A large cream self with a striking purple eyezone and thick purple picotee above a green throat. Tetraploid. 'Cindy's Eye' × 'Daring Deception'. Honorable Mention 2002. Don C. Stevens Award 2002.

'Shadows Within' (Ted Petit, 1999). Semi-evergreen. Scape 25 in. (63.5 cm); flower 6 in. (15.2 cm). Midseason. A peach to salmon, consistently double flower with a large, dark purple eyezone and a wire gold edge. Tetraploid. (('Wayne Johnson' × 'Rosetta Stone') × ('Wayne Johnson' × 'Rosetta Stone')) × 'Tet. Exotic Echo'.

'Shadows of the Pyramids' (John Peat, 2001). Semi-evergreen. Scape 19 in. (48.3 cm); flower 6 in. (15.2 cm). Early midseason. A golden yellow with a complex, triple-banded eyezone of shades of rose-burgundy above a green throat. Tetraploid. 'Raspberry Candy' × Seedling.

'Shake the Mountains' (Jamie Gossard, 2001). Evergreen. Scape 40 in. (101.6 cm); flower 8.5 in. (21.6 cm). Midseason. A large golden yellow with a striking patterned eyezone on both the petals and sepals. Tetraploid. 'Moonlit Masquerade' × 'Boney Maroney'.

'Shark Bite' (Patrick Stamile, 2001). Evergreen. Scape 28 in. (71.1 cm); flower 7 in. (17.8 cm). Early. Pink with a darker rose eyezone and picotee edges surrounded with gold, tendril-like shark's teeth above a super green throat. Tetraploid. (('True Grit' × 'Admiral's Braid') × (Seedling × 'Song Without Words')) × 'Tet. Green Widow'.

'Shirley Temple Curls' (John J. Temple, 1996). Evergreen. Scape 24 in. (61.0 cm); flower 10 in. (25.4 cm). Early midseason. A light orange-red spider with a burgundy eyezone above a deep green throat. Very curled and twisted. 5.6:1. Diploid. ('Lines of Splendor' × 'Garden Portrait') × ('Rainbow Spangles' × 'Lois Burns'). Honorable Mention 2001.

'Small Tempest' (Elizabeth Anne Salter, 2000). Semi-evergreen. Scape 22 in. (55.9 cm); flower 3.5 in. (8.9 cm). Midseason. An ivory-cream-yellow with a huge, bright, circular, red eyezone above a bright yellow to green throat. Tetraploid. 'Tet. Dragons Eye' × 'Witches Wink'.

'South Beach Sunset' (John Peat, 2001). Dormant. Scape 20 in. (50.8 cm); flower 6 in. (15.2 cm). Midseason. An iridescent orange with a large red eyezone above a green throat. Nicely ruffled with a wire red picotee edge. Tetraploid. 'My Pirate Days' × 'Marilyn Siwik'.

'Spice Hunter' (Dan Trimmer, 2002). Evergreen. Scape 28 in. (71.1 cm); flower 6 in. (15.2 cm). Midseason. A dark peach flower with rose-cranberry-red eye and a half-inch, red picotee edge. Tetraploid. 'Pumpkin Moonshine' × 'Raspberry Beret'.

'Spoons for Escargots' (John Peat, 1999). Semi-evergreen. Scape 28 in. (71.1 cm); flower 7 in. (17.8 cm). Midseason. A rose flower with a large, deep rose eye displayed on both the petals and sepals. The sepals are both quilled and spatulate. Tetraploid. (('Lin Wright' × 'Mardi Gras Ball') × 'Swirling Spider') × 'Misty Memories'.

'Steve Trimmer' (Dan Trimmer, 1999). Semi-evergreen. Scape 28 in. (71.1 cm); flower 5.25 in. (12.7 cm). Early midseason. A pale yellow with a plum eyezone and edge above a yellow to green throat. Tetraploid. 'Kisses Like Wine' × 'Calico Jack'.

'Strawberry Lightning' (Ted Petit, 2001). Evergreen. Scape 23 in. (58.4 cm); flower 6 in. (15.2 cm). Midseason. A large rose bloom with a red eye and green throat. The bold flowers are surrounded by a red picotee and a gold edge. Tetraploid. ('Misty Memories' × 'Splendid Touch') × 'Only Believe'.

'Through the Looking Glass'. Photo by Ted Petit

'Strawberry Lightning'. Photo by Ted Petit

'Swashbuckler Bay' (Jeff Salter, 1999). Semi-evergreen. Scape 29 in. (73.7 cm); flower 6 in. (15.2 cm). Midseason. A bright salmon-coral flower with a large, triangular, black eye and matching picotee above a green throat. Tetraploid. Parents unknown.

'Through the Looking Glass' (Ted Petit, 2001). Semi-evergreen. Scape 24 in. (61.0 cm); flower 6 in. (15.2 cm). Midseason. A salmon-pink self with a complex, patterned eyezone made of many intricate layers above a deep green throat. Tetraploid. 'Opal Ring' × ('Forest Phantom' × 'Rainbow Eyes').

'Time for Eternity'. Photo by Ted Petit

'Time for Eternity' (Ted Petit, 2002). Semi-evergreen. Scape 26 in. (66.0 cm); flower 6 in. (15.2 cm). Midseason. Large, showy, cream-pink flowers with a patterned eyezone. The pattern continues along the extremely ruffled petal edges as a multiple picotee. Tetraploid. 'Opal Ring' × 'Living on the Edge'.

'Uppermost Edge' (Mort Morss, 1994). Semi-evergreen. Scape 21 in. (53.3 cm); flower 5 in. (12.7 cm). Midseason. Pale apricot with a purple edge and eyezone above a yellow to vivid green throat. Tetraploid. ('Wedding Band' × 'Mediterranean Mood') × 'Angel's Smile'. Honorable Mention 2001.

'Violet Reflections' (Ted Petit, 2003). Semi-evergreen. Scape 25 in. (63.5 cm); flower 5.5 in. (14 cm). Midseason. A mauve-peach flower with a striking, violet-blue, patterned eyezone and a matching wire edge above a green throat. Tetraploid. 'Shadows of the Pyramids' × 'Clothed in Glory'.

'Visual Intrigue' (Jeff Salter, 2000). Semi-evergreen. Scape 29 in. (73.7 cm); flower 6 in. (15.2 cm). Early midseason. A pale ivory-cream with a complex, blue-violet eyezone that appears on both the petals and sepals. Tetraploid. Parents unknown.

'Vivacious Pam' (John Peat, 2002). Semi-evergreen. Scape 25 in. (63.5 cm); flower 6.25 in. (15.2 cm). Early midseason. A large pink bloom with a brilliant red eye and picotee edge, red veins, heavy ruffling, and a wire gold edge. Tetraploid. (('Kyoto Garden' × 'Creative Edge') × 'Mardi Gras Ball') × ('Pirate's Ransom' × 'Mardi Gras Ball').

'Vivacious Pam'. Photo by John Peat

'Way Out Yonder' (Elizabeth Anne Salter, 2002). Semi-evergreen. Scape 18 in. (45.7 cm); flower 3 in. (7.6 cm). Midseason. A light to medium lavender-rose flower with a deep blue-violet, complex eyezone surrounding an intense green throat. Diploid. Parents unknown.

'Wild Horses' (Dan Trimmer, 1999). Evergreen. Scape 37 in. (94.0 cm); flower 7 in. (17.8 cm). Early. A cream-yellow with a black-purple halo above a yellow to green throat. Tetraploid. 'Moonlit Masquerade' × 'Tet. Cleopatra'. Honorable Mention 2002.

'Wild and Wonderful' (Patrick Stamile, 2002). Evergreen. Scape 36 in. (91.4 cm); flower 8.5 in. (21.6 cm). Early. A beige-pink spider with a large, fern-green throat and a huge, red, chevron-shaped eye with sepals that twist and curl. 2.8:1. Tetraploid. 'Waiting in the Wings' × ('Lavender Arrowhead' × 'Jabberwocky').

'Wild and Wonderful'. Photo by Patrick Stamile

'Wisest of Wizards' (Jeff Salter, 1994). Semi-evergreen. Scape 26 in. (66.0 cm); flower 5.5 in. (12.7 cm). Early midseason. Large ivory self with a pale rose eyezone and matching rose and gold, ruffled edge. Tetraploid. Parents unknown. Honorable Mention 2000.

'Zinfandel Blush' (Ted Petit, 2001). Evergreen. Scape 30 in. (76.2 cm); flower 5 in. (12.7 cm). Midseason. A soft peach-pink with a distinctive, multiple, rose eyezone and picotee edges surrounded in ruffled gold. Tetraploid. 'Mardi Gras Ball' × Seedling.

CHAPTER 6

Landscaping with Daylilies

by Melanie Vassallo

Daylilies in the Garden

Tolerant of a wide variety of climate zones and soil conditions, the modern daylily is an ideal garden plant. Due to the invasive nature of many species daylilies, they were once mostly relegated to roadside plantings or out of the way locations—thus they earned nicknames such as ditch lilies or outhouse lilies. In comparison, the modern daylily is a well behaved garden perennial. Hybrid daylilies no longer spread underground stoloniferously but instead multiply at the crown, sending up new fans alongside existing ones. Or sometimes single fans split in two during bloom season. Such a desirable growth habit makes the modern daylily suitable for almost any type of garden.

The available multitude of sizes, colors, and shapes of daylilies will add to any planting, whether a new garden or an existing one. Although tolerant of shade, daylilies bloom better with more sun, especially the further north they are grown. Ideally they should be incorporated into gardens with at least four to six hours

The Blaybrough Garden, Massachusetts. Photo by Melanie Vassallo

Harbe's Farm Stand, Long Island, New York. Photo by Melanie Vassallo

of direct sunlight. Less light will cause diminished bloom output and scapes will become gangly, leaning toward any available light.

The perennial border is a perfect location for daylilies. Many perennials bloom in the spring before the daylily season, and adding daylilies extends the flowering time for the whole planting. Varying the selection of daylilies can then extend the bloom time even further. Some gardeners choose one type of daylily—for instance a midseason, round, pink bloom, 22 in. (55.9 cm) high—but the great variety available makes easy work of forming a pleasing garden display. Generally, plant shorter daylilies at the front of the border and the tallest ones in the back. An occasional medium to a tall daylily, especially one with a small flower on a tall scape or an airy spider daylily, can be stunning close to the front edge.

Daylilies are excellent in cottage gardens, too, with their exuberance of brilliant colors. The rugged toughness of a good hybrid daylily ensures that it will continue to grow and thrive even as aggressive annuals and biennials self sow in the same area. Strong colors such as the coral-pink of 'Jeanne Fitton' (George Rasmussen, 1991) or the deep purple of 'Forbidden Desires' (Ted Petit, 1995) hold their own among the magentas and yellows that are prevalent in many cottage gardens. The bold spider forms such as the yellow 'Spider Miracle' (W. B. Hendricks, 1986) and the dusky purple 'Eggplant Escapade' (Margot Reed, 1996) will tame the wild abandonment of the cottage garden.

All daylilies may not be appropriate in a formal garden, but many selections would be stunning if given a bit of forethought. Formal gardens need good, clean foliage; strong, straight scapes; and reliable blooms. Many of the modern tetraploids would be ideal.

The collector's garden, of course, could be overflow-

The Darrel Apps garden, New Jersey. Photo by Melanie Vassallo

ing with modern daylilies. With thousands and thousands of named hybrids available, today's plant collector has a mind-boggling array of daylilies to choose from. To help narrow the choices, many collectors spotlight a specific type of daylily, such as tetraploids with strong eyes and edges; doubles; miniatures; or round, ruffled, pastel confections. Collections of daylilies by specific hybridizers, award winners such as Stout Medal winners, or heritage collections are all very popular. In these cases a collection could contain a wide variety of sizes, forms, and colors.

For the family garden modern daylilies can be a joy. They grow extremely well in an organic situation with no pesticides or chemical fertilizers. Children adore the names that spark their imagination, such as 'Spiderman' (Kenneth G. Durio, 1982), 'Piglet and Roo' (John Peat, 1998), 'Little Whipper Snapper' (Grace Stamile, 2002), or 'Wiggle Worm' (Bobby Baxter, 2002). Adults, too, will find names that tickle their fancy, such as 'Scorpion's Dance' (Geraldine L. Couturier, 1995), 'Dottie's Rompers' (Ra Hansen, 1996), 'Radiation Biohazard' (Jamie Gossard, 2000), or 'Twisted Sister' (Bob Schwarz, 1999).

Though rarely mentioned, the fact that every part of the daylily is edible and not poisonous to humans—provided no pesticides or chemicals have been used—is

another draw to the family garden. Since a new daylily bloom will open each day, it does no harm to pluck today's flower and make it a part of a meal. Tell a child that they can have a scoop of ice cream in their choice of daylily bloom and they will spend half an hour in the garden selecting the bloom that holds the largest scoop. An elegant addition to any garden party would be daylily blooms stuffed with chicken, tuna fish, or seafood salad, all served on a bed of lettuce.

Hobbyist gardeners, who enjoy many facets of gardening including growing plants from seed, would find hybridizing daylilies and harvesting their seed extremely easy and rewarding. Hybridizing is explained in more detail in Chapter 9, but I encourage hobbyist gardeners to try it.

Old-fashioned gardens that usually feature the full blooms of roses, peonies, and irises appreciate the full formed blooms of double daylilies. They come in small, "popcorn" sizes, large, "softball" sizes, and everything in between. The creamy pastels can be used to echo the earlier show put on by roses, azaleas, and peonies.

Low-maintenance or weekend gardeners would do well to add daylilies to their landscapes. Avid daylily collectors are quick to point out the many hours they spend grooming their plants, but in truth the modern daylily grows quite well even if neglected. Daylilies will thrive in sandy soils and tolerate hard clay conditions. Planted along a pond or stream, they will live through floods that cover their crowns for long periods of time. Similarly, a well established clump of daylilies will also survive a long period of drought, although bloom size and bud count will be diminished. Daylilies do appreciate a simple regime of incorporating compost or well rotted manure once in the spring and again after bloom is finished. Gardeners who do not have these products available can also use slow-release fertilizers. Even leftover lawn fertilizer will do. If rain fall has been low, a deep watering of an inch or more twice a week will keep daylilies thriving.

When choosing a location for a new daylily garden, one must take into account several factors. As I mentioned, daylilies require four to six hours or more of direct sunlight in USDA Zone 5a or warmer. Regions further north and in colder climatic zones should strive for locations with full-day sun. The proximity to water, either from underground sprinklers or hose connections, is important to avoid having to lug large amounts of water to new plants. Also consider that daylily blooms face the sun as they open. Gardens planted along the sides of man-made structures such as houses, garages, sheds, or barns work well because the blooms are sure to face outward toward viewers. Stockade fences or evergreen hedges work the same way. The blooms of daylilies planted in beds out in an open field, yard, or lawn will generally face southeast, south, or southwest. In this situation, remember to place markers recording the names of the daylilies on the southern side of the plants. Markers placed north of a daylily clump will cause visitors to forever circle a bed, first looking at the bloom and then searching for the name.

Peak daylily bloom time in northern portions of the United States and throughout Canada tends to be during the summer months. Due to rebloom, even southern locations experience bloom in the summertime. This timing makes daylilies ideal to add around swimming pools, decks, patios, and playgrounds. With their rugged nature, even if a ball lands in the middle of a clump or a wagging dog tail snaps off the top of a bloom scape, the daylilies will continue to grow and flourish. They will survive and even thrive when planted in large planters or containers.

Modern daylily cultivars that reliably rebloom are best for gardens in warmer zones and southern locales.

The Marion Miller garden, North Stonington, Connecticut. Photo by Melanie Vassallo

A garden in the Carolinas. Photo by Melanie Vassallo

These daylilies can offer months of beauty. Gardeners in cooler temperature zones, however, should not count on rebloom. Depending on the weather, a cool wet spring or an early frost, rebloom can be very sporadic. Northern gardens benefit more from cultivars with high bud count, but also consider how well a bloom opens under cool nights. A high bud count would be of little advantage if the blooms themselves struggle to open.

Visiting daylily gardens in your climate zone is an excellent way to locate those selections that thrive in local growing conditions. The American Hemerocallis Society (AHS) has hundreds of daylily display gardens throughout North America. A quick visit to the Internet at www. daylilies.org will show a listing of gardens in the various regions of the AHS. Just a short phone call is usually enough to schedule a tour.

After several years of growing daylilies, gardeners will find themselves with a delightful dilemma. Individual daylily clumps will need to be divided after three to five years in warmer zones and five to seven years in colder locations. Signs that a daylily is in need of division include crowded foliage and fewer bloom scapes. This is also the ideal time to refurbish the soil before replanting a smaller division of the daylily. If the clump yields a large number of divisions, replant them in an attractive arrangement of three pieces containing three to five fans each. Dig one large hole, add the soil

amendment of choice, and then arrange the three pieces in a triangle, leaving 12–15 in. (30.5–38 cm) between each piece. This arrangement makes it easy in the future to lift one of these pieces while keeping an established plant in the ground.

Gardeners with large tracts of land might gladly plant any excess divisions in new locations on their property. Urban and suburban home owners, though, with smaller pieces of land, will soon find themselves with more daylilies than garden space. Luckily these easy-to-grow plants are excellent for sharing with other gardeners. Daylilies donated to gardens planted at churches, firehouses, schools, and town plantings are always highly appreciated.

Companion Plants

Accepting of such a varied range of growing conditions, the modern daylily is the ultimate companion plant. Annuals, biennials, perennials, tropicals, bulbs, shrubs, and even decorative trees combine beautifully with daylilies.

Daylily collectors and hybridizers can easily become entrenched in monocultures, growing only daylilies. Not only can a monoculture be boring but it might also prove unhealthy. A monoculture, a garden that grows only a single plant type, easily attracts pests. Imagine an insect that feeds on daylilies flying over a field of daylilies—it would be like a bullhorn shouting "come

A garden in Connecticut. Photo by Melanie Vassallo

and get it." A diverse garden with many different plants makes it harder for pests to find their favorite meal. Also, many plants invite beneficial bugs into the garden, bugs that often will eat the pest bugs.

If a gardener wanted to choose only one companion plant to grow with their daylilies, I recommend yarrow (*Achillea millefolium*). Yarrow attracts a beneficial insect named *Orius insidiosus*, also known as minute pirate bug. This insect feeds on thrips, spider mites, aphids, and insect eggs. When insects are not available, they feed on pollen.

The number of companion plants that will beautify and enhance a daylily garden is staggering. Many people do not consider daylily foliage extremely attractive, so adding companions hides this aspect. Also, the daylily bloom season is quite specific; gardeners looking for longer seasonal interest should consider a large amount of companion plants.

Early spring is an exciting time in the garden, but daylilies make no impact at all at this time. Early blooming bulbs such as crocuses, hyacinths, tulips, daffodils (*Narcissus*), and grape hyacinths (*Muscari*) add color to the garden. The foliage must be left on these bulbs after they bloom for them to return in future years. Daylily foliage quickly grows and hides the dying foliage of the spring bulbs.

Early spring perennials are also an important part of the daylily garden. Blooms of lungwort, (*Pulmonaria*), snow in summer (*Cerastium tomentosum*), columbine (*Aquilegia*), pasque flower (*Pulsatilla vulgaris*), and more, will signal that spring has finally arrived. For semi-shaded beds the many species of *Helleborus* will begin blooming as early as late winter and continue through spring. Even after blooming their foliage is attractive, and best of all, deer will not eat hellebores.

Mid to late spring brings an even larger selection of companion plants. Numerous species of oriental onions (*Allium*), including chives, onions, and garlic, are available with different-sized blooms in shades of

lavender and white. Again, the daylily foliage will artfully hide the spent foliage of these bulbs. Perennial geraniums are easy to grow and many varieties thrive in the same conditions as daylilies. With almost evergreen foliage, crane's bill (*Geranium ×cantabrigiense* 'Biokovo') is just wonderful planted in front of daylilies, as is another ground cover, the tiny, creeping *Veronica* 'Waterperry Blue'.

Golden oregano (*Origanum vulgare* 'Aureum') is grown for its showy golden foliage. Combined with some of the purple-leafed coral bells (*Heuchera*), also known as alumroot, such as *Heuchera* 'Pewter Veil', tiny crested iris (*Iris cristata*), leopard's tongue (*Mazus rep-*

The Taylor garden in the Carolinas. Photo by Melanie Vassallo

The Jeffcoat garden, South Carolina. Photo by Melanie Vassallo

tans), and dew-studded lady's mantle (*Alchemilla mollis*), the garden will have a lovely front border to set off the lower growing daylilies. The little known compact goat's beard (*Aruncus aethusifolius*) has a lovely bloom and extremely attractive foliage. It stays perfectly in its boundaries and makes an excellent companion for daylilies, particularly in front of the miniature varieties. Semi-shade locations can also feature *Corydalis lutea*, bugleweed (*Ajuga reptans*), and the newer dead nettle hybrids (*Lamium maculatum*). *Liriope muscari* is also considered an excellent edging plant for daylilies, but it does not begin to put on a show until later in the season.

Bleeding hearts (*Dicentra*), bearded iris (*Iris germanica*), foxgloves (*Digitalis*), lupine (*Lupinus*), spider-wort hybrids (*Tradescantia*), cushion spurge (*Euphorbia polychroma*), and meadow rue (*Thalictrum aquilegiifolium*) all add some height to the late spring garden just as the daylily foliage is putting on heavy growth.

Perennials for the middle of the daylily border that flower just before daylily season include the shrub-like false indigo (*Baptisia*), poker lily (*Kniphofia*), Maltese cross (*Lychnis chalcedonica*), big betony (*Stachys macrantha* 'Superba'), sundrop (*Oenothera* 'Cold Crick'), lamb's ears (*Stachys byzantina*), and peach-leafed bellflower (*Campanula persicifolia*). All of these appreciate the full sun conditions that daylilies thrive upon.

For the height of daylily season choose companion plants that will enhance the daylilies. Perennials in colors not available yet in the daylily world are excellent choices. The dark blues, purples, and lavenders of

Japanese irises (*Iris ensata*) are spectacular companions for daylilies. Tall, stunning blooms on *Iris ensata* 'Aka Fur' or 'Pleasant Journey' can be showstoppers. The thread-leafed tickseed varieties (*Coreopsis verticillata*) are very popular now in gardening circles but are not always hardy where daylilies grow. Southern gardens will appreciate *Coreopsis* 'Sweet Dreams' and 'Limerock Ruby', while cooler climates would do better with *C. verticillata* 'Zagreb' and 'Moonbeam'. Lance-leafed coreopsis (*C. lanceolata*) is a short-lived, self-sowing perennial that will thrive in daylily gardens. Catmints (*Nepeta*) are stellar companions for daylilies. They peak just as the daylilies begin to bloom and attract a host of butterflies to the garden. The pink-blooming *Nepeta grandiflora* 'Dawn to Dusk' is enchanting while the tall *N.* 'Six Hills Giant' puts out a cloud of frothy blue flowers.

Hostas, so often relegated to the shade garden, are a favorite companion plant for daylily gardens that are not planted in full sun. Quite tolerant of full sun, especially if there is plenty of moisture, hostas will enhance a daylily planting and delight the collecting gardener's nature. The light chartreuse foliage of *Hosta* 'Sea Fire' or the light variegated foliage of 'Spritzer' will add zing to a sea of daylilies. Stonecrop (*Sedum*) is another collector's plant that is available in many different types. Insisting on full sun and tolerant of less than desirable conditions, they are a must as companions for daylilies. Some varieties creep along the ground and should be used along the front edges. Some varieties are upright and bloom along with the daylilies, such as the charming yellow *Sedum* 'Lemon Snowflakes' and the cool creamy *S. telephium* subsp. *ruprechtii*, which also showcases blue foliage. And do not ignore the late-summer- and early fall-blooming varieties, such as *S. telephium* 'Matrona', *S.* 'Herbstfreude' (previously known as 'Autumn Joy'), or *S. spectabile* 'Brilliant'.

To add much beauty during the daylily bloom season, consider the gorgeous flowers of *Phlox paniculata*, purple coneflower (*Echinacea*), globe thistle (*Echinops ritro*),

Salvia sylvestris 'Mainacht' (May night), *Liatris*, balloon flower (*Platycodon*), lady's bells (*Adenophora*), butterfly weed (*Asclepias*), *Astilbe*, bee balm (*Monarda*), and Stokes' aster (*Stokesia laevis*). Choose color combinations that will enhance the neighboring daylily blooms.

Once the daylilies begin to wind down, mid to late summer bloomers are also valuable additions to the garden. Choices among bulbs and tubers include the beauty of the Asiatic lily (*Lilium candidum*), the sword-like *Crocosmia* ×*crocosmiiflora*, the tropical foliage and blooms of cannas, and the floriferousness of dahlias. Among perennials, warm autumn colors in the blooms of chrysanthemums (*Dendranthema* ×*grandiflora*), asters, sneezeweed (*Helenium*), and hardy fuchsias, often called lady's eardrops, keep the magic alive. The genus *Rudbeckia* offers several useful daylily companions. Giant coneflower (*R. maxima*) is a good addition to achieve tall punctuations in the daylily garden. It stays in a clump and is a slow grower. Black-eyed Susan, or golden coneflower (*R. fulgida* var. *sullivantii* 'Goldsturm'), is also a beautiful daylily companion, but it can be invasive. *Rudbeckia laciniata* 'Herbstsonne' is a more vigorous, tall variety but not at all invasive. Combine it with tall, late blooming daylilies for a stunning display.

Annuals, too, make great additions to the daylily garden. Many varieties will scatter enough seed that they

The Marion Miller garden, North Stonington, Connecticut. Photo by Melanie Vassallo

will return from year to year. Sweet alyssum (*Lobularia maritima*) will create a frothy white front border as the summer progresses. Catchfly (*Silene armeria*) puts forth tons of hot pink blooms and will return in waves. Cosmos and spider flower (*Cleome hassleriana*) add height and beautiful colors to the daylily garden.

Shrubs that work as companions to daylilies could take up another whole chapter, but I will mention just a few stellar performers here. The small Japanese spireas, such as *Spiraea japonica* 'Alpina Little Princess', will bloom during early daylily season. Blue mist shrub (*Caryopteris*) adds a wonderful foliage background and then clouds of blue flowers when the daylilies are done blooming. Another excellent backdrop comes from hy-drangeas, which bloom in blue to rose colors at the same time as daylilies in warm climates. Hardy hibiscus cultivars, such as *Hibiscus moscheutos* 'Kopper King', carry attractive foliage and large tropical blooms. With *H. syriacus* (rose of Sharon), hardy to Zone 5, and its cultivars, almost everyone can find a hibiscus for their garden. Butterfly bush (*Buddleja davidii*) is an excellent shrub to keep in the back of a daylily border. Not only are the foliage and flowers beautiful, but the added attraction of butterflies makes it a spotlight in the garden. In southern gardens, gardenias bloom at the same time as daylilies, and their strong sweet scent can perfume an entire garden. Finally, the variegated dogwood shrub (*Cornus alba* 'Elegantissima') can be grouped with a tall

The Watts garden, Mississippi. Photo by Melanie Vassallo

A garden in the Carolinas. Photo by Melanie Vassallo

catmint (*Nepeta*) and a ruffled pink daylily, such as 'Pacific Princess' (Ted Petit, 2000), and visitors will heap on the compliments.

I have not yet mentioned ornamental grasses, but they are highly attractive companions to daylilies. Small grasses such as blue fescue (*Festuca cinerea*), black mondo grass (*Ophiopogon*), and tufted grass or sedge (*Carex stricta*) look lovely weaving in and out toward the front of the daylily garden. The variegated Hakone grass (*Hakonechloa macra*) works in this location, too. Midsized grasses such as zebra grass (*Miscanthus sinensis* 'Morning Light') or fountain grass (*Pennisetum alopecuroides* 'Hameln') will echo the structure and form of the daylily clump. The tall grasses *Miscanthus sinensis* 'Strictus' and 'Gracillimus' add strength and backbone to the rear of the daylily garden.

Selected combinations of the plants mentioned in this chapter are sure to be pleasing. Keep in mind the various sizes, bloom seasons, and colors when grouping plants. Remember that most of these plants will be forgiving if gardeners find it necessary to rearrange the planting pattern. The most important advice I have for gardeners choosing daylily companions is to look for plants that show off attractive foliage for most of the growing season. Also, plants with easy going natures, like daylilies, will make a gardener's life easier. Finally, select plants with long bloom seasons to add interest and seasonal color to the garden.

CHAPTER 7

Daylily Cultivation

As we have mentioned, daylilies are among the most carefree perennials in gardens today. Compared to many other garden plants, the horticultural requirements of the modern daylily still remain minimal. Sunlight, soil, and water are the few primary requirements to consider when planting a new daylily or moving or dividing an old one. The previous chapter on landscaping touched upon some general preferences of daylilies, but this chapter will discuss them in more detail.

Sunlight and Choosing a Planting Site

Daylilies prefer full sun, although they will grow happily in partial shade. A minimum of four to six hours of direct sunlight, preferably in the morning, is generally recommended in USDA Zone 5a or warmer. Daylilies will usually survive in full shade but will produce fewer flowers or none at all. Signs of too little direct sunlight are lanky foliage and unusually tall flower scapes that tend to lean toward the sun. The colder the climate—and, therefore, the weaker the sunlight—the more direct sun the plants will need. In very cold climates,

colder than Zone 5a, plant daylilies in an area where they will receive full sun for most of the day. In warm, sunny climates daylilies can tolerate less sun.

The flowers themselves benefit most from a little shade in midday to late afternoon, when the sun is at its hottest, particularly in hot, sunny climates and with dark-colored flowers, such as reds, purples, and blacks. These richly colored, dark flowers absorb the heat from the sun and will often scorch in full, hot sun. Shade during the hottest period of the day will keep these flowers looking their best. Also remember that daylily flowers tend to open facing the sun, so plant them where the flowers will face viewers.

Soil and Planting

We have observed daylilies growing in virtually every type of soil, from Florida sand to heavy clay. Daylilies are not overly particular about soil conditions, although they do perform best in moist but well drained soil. Daylilies also love loose soil with lots of aeration, rather than soil that is densely packed. Loosen the soil prior to planting, as you would for any plant. Adding organic matter is always a good idea, such as manure, rotted leaves, compost, and so on. Many gardeners have found that daylilies thrive with fine pine bark worked into the soil; it works extremely well to keep the soil aerated. Remember, however, that any decaying organic matter requires nitrogen to decay and will deplete it from the soil. If you use uncomposted organic matter, be sure to compensate by increasing the amount of fertilizer.

Before planting, prepare a hole large enough to accommodate the plant and form a mound at the bottom of the hole on which to set the plant. Then set the plant to the same height as it was in the soil before—note the difference in the color of the leaves. They will be green where they were above ground and white where they were below. For newly purchased plants, plant them immediately and water them in well, or if they appear dry, place them in water overnight to saturate them prior to planting. Always leave the root system intact. Since the plant is depending on the roots to obtain its water and nourishment, do not trim them.

Spread the roots out in all directions in the planting hole before covering them, particularly in environments frequented by freeze-thaw conditions. Spreading the roots out over a wider area, reduces the likelihood of "winter heave," where plants literally lift out of the ground, and increases the probability of winter survival.

Although daylilies are tolerant of a wide soil pH range, ideally they prefer neutral to slightly acidic conditions. Daylilies usually flourish in the average garden despite imbalances in soil pH; however, if plants fail to thrive despite your care, consider having the soil tested for pH by a local agricultural agent.

Water

Daylilies prefer moist but well drained soil. Although they are very drought resistant and can survive under conditions that overtake most other plants, they perform much better when well watered. At the other extreme, though they are often seen growing in ditches and can withstand flooding better than most other plants, they do not do well with prolonged periods in standing water. Daylilies growing in colder climates must not be left in standing water over winter. The

The parts of a daylily plant. Watercolor by Lesa Peat

freezing and thawing action of the water will often kill the plants. In hot climates, standing water during the heat of summer increases the risk of diseases that can cause the plants to develop crown rot.

Daylilies particularly enjoy lots of water during the bloom season in order to produce large, voluptuous blooms. Locate plants where they can receive an ample supply of water when blooming. Mulching with some organic matter is not required but it helps to retain water, keeping the soil moist and cool. The particular type of mulch is not important, but be aware that mulch can cause an increased risk of slugs in some climates.

Fertilizer

Like all other perennials, daylilies enjoy some fertilizer. It is not absolutely necessary, but in order to get the maximum enjoyment out of your daylilies, some fertilizer is beneficial. Any balanced fertilizer is adequate, such as 6-6-6 or 20-20-20, which can usually be purchased in a local garden center. For the modern hybrids, many growers are finding that slow-release fertilizers produce the best performance, often causing the growth of large, leek-sized fans and increasing flower-bud production. Daylilies seem to respond well to small amounts of fertilizer applied continuously throughout the growing season in cold climates and year-round in warm climates. Though this is certainly not necessary for backyard gardeners, it does result in larger plants with more opulently and exotically displayed blooms. Generally, an application of fertilizer in the spring and another prior to bloom is

Evergreen daylily foliage in early spring. Watercolor by Lesa Peat

Semi-evergreen daylily foliage emerging in early spring. Watercolor by Lesa Peat

sufficient to ensure good growth and healthy bloom. Daylilies will grow as naturalized plants with little care, but a continuous, slow-release fertilizer and adequate water will bring out the best in the modern hybrids.

Climate and Evergreen vs. Dormant

Daylilies will thrive in virtually any climate. While most do well across a large climate range, certain varieties do perform better in the extreme climatic zones. For example, in very cold climates, such as Canada, dormant daylilies are able to perform well since they get the sufficient chilling they need. Even in locations that receive only mild frosts, however, many dormant daylilies will also perform very well. Some pure evergreens are not cold hardy and may not be able to survive in the most extreme cold areas; however, most modern evergreens are quite cold hardy and will also thrive in these conditions. In very hot climates, such as the deep, southern United States and northern Australia, evergreen varieties generally tend to perform better.

Although most daylilies require some degree of winter chilling in order to survive or bloom, some varieties perform well even in frost-free climates. Dormants do require some degree of winter chilling in order to sur-

Dormant daylily foliage emerging in early spring. Watercolor by Lesa Peat

vive and bloom. Pure evergreens do not require any chilling to survive, but may require some to bloom, depending on the cultivar. Most plants today, however, come from a heritage including both dormant and evergreen parents and themselves vary in degree of semi-evergreen. Hybridizers have been breeding evergreen and dormant plants for so many generations that few modern daylilies are purely evergreen or dormant plants. The advantage is that, with few exceptions, most daylilies today thrive across a very wide climatic extreme. Semi-evergreen to dormant daylilies are generally recommended for Zone 4 and colder, although most evergreen varieties also do very well in these regions. In Zones 9a–11 some very hard dormants, such as 'Stella De Oro', are used as annuals in the landscape trade; however, the vast majority of dormants do very well in these warm climates.

Winter Care

Most authorities generally recommend that gardeners mulch daylilies prior to the onset of winter in colder climates. Although not absolutely necessary, mulching will increase their survival rate, particularly of recent additions to the garden that are not yet well established. Apply mulch after the first major freeze, locking the cold into the soil and preventing freeze-thaw cycles. When spring arrives with its cool, wet rains and the last killing frost has past, rake the heavy mulch off the daylilies. Removing the mulch also removes the envi-

ronment in which slugs, earwigs, and other pests thrive. These pests can affect or inhibit new growth of the daylily leaves. The raking action is also beneficial in that it removes old evergreen foliage that has frozen and become damaged over the winter, allowing the unrestricted growth of new foliage. Once the rainy season has subsided, reapply a lighter mulch to help retain moisture and keep the soil temperatures cool.

Dividing and Propagating

After daylilies have been growing for a few years, they probably will have formed large clumps. Daylilies typically increase from one "fan," or plant, into several during the average season, forming a clump after a few seasons. Eventually you may notice a decline in the quality of flowers as the plants become root bound. Large clumps left undivided for years generally produce fewer blooms of inferior quality. For optimal enjoyment of your daylilies, divide the clumps periodically.

Late summer to early fall is the ideal time to divide daylily clumps, since it gives the newly planted fans enough time to become fully established prior to next season's bloom time. Six weeks prior to the first frost is generally recommended. In colder climates, do not wait until too late, since the plants need to establish before the onset of winter. If you are concerned about possible winter losses, spring is also an excellent time for planting and dividing in colder climates. In hot climates, because of the possibility of losing plants to extreme heat, the cooler fall weather is better for dividing daylilies.

Plants can be divided into single fans, but the flowers often look better from small clumps of two to three plants. These small clumps allow the growth of a large healthy root system to support the plants and produce the most attractive flowers. A newly divided clump or newly acquired plants take one to three years to fully establish and show their full potential.

To divide a clump, first dig it up and remove as much soil as possible from the root mass by spraying it with a garden hose. This cleaning allows you to see more clearly the individual plants and their root mass. Often a clump will have separated into more than one crown on its own, allowing you to simply pry the plants apart, although this apparently simple task can be arduous, since the roots are typically tangled. If the plants do not pull apart by hand, use a knife to divide them. If you need to cut the clump, make sure that each plant has some roots attached to it. Also, cutting a plant makes it susceptible to fungus infection on the open wounds, leading to rot. Avoid cutting plants during the hot summer months, for fear of losing them. If you must divide daylilies in the heat of summer, soak the plants for a few minutes in a fungicide or apply a dry fungicide to the wound prior to planting.

Trim the leaves on newly divided plants back to approximately one-third to one-half their original size. Since the roots have been disturbed, the plants are less capable of supplying the leaves with water and nutrients. This trimming allows the plant to survive while it reestablishes its root system. Using a fertilizer with high phosphorus with minors, such as 10–52–10, promotes rapid root growth after transplanting.

Plant daylilies 18–36 in. (46–91 cm) apart, depending on how long you plan for them to remain there. If you would like an immediate display of color, plants can be spaced close together; however, they will need to be divided sooner than those spaced farther apart.

Some daylilies develop "proliferations," or small plants on the flower scapes. Although they typically do not form roots, proliferations are capable of forming roots and often do so during prolonged rainy weather. Proliferations can be removed from the scape and treated like any other small plant or cutting. Induce the plant to form new roots by placing it in a glass of water or treating it as you would a cutting. Another method of inducing root growth is to remove the bract (see the figure on parts of the daylily in Chapter 7), then fill a small piece of plastic wrap with potting soil, and tie it to the scape at the base of the proliferation. This keeps the base of the proliferation moist and encourages its root formation. Applying a rooting hormone will increase the chances of the proliferation forming roots. Once several roots have formed on the proliferation, it can either be planted directly in the ground in late summer, or potted and grown as a houseplant over winter. The resulting plant will be identical to the mother plant from which it was removed.

CHAPTER 8

Daylily Pests and Diseases

with Sue Bergeron

Gardeners who grow a few daylilies among their other plants probably will not notice much in the way of pest and disease problems. Most readers of this book, however, have likely succumbed completely to the daylily's charms and progressed into the collecting mode. You will be bringing plants in from various sources, perhaps growing them in daylily-only groups, and the numbers of specimens will begin mounting. The chance that you may be presented with a pest or disease problem of some kind will also increase.

Minimize potential problems by ensuring good growing conditions. Providing adequate water, fertilizing when necessary, and keeping weeds under control will help give daylilies the upper hand. But do not get over-enthusiastic with fertilizer, as this can predispose plants to pest and disease problems. Too much fertilizer can also directly damage plants. Another healthy practice is to water thoroughly at intervals rather than applying small amounts frequently. If you irrigate with overhead sprinklers rather than soaker hoses, do so early in the day. Because fungal diseases generally ap-

preciate wet leaves, make conditions more difficult for them by giving the foliage enough time to dry before nightfall.

Should a disease problem occur, correctly identifing the culprit is important so that you can apply the most effective control method at the most appropriate time. Brown spots on leaves may indicate either disease or insect problems. The different feeding habits of different pests can help ascertain the perpetrator. Some, such as slugs and earwigs, chew pieces out of the leaves or flowers. Others, such as aphids, have "beaks" that pierce plant tissue, allowing the pests to suck out the juices. Diseases may attack leaves, scapes, roots, or the crown. Leaf damage is obvious, but if the problem is below ground you may see just an unhealthy-looking plant. Listed here are the major pest and disease problems for daylilies, categorized by symptoms and signs.

Daylily Rust

A yellow or orange powdery substance that comes off when touched is likely to indicate daylily rust, caused by the fungus *Puccinia hemerocallidis.* This disease does not occur in all countries, and first arrived in North America in 2000. It is, therefore, not fully understood. *Patrinia* and daylilies are the only plants currently proven to be affected by this disease. *Patrinia*, currently relatively uncommon in North American gardens, theoretically may enable daylily rust to overwinter in colder zones, although at this time no evidence exists to support this and the possibility is still being researched. Daylily rust can persist from year to year on daylilies alone in mild winter areas, but it is killed during winter in cooler climates. Even if a plant becomes infected with rust, the rust will not overwinter in areas that receive prolonged freezing temperatures. In North America, rust cannot survive winters north of Georgia; thus, daylily rust is only a problem for southern gardeners.

It has become clear that different daylily cultivars show tremendous differences in susceptibility to rust. While some southern gardeners have chosen to spray fungicides to control rust, many others have chosen to compost the most susceptible plants. Once these plants are gone, the remaining daylilies show relatively little damage from rust, with most of the damage occurring on the lower, senescent leaves, having little effect on the overall garden appearance of the plants. Also, some major daylily hybridizers are creating new daylily hybrids that are increasingly resistant to rust.

Rust appears to be worst during mild to warm rainy weather, showing little evidence during extreme heat or cold. For those who insist on perfectly groomed gardens, with no trace of disease or damage, daylily rust can be controlled with fungicides. Check with a local extension service or equivalent for the latest control recommendations. During this period of culling highly susceptible cultivars and breeding more rust-resistant ones, some gardeners have chosen to spray only occasionally during spring and fall, when the symptoms are worst. Other gardeners simply destroy the most susceptible plants and ignore it on the rest.

Aphids

A number of loose, white flecks, often described as dandruff on leaves, that can be somewhat sticky, probably signifies the presence of aphids. Aphid feeding may sometimes result in brown spots, occasionally leading to confusion with daylily rust. If you part the leaves and look down into the depths of the plant, where aphids like to congregate while enjoying lunch, you should be able to see them. If the aphid population builds up significantly, plants may grow with less than their normal enthusiasm and the leaves may appear yellow. Aphids can usually be controlled by spraying the plants with a water hose. If they become a nuisance, a number of insecticides are readily available in garden centers for their control.

Spider Mites

White and yellow speckles on leaves, especially indoors or during dry weather, may point to the presence of spider mites. Spider mite injury can also result in brown spots or areas on the leaf, leading to confusion with signs of daylily rust. Look for webbing underneath the affected leaves, and you might even be able to observe the tiny mites moving. A magnifying glass will help and may allow you to see the tiny round mite eggs, as well as determine whether any brown spots have yellow-orange, powdery rust spores. The undersides of the leaves, where the mites most often eat, sometimes also have a dried, silver to gray cast, along with the possible yellow to brown spots. Many gardeners merely spray plants with water frequently, especially the under sides of the leaves, to discourage spider mites. For those preferring stronger stuff, bear in mind that using the wrong pesticide can even increase spider mite damage. In larger applications, spider mites can quickly become resistant to specific chemicals, so rotating among different chemicals becomes important. The home gardener, however, can best attack these pests with the garden hose.

Leaf Streak

If leaves have yellow and brown streaks, especially along the midrib, the problem is likely to be leaf streak, a fungal disease caused by *Aureobasidium microstictum.* Affected leaves may die. Some gardeners report success with fungicides, others rely on cleaning up old foliage in the fall to reduce infective material. However, leaf streak does little apparent harm to the plant, so most gardeners simply ignore it.

Crown Rot

Wilting, possibly yellowing leaves with disintegrating plant tissue at or below soil level may signify infection by a rot-causing fungus or bacterium. When a leaf is pulled from the sick plant, the infected tissue may emit a strong, unpleasant odor in some cases, particularly with bacterial soft rot, but other types of rot are not as odoriferous and one's nose should not be the only diagnostic tool. Environmental factors, pest injury, and gardening practices can all influence the development of rot. If plant losses are significant, contact a diagnostic service through the local extension office or equivalent so that any fungi, bacteria, pests, or other contributing factors can be identified and a solution recommended.

Rot is most common in warm climate areas during hot, wet periods. The entire plant will generally turn yellow, at which point the rot has probably invaded the crown and little can be done to save that fan. If the fan is part of a clump, the rot can spread to the rest of the clump or may stop with the single fan. If the plant is important and you wish to save it, dig up the clump, clean off any deteriorating tissue, and soak the remaining plants in a systemic fungicide or a combination of systemic and contact fungicides. Often, simply drenching the clump in a combination of systemic and contact fungicides is sufficient to stop the progression of crown rot into the remainder of the clump.

Spring Sickness

Stunted fans early in the season, often growing sideways with brown, "saw-tooth" leaf edges and holes, could signify spring sickness. It may affect only one or two fans in a daylily clump, or several. These fans may or may not start growing normally later in the season, but some do manage to bloom. This disorder has been a puzzle for decades and no method is currently established for prevention or control. Since spring sickness rarely occurs in climates with mild winters, growers generally assume it to be the result of winter damage and some advantageous fungus. When daylily gardeners are confronted with this affliction, a common course of action is to either ignore it or cut off the offending fans at ground level. Do not decapitate them too late, though, or you may inadvertently remove the developing flower scape as well.

Thrips, Tarnished Plant Bugs, and Earwigs

Silvery streaks and spots on leaves, or distorted flowers and buds that drop, could indicate the presence of thrips. Tarnished plant bugs may also damage daylily flower buds. Thrips are very small, elongated insects, whereas tarnished plant bug adults are larger—about 0.25 in. (0.64 cm) long and brownish—and are very adept at ducking under a flower bud or leaf when they think you are looking at them. Baby tarnished plant bugs resemble green aphids, but they move a lot more quickly. In addition to bud dropping, thrips are reputed to cause misshapen, discolored, and gnarled areas on flower blooms. They are also sometimes blamed for pale marks on flowers, although if the lighter mark is circular, and there may be a number of them, this is more likely the result of water spots in partially open buds. Thrips are generally worse in cool weather. When the surface of the bloom has literally been chewed away leaving white patches, the culprits are probably earwigs.

Snails and Slugs

Snails and slugs can become pests, especially in cool, damp climates. They most commonly attack newly emerging leaves, chewing ragged notches in the sides of the leaf, causing them to appear frayed on the edges. You can sometimes see the telltale shiny slime tracks. In cases of an extreme infestation, they can also eat holes in the middle of the leaf and even attack the flowers.

Snails and slugs generally feed at night and find refuge during the day under mulch and debris. Removing any dead organic material close to the daylilies is generally the best course of action to prevent their damage. In extreme cases, slug bait can be purchased at most garden centers.

Gall Midge

If flower buds become unusually swollen or distorted and contain tiny, whitish maggots, your daylilies may have been visited by another pest new to North America, currently reported only in British Columbia. The maggots are the larvae of a small fly, *Contarinia quinquenotata*, commonly called the hemerocallis gall midge. If you believe your daylilies have this pest, have a local diagnostic laboratory familiar with them confirm their identification and advise you of appropriate action. Contacting local agricultural authorities will also help track its spread within the continent.

The gall midge is well known in Europe, but its introduction to North America is too recent to indicate to what extent it will be a problem here. Control of this pest is easy if gardeners are diligent in looking for the problem. In British Columbia, the adult fly lays her eggs in mid May, with the larvae hatching out and crawling into one or two of the largest buds on a flowering scape. The damage caused by their presence is clearly evident by mid June, and any affected buds should be picked off and destroyed. Since this insect has only one generation per year, destroying affected buds cuts the life cycle for that year and will significantly reduce the numbers for the following year.

Despite these few pests and diseases that attack modern daylilies, most of them do little overall damage to the plant. Except in extreme circumstances, most of them require little or no attention from backyard gardeners, as daylily clumps thrive in natural settings. Typically, the few problems that might appear require only a good spraying from a water hose. Even with the new daylily rust, the most effective treatment is to simply compost the most vulnerable plants and ignore it on the rest. The daylily continues to be a most maintenance-free perennial for the garden, and with reasonable care, one that should not require chemical sprays or treatments from average gardeners.

CHAPTER 9

Hybridizing Daylilies

One appealing and exciting quality of daylilies is the ease with which any gardener can cross-pollinate flowers, set seed, and raise seedlings to blooming plants in a short time. We spend a great deal of time speaking at different clubs and societies, where we always encourage gardening enthusiasts, young and old, to join us in creating new flower faces. It is a fun and fascinating part of gardening that most backyard gardeners have never tried but often fall in love with once they begin.

Why Hybridize?

Many people ask, "Why should I start hybridizing at this stage in the evolution of the daylily? What is left to do?" Quite simply, the possibilities are endless. For example, only recently did two categories come into being in the Awards and Honors System of the American Hemerocallis Society (AHS). The Lambert/Webster Unusual Forms Award for exotic and unusual formed daylilies was created in 2000, a clear indication that this type of flower is still in its infancy. The R. W. Munson Jr. Award for patterned daylilies is the newest of the

awards, created in 2001. Bill Munson choose this type of flower to receive an award carrying his name because he felt that the potential for patterns in daylily flowers is virtually limitless, and that we have only just begun to explore the possibilities. These are just two new areas of interest. Polytepals are also just beginning, and many other novel facets are open for exploration, such as the new three-dimensional carving, shark's tooth edging, patterns that surround the petal edges to form multiple picotees, and formal hose-in-hose doubles, just to mention a few.

To begin, ask yourself what type of daylily you find most beautiful. This is not a difficult question; simply look at the daylilies you already have in your garden. You chose them because they have something that appeals to you, be it their color, size, form, and so on. Begin your hybridizing efforts by crossing them, and move further in that direction. Every generation will give you new ideas, as new daylily faces emerge from your "painting with pollen." If you want to make your seedlings look more modern, consider purchasing just one cutting-edge daylily to add to your gene pool. You will probably be astonished at the flowers you create.

Another typical question is, "Why should I hybridize when I can't compete with the large Florida hybridizing nurseries?" This is somewhat like asking why should you have children, the Kennedys have already had some, and it will be difficult for your children to compete with theirs. But, you do not have to compete. Every artist paints with a different style, and your living paintings will reflect your style. Every child is different and brings joy to their parents; so it is with gardening creations.

Also, gardeners in warm climates do not always have an advantage. For example, in warmer climates most tetraploid daylilies have difficulty setting seed, especially the spiders. Hybridizers have speculated that the pistils of the large-flowered spiders are so long that the pollen cannot reach the ovary to fertilize it before the ovary becomes senescent. Daylilies set seed more readily in cool weather, so spider and spider variant daylilies are a dream come true for gardeners in colder climates.

Another concern we often hear is that gardeners do not have the time to hybridize, because they have to leave for work early in the morning before pollen sacks are open. This hurdle can easily be overcome by storing pollen from your favorite daylilies. Simply pick the blooms you wish to use as pollen parents and place them in a cup of water in the refrigerator. You will find that the pollen is fresh and ready to use the next morning. As long as it is kept dry, pollen can be stored in the refrigerator for days before use, with no loss in vitality. Some hybridizers have even begun trading special or difficult-to-obtain pollen with friends in distant places, using overnight courier services.

Gardeners really have no reason not to hybridize daylilies. It does not take a large garden. Sometimes only a few seedlings from your favorite cultivars can add untold enjoyment to your gardening time. Simply watching your own creations grow, and the anticipation of seeing what their flowers ultimately will look like,

will probably have you rushing to your garden every morning like a child at Christmas.

Hybridizing Techniques

The specific technique of hybridizing is a simple one that anyone can do. Simply take the pollen from one flower, dab it onto the pistil of another, then harvest and plant the seeds when they ripen. Within nine months to two years, a newly created daylily will bloom. Hybridizing is as simple as that, although some do embellish on the technique. And there is no such thing as a mistake. The results of any cross can be diverse and unexpected. Even if the same two plants are used by different hybridizers, the resulting progeny is always somewhat different.

One critical component in any attempt to hybridize daylilies is ploidy: diploid daylilies cannot be crossed successfully with tetraploid daylilies. (Please see Chapter 3 for an explanation of diploid and tetraploid and why they are not compatible.) To find out whether plants are diploid or tetraploid consult the AHS cultivar checklists, the *Eureka Daylily Reference Guide*, the supplier of the particular daylily, or the Internet. (To order the AHS cultivar checklists, contact Jimmy Jordan at 276 Caldwell Dr., Jackson, TN 38301, tel 731-422-2208; http://www.daylilies.org/ahs/. To order the *Eureka Daylily Reference Guide* contact Ken Gregory at Box 7611, Asheville, NC 28802, tel 828-236-2222; http://www.gardeneureka.com/.) Once you determine the ploidy of the plants you wish to breed, be sure to cross diploids with diploids and tetraploids with tetraploids. If you cannot determine a plant's ploidy, the worst that can happen is that the flowers will not set seed pods, or any pods it does set will abort before the seeds ripen.

To begin hybridizing, be aware of the basic parts of the daylily plant, shown in Chapter 7. The simplest method is to begin by removing a stamen, the male flower part, from one flower. At the end of the stamen is the anther, which contains the yellow to gold pollen sacs. Hold the stamen and brush its pollen onto the pistil, the female part, of another flower. Since the pistil of the daylily is usually much longer than the stamens, most hybridizers do not bother covering the pistil to prevent bees, butterflies, or other insects from pollinating the flower. If the two flowers that you wish to cross are not open on the same day, refrigerate the pollen. For longer term storage, pollen can be frozen.

Freezing pollen involves gently removing, or "popping off," the anther into a container using a pair of tweezers or your fingernails.

The container can be as simple as a folded piece of aluminum foil, a film cannister, or contact lens cases. Freeze

Pollen being applied to the pistil of a daylily flower during hybridizing. Watercolor by Lesa Peat

pollen while it is still fresh, and always keep it dry, especially when removing it from the freezer. Since condensation typically forms on the outside of the container, allow it to reach room temperature and dry before opening it. Frozen pollen can be defrosted and refrozen for use anytime, including the following spring, or even years hence. When ready to make the cross, take the pollen sac from the container—a pair of reverse tweezers works most easily—and use it as you would fresh pollen. If you need only a small amount of pollen, a small artist's brush can pick up just a few grains of pollen. Be sure to always clean the brush between uses of different types of pollen.

Most pollen is fertile, with a few exceptions. The pollen from tetraploids converted from diploid plants can be extremely difficult to use, since it is often not very fertile. Also, some cultivars have pollen that is white, crystalized, or clumped in appearance; this pollen is typically hollow and will usually not set a seed pod. It is not completely impossible to set seeds from such pollen—a few viable pollen grains are often mixed in with the sterile pollen. Also, if the pollen from a plant is not viable, you can often still get seed from the plant by using it as the pod parent. Even with deliberate pollination, many crosses do not take, and seed pods do not form. To help bring about a success, make crosses in the cool, moist period of early morning. Successful crosses become less and less likely as the day progresses and the temperature rises. On cool, overcast days, though, pollination can be successful well into the afternoon.

Recording the pod and pollen parents of crosses and keeping careful records is important. The most common method is to use white paper "jewelers' tags," those generally used for marking prices. They are readily available in most office supply stores. Always use a

waterproof permanent marker to write on the tags. The lettering must be able to withstand rain and watering over the six to eight weeks until seed harvest.

Daylily flower following pollination showing newly forming seed pod and parentage tag. Watercolor by Lesa Peat

A few days after pollination, the daylily flower will drop off. If pollination was successful, a very small green seed pod will be at the base of what was once the flower. The seed pod will slowly enlarge and mature within six to eight weeks. A mature seed pod will turn brown and split open to reveal round, glossy black seeds. Keep a close watch on the seed pods as they mature, since once they crack open the seeds are easily scattered by wind and rain.

After collecting the seeds store them in containers, such as envelopes or Ziploc bags, labeled with their parentage and place them in the refrigerator for a period of chilling. For maximal germination, particularly if the parent plants have some degree of dormancy, refrigerate the seeds for a minimum of three weeks. Most hybridizers attempt to keep the seeds moist during chilling. Some research suggests that completely dried out seeds do not receive the benefits of refrigeration. We place a small amount of a mild fungicide and water mixture into the Zip-loc bags before sealing, to both moisten the seeds and prevent fungi from growing and causing the seeds to rot.

Immature daylily seed pods and parentage tags during ripening stage. Watercolor by Lesa Peat

Fully mature seed pod containing black seeds ready for harvest. Watercolor by Lesa Peat

Following the refrigeration period, daylily seeds may be planted outside in the fall or spring, or started inside. Simply treat them as you would any other seeds. Daylily seeds sown outdoors in the fall in cold climates do not need to be refrigerated, since they will be chilled naturally. However, if they sprout before the onset of winter, the plants may not reach sufficient maturity before the cold sets in and they may be lost. Also, as the grower you lose the benefit of the winter growing time. Most hybridizers and gardeners in cold climates start their seedlings inside and overwinter them in a greenhouse, sunny window, or under grow lights in the basement. Then, when spring arrives, they plant the young seedlings in the garden.

Though not necessary, many hybridizers in warmer climates have found it best to start seeds in trays indoors, as optimum germination occurs at 78°F (25.6°C). Often in late summer the temperature outdoors is in the upper 80s to 90s (29–37°C), which can reduce seed germination and increase the likelihood of a fungus causing the seeds to rot. Indoors or out, germination usually takes place within two weeks, although some seeds can be slow to germinate.

When planting seedlings outdoors, space them a minimum of 4 in. (15 cm) apart in rows 12–18 in. (30.4–45.7 cm) apart, depending on how long you plan to leave the plants undisturbed. They should have ample room in this space for about two years. If you do not wish to move the plants for several years, you must allow them more space to grow during this period without becoming over crowded. Also, be sure to transfer the parentage information to the garden with the plants. Again, remember to use some material that will withstand the weather during the period between planting and blooming. Over a nine-month to three-year period, paper and wood deteriorate, and even permanent waterproof ink fades. Metal garden markers are excellent, and simple pencil on plastic tags lasts for years.

Once out in the garden, plants will take from one to three years to flower. In warm climates or in a greenhouse, if the seeds are planted early and the plants are fertilized heavily, they can bloom the following spring, or within nine months.

CHAPTER 10

A Look to the Future

Daylilies are constantly evolving, not only in terms of new colors and color combinations, but the flower shapes and sizes are also taking on new looks. Although difficult to visualize from close-up photographs, some daylilies are more than 15 in. (38 cm) in diameter, while others are a mere 0.87 in. (2.2 cm) in diameter, the size of a US quarter. The variations in shapes and sizes of the modern daylily are so great that it is difficult to imagine that such diverse flowers comprise a single genus.

With tens of thousands of new daylilies bred, and more than a thousand new daylilies registered with the American Hemerocallis Society (AHS) each year, many new flower styles, colors, and sizes are certain to emerge in the future. The competitive nature of daylily hybridizing compels many breeders to push their favorite type of flower to its next logical, or often not-so-logical, step, producing an ever increasing diversity in flower form. These new, cutting-edge flowers are presented in this chapter. Most flowers in this chapter are so new that they have not yet been named, and at the time of this writing can only be found in the gardens of the hybridizers who created them. However, over time these plants will be named and released to the public.

Determining the "new directions" that daylilies are taking is a difficult task, since every year more new breaks occur that seemed to be completely unpredictable or unimaginable only a year earlier. Some trends seem to be emerging, though, and some directions seem likely to continue, such as increased gold edging and the search for the color blue.

The gold-edged daylilies became increasingly prominent during the 1980s and '90s. At first the gold edge was very tiny, and often the viewer had to have a good imagination to see it. Today, the gold edges on some flowers, such as 'Gary Colby' (Ted Petit, not yet registered), are greater than 1 in. (2.5 cm) wide. Along with heavy gold edges, the ruffling on the petals has also become more and more pronounced, with ruffles more than 1 in. (2.5 cm) wide, taking up most of the petal surface.

Breeders have also been working to increase the size of the daylily flower. Tetraploid spiders are approaching 16 in. (40.6 cm) in diameter. Full-formed flowers now exceed 8 in. (20.3 cm) in diameter. In the other direction, hybridizers have now bred daylilies less than 1 in. (2.4 cm) in diameter.

In terms of color, daylilies are becoming much more richly saturated with bold and dramatic eyes and edges in virtually every color. The color blue has clearly emerged in the eyezone, and new and richer shades of blue are appearing. The color patterns found in daylilies are becoming increasingly complex, not only in the eyezones but in the entire flower. These patterns are beginning to encircle the entire petal edge, giving rise to multiple-edged flowers. With the increasingly vivid colors, the flowers have also taken on heavier and heavier substance. In some flowers this heavy substance is also associated with deep carving that adds a three-dimensional effect to the flower.

As the flowers pictured in this chapter show, the future of the daylily continues to be very bright. These daylilies represent only a few of the many new directions being taken by breeders today.

'3265-A' (Patrick Stamile) A lightly ruffled, patterned flower with a cream base. A slate-gray-blue eyezone is surrounded by a lighter, bluish band, which in turn is surrounded by a darker purple band that is repeated out on the petal edges as a picotee. Tetraploid.

'3265-A'. Photo by Patrick Stamile

'Spacecoast Royal Ransom' (John Kinnebrew) A highly ruffled, dark purple flower with an extremely ornate, heavy gold edge and a small, lighter watermark above a green throat. Tetraploid.

'Spacecoast Royal Ransom'. Photo by John Kinnebrew

'3262-D' (Patrick Stamile) A cream, faintly lavender flower with a complex eyezone of navy blue, slate-gray, and purple above an emerald-green throat. The pattern of the eyezone is also mimicked on the sepals. Tetraploid.

'3262-D'. Photo by Patrick Stamile

(Ted Petit) A large, wide-petaled, heavy-substanced, golden yellow flower with extraordinarily wide, heavy ruffling that takes up most of the petal surface. Tetraploid.

Hybridizer, Ted Petit. Photo by Ted Petit

(Dan Trimmer) A cream-peach flower with a huge, dark purple eye and wide purple picotee surrounded by a wire white, serrated edge with tiny shark's teeth. Tetraploid. 'Calling All Angels' × 'Jane Trimmer'.

Hybridizer, Dan Trimmer. Photo by Dan Trimmer

'Kay Day' (David Kirchhoff) A ruffled, clear pink double with a wire gold edge. Tetraploid.

'Kay Day'. Photo by David Kirchhoff

'Bonnie Holley' (Jeff Corbett) A heavy-substanced, peach-orange flower with deep sculpting above a green throat. Large, flowing, darker ruffles surround the wide petals. Tetraploid.

'Bonnie Holley'. Photo by Jeff Corbett

(Ted Petit) A nine-petaled, hose-in-hose, pink flower with a darker burgundy-pink eye-zone and wire picotee surrounded with a narrow, lightly ruffled, gold edge. Tetraploid.

Hybridizer, Ted Petit. Photo by Ted Petit

'6902' (Karol Emmerich) An unusual flower with pinched petals of cream-yellow and a dark purple eyezone and picotee edge. The darker eyezone is mimicked on the sepals, forming a large, unusual pattern. Tetraploid.

'6902'. Photo by Karol Emmerich

'Isle of Wight' (Dan Trimmer) A heavily ruffled, clear baby-ribbon-pink with a deep green throat. The petals are very wide, showing a beautifully symmetrical, very round flower. Tetraploid.

'Isle of Wight'. Photo by Dan Trimmer

(John Kinnebrew) A burgundy-purple, velvety flower with a large, near black, dark purple eyezone and picotee edge above a dark green center. Tetraploid. 'Spacecoast Shiner' × 'Mister Lucky'.

Hybridizer, John Kinnebrew. Photo by John Kinnebrew

D20243B (Grace Stamile) Semi-evergreen. Scape 18 in. (45.7 cm); flower 3.5 in. (8.9 cm). Early. A cream-pink with a complex, slate-gray-violet eyezone with patches of navy blue and a purple band surrounding the eyezone above a lime-green throat. The eye is mimicked on the sepals. Diploid.

D20243B. Photo by Patrick Stamile

(Ted Petit) A salmon-peach, wide-petaled flower with a dark purple eyezone and a very wide, dark purple picotee surrounded by a wire gold edge above a yellow to green throat. Tetraploid.

Hybridizer, Ted Petit. Photo by Ted Petit

(John Peat) A large rose-pink with a diamond-dusted, ruffled, gold edge and a faint, lighter pink watermark above a green throat. The flowers are very heavy with a thick, waxy substance. Tetraploid.

'13500' (Karol Emmerich) A lavender-rose with a tightly crimped, heavy gold edging and a yellow-gold watermark above a green throat. Tetraploid.

Hybridizer, John Peat. Photo by John Peat

'13500'. Photo by Karol Emmerich

(Ted Petit) An extremely wide-petaled, round, thick, waxy, cream-pink self with a solid, ruffled, gold edge above a grass-green throat. Tetraploid.

Hybridizer, Ted Petit. Photo by Ted Petit

(Ted Petit) A nine-petaled, hose-in-hose red with a beaded, lightly ruffled, gold edge above a dark green throat with a faint watermark surrounded by a wire red eyezone. Tetraploid.

Hybridizer, Ted Petit. Photo by Ted Petit

(Barry Matthie) A flesh-pink with a darker rose-pink eyezone above a large green throat. The sepals are twisted and spooned, giving this flower the appearance of motion, thus making it an unusual form. Tetraploid. 'North Wind Dancer' × 'Starmans Delight'.

Hybridizer, Barry Matthie. Photo by Barry Matthie

(John Peat) A cream-pink flower with a large, candy-apple-red eyezone broken up with a circular pink wire watermark above a green throat. The pattern varies from day to day, showing a very different flower from one day to the next. Tetraploid. 'Altered State' × 'Avante Garde'.

Hybridizer, John Peat. Photo by John Peat

'2179' (Patrick Stamile) A large, wide-petaled, dimpled, pink flower, very round in appearance and surrounded by a tightly crimped, ruffled, gold edge. A dark green center lies below the large yellow watermark. Tetraploid.

'2179'. Photo by Patrick Stamile

'373-A' (Patrick Stamile) A very narrow-petaled, cream-pink spider with an extremely large lime-green throat. The petals and sepals are twisted and curled, also making it an unusual form. Tetraploid.

'373-A'. Photo by Patrick Stamile

'22-A' (John Peat) A dark burgundy-purple flower with heavy, tightly ruffled edges. Often extra gold tissue forms "wings" that jut out from the midribs. Tetraploid. 'Eternity's Shadow' × ('Sultry Smile' × 'Sultry Smile').

'35502'. Photo by Karol Emmerich

'35502' (Karol Emmerich) A large, dark burgundy-purple with a lighter watermark above the yellow to green throat. The ruffled edge is of white-gold with many hocks, knobs, and teeth. Tetraploid.

'22-A'. Photo by John Peat

(Ted Petit) A cream-pink flower with a striking, burgundy-red eyezone and picotee edge above a crabapple-green throat. The flower is further enhanced by a ruffled, gold edge with tiny teeth, making a very striking display. Tetraploid. 'Only Believe' × 'Mardi Gras Ball'.

'22-B'. Photo by John Peat

'22-B' (John Peat) A large rose-lavender flower with a half-inch, rubbery, tangerine, diamond-dusted edge. The edge often takes up most of the petals, leaving very little rose-lavender color. Tetraploid. 'Eternity's Shadow' × ('Sultry Smile' × 'Sultry Smile').

Hybridizer, Ted Petit. Photo by Ted Petit

(John Kinnebrew) A cream with a striking, lime-yellow-green, applique throat below a very dark purple eyezone and picotee edge. The throat forms an interesting pattern of ridges as it bleeds out into the eye. Tetraploid. 'Catcher in the Eye' × Seedling.

'0-106'. Photo by Dan Trimmer

Hybridizer, John Kinnebrew. Photo by John Kinnebrew

Hybridizer, Ted Petit. Photo by Ted Petit

(Ted Petit) A rose-lavender with wide, raised, vertical, gold, ruffled edges. A second, chartreuse edge surrounds the gold edge. Tetraploid.

'D398J'. Photo by Patrick Stamile

'0-106' (Dan Trimmer) A cream-white with a large, complex eye of red. The grass-green throat draws viewers into the complex eyezone while offering a cool contrast to the huge red eye. The petals are surrounded by a ruffled, red, picotee edge. Tetraploid.

'D398J' (Grace Stamile) A miniature cream-purple with a dark purple eyezone. An adorable popcorn double with darker veins of purple. Diploid.

(Ted Petit) A cream-pink flower with a large, candy-apple-red eyezone and very wide, matching picotee surrounded by a wire gold edge. The eye and picotee are so large and wide that very little of the petal self is visible. Tetraploid.

(Dan Trimmer) A golden yellow with an extremely wide, burgundy-purple picotee edge and eyezone. The heavily ruffled picotee is also surrounded in gold. Tetraploid. 'Spice Hunter' × 'Calling All Angels'.

Hybridizer, Ted Petit. Photo by Ted Petit

Hybridizer, Dan Trimmer. Photo by Dan Trimmer

Hybridizer, John Peat. Photo by John Peat

(Ted Petit) A soft violet-pink flower with very wide and heavy, gold, ruffled edges. Tetraploid.

Hybridizer, Ted Petit. Photo by Ted Petit

'GDOT641' (George Doorakian) A narrow-petaled, cream-yellow flower with a dramatic, dark green, tightly crimped, ruffled edge. Tetraploid.

'GDOT641'. Photo by George Doorakian

(John Peat) A soft baby-ribbon-pink with a tightly ruffled, gold edge above a deep lime-green throat with extremely heavy substance. Tetraploid.

'22-C' (John Peat) A dark burgundy-purple with a large orange throat above a green heart. A wide, very ruffled,

rubbery, tangerine edge surrounds this 6.5 in. (15.2 cm) flower. Tetraploid. 'Eternity's Shadow' × ('Sultry Smile' × 'Sultry Smile').

'22-C'. Photo by John Peat

'22-D' (John Peat) A wide-petaled, pink-lavender-rose self with a tightly crimped, diamond dusted, rubbery edge of tangerine-orange with a matching tangerine eyezone above a green throat. Tetraploid. 'Eternity's Shadow' × ('Sultry Smile' × 'Sultry Smile').

'22-D'. Photo by John Peat

'Lemon Spritzer' (Bob Schwarz) A golden yellow, unusual formed, narrow-petaled flower with a large green throat. The sepals are spooned and rolled with the petals bending and curling gently, giving the appearance of motion. Tetraploid.

'Lemon Spritzer'. Photo by Bob Schwarz

'D20243A' (Grace Stamile) A dark purple peony double with a complex eye in shades of gray and blue above a dark green throat. Diploid.

'D20243A'. Photo by Patrick Stamile

'Emerald Starburst' (George Doorakian) A dark black-purple with a huge, emerald-green, chevron-shaped throat. The throat extends far out on the petals and is a darker emerald-green toward the center. Diploid.

'Emerald Starburst'. Photo by George Doorakian

'Gary Colby' (Ted Petit) A burgundy-purple with ruffled folds of gold in the edge that is wider than 1 in (2.54 cm). A very large, 8 in. (20.3 cm), heavy flower with a yellow watermark and a deep green center. Tetraploid.

'Gary Colby'. Photo by Ted Petit

'3262-B'. Photo by Patrick Stamile

(Mort Morss) A cream-purple with a complex, bluish eyezone above a large green throat. The complex eyezone continues out around the petal edges, which are surrounded in knobby gold and adorned with small tentacles. Tetraploid.

Hybridizer, Mort Morss. Photo by Mort Morss

'3262-B' (Patrick Stamile) A violet-peach flower with a huge, complex, blue and purple eyezone above a deep green throat, with a wire blue and purple picotee surrounding the petal edges. The complex eye is also found on the sepals. Tetraploid.

'Tony Thompson' (John Peat) A large, 7.5-in. (19.1-cm), wide-petaled, salmon-pink flower with large,

spooned sepals. A burgundy eyezone and picotee are surrounded by heavy, diamond-dusted edges of gold. Tetraploid. 'Reyna' × 'Mardi Gras Ball'.

'Tony Thompson'. Photo by John Peat

'2-39' (Dan Trimmer) A very wide-petaled, dark purple flower with ruffled and looped edges of golden

'2-39'. Photo by Dan Trimmer

white. A darker purple eyezone shows above the lime-green throat. Tetraploid.

(David Kirchhoff) A cream-white peony double carrying a complex, bluish purple eyezone with purple veins streaking through it, making an interesting pattern.

Hybridizer, David Kirchhoff. Photo by David Kirchhoff

(Ludlow Lambertson) A lavender-purple flower with a huge gray watermark above a yellow to green throat. The edges are gold with striking, sharp, tooth-like tentacles. Tetraploid.

Hybridizer, Ludlow Lambertson. Photo by Ludlow Lambertson

(Ludlow Lambertson) A dark burgundy-red, narrow-petaled flower with a yellow to green throat. The edges carry toothy, pointed tentacles that surround both the petals and the sepals. Tetraploid.

Hybridizer, Ludlow Lambertson. Photo by Ludlow Lambertson

(Les Holton) A cream flower with a bold and dramatic, thick, ruffled, knobby, bright red edge. The large candy-apple-red eyezone above the green throat is brilliant, and combined with the picotee edge forms a fabulous contrast in colors. Tetraploid.

Hybridizer, Les Holton. Photo by Les Holton

'34-F' (Gunda Abajian) A cream flower with a complex, patterned, bluish eyezone and darker purple picotee. The eyezone is broken up with fish-scale-like patterns. Tetraploid.

'3K33'. Photo by Gunda Abajian

'34-F'. Photo by Gunda Abajian

'3K33' (Gunda Abajian) A golden orange, extraordinarily ruffled flower, with ruffles on top of ruffles. They are gold, folded, and crimped. Tetraploid.

CHAPTER 11

Exhibiting Daylilies in Shows

by Betty Roberts

Exhibiting daylilies in shows accredited by the American Hemerocallis Society (AHS) is a fun and exciting aspect of growing daylilies. It has a natural appeal to most gardeners, and adds a delightful element of friendly competition to gardening. However, at no time does a daylily come under such intense scrutiny as when it is on the show bench being examined by a team of three AHS-accredited judges. Exhibitors who want to be consistent winners should take a cue from the judges. Knowing what they look for will increase the chances of getting a high-scoring ribbon and then being considered for the AHS Rosettes, which are awarded to the top winners in each section (the various awards are described below).

Before proceeding any further, I would like to champion all plant society and garden club shows from the standpoint that the primary purpose of a show is to educate the public, awards and recognition to the exhibitors notwithstanding. As a National Garden Clubs flower show judge, as well as a daylily, rose, and iris judge, I have more than thirty years of judging experience to help increase readers' awareness of the judging process.

Daylilies are placed in shows by type or size, in nine different sections in a show. The most common section is the large type—those 4.5 in. (11.4 cm) in diameter or larger. The other sections are the spider or spider variants, unusual form flowers, small flowers of more than 3 in. (7.6 cm) but less than 4.5 in. (11.4 cm), miniatures of less than 3 in. (7.6 cm), doubles, seedlings, the Regional Popularity Poll winners, and a youth section. From these nine sections, judges select a winner of each section, which receives an AHS Rosette, and then from these rosette-winners they select the Best-in-Show exhibit by written secret ballot.

All flower show judges use a scale of points to help evaluate a specimen and make the judging process as fair and unbiased as possible. Judges evaluate a daylily exhibit using one of three scales of points—one for flowers on scape, one for seedlings, and one for flowers not on scape. In each instance, the highest number of points is based on qualities of the flower itself. Judges are not allowed to touch the bloom in any way, not with fingers, pencils, cotton swabs, or anything else. They also may not lift a bloom out of its container. When members of a judging team feel it necessary to move or lift an exhibit, they are obliged to call on a member of the clerking team.

What qualities make up a good flower? Many judges are influenced more by the color of a flower than by any other quality. Just as a clear, vibrant, beautiful daylily can beckon to you in the garden, it can also "woo" you on the show bench. Color is so compelling that judges have to be careful to avoid giving or deducting points based strictly on liking or disliking a particular color.

The "form" of the flower is the next most important attribute. Being a lover of all types of flowers, I am particularly interested in the form of the daylily. Today we are fortunate to have daylilies of every conceivable shape. There are pretty, petite doubles to fill a spot in the rockery; round, ruffled beauties to satisfy the daylily connoisseur; spiders, spider variants, and unusual forms to entice the adventurous; and polytepals to fulfill the quest of tomorrow's advocate. Judging the varied forms can be a challenge and requires an open mind and an adventurous spirit, willingness to learn, and the will to be impartial.

The round "bagel" type of daylily flower is probably the easiest to judge for form. The most important quality in judging this type of flower is symmetry. Do all the petals and sepals form a pleasing, consistent pattern, or is one petal out of synchrony, ruining the symmetry? Are all three petals and three sepals present? Does the flower have six stamens and one pistil? Believe it or not, unless a judge is designated to check to make sure all flower parts are present, a top prize could easily go to a bloom that has no pistil.

Besides form, flower judges consistently use two other terms to describe a flower: texture and sub-

stance. Texture has to do with the surface quality of the bloom. *Webster's New Universal Unabridged Dictionary* (1996) defines texture as "the visual and especially tactile quality of a surface," and in another sense, "a rough or grainy surface quality." Since judges are not allowed to touch the bloom, they must determine the surface quality solely on the basis of sight. Drawing comparisons to fabric helps in framing the terminology of this elusive quality. Is the flower smooth, like satin or velvet, or rough, like corduroy? Does it have crinkled stripes like seersucker? Judges need to know this terminology since they need to discuss a bloom in precise terms.

In defining substance, *Webster's* states that it is a "substantial or solid character or quality." Substance is an inherent quality that allows a flower to look crisp and turgid. A lack of substance causes "thinning" or wilting. As you might guess, a bloom that has thin substance or is losing substance, its petals thinning and weakening through the day due to water loss, will also lose judging points.

Condition is another important aspect of judging a specimen. Is the exhibit clean and free of dust, insects, pollen, spider webs, and physical damage? Both the bloom and the scape are evaluated for presentation qualities. Dust, insects, and pollen can be easily removed by swabbing gently with a cotton swab. Because daylilies can be difficult to transport, a tear can sometimes develop in the petals. If the tear is very small, it can be removed with a pair of cuticle scissors. Judging points will still be lost; however, the deduction will not be as severe as when the tear is quite noticeable.

A specimen with two or more open blooms will receive a high score, providing both blooms are in excellent condition. Each bloom should be evaluated as though it were a single specimen. Multiple blooms should not touch each other or any flower buds, as these will interfere with the flowers' form. A bud and even a bloom may be very carefully removed to improve the overall presentation of the exhibit. A judge should be careful not to deduct too many points for insignificant faults of multiple bloom specimens. Generally speaking, a daylily with two or more blooms can be quite spectacular, and a judge should evaluate accordingly.

Daylily blooms should be well supported by a scape that is in proportion to the size of the bloom. A large bloom demands a strong, upright scape of adequate height—a large, robust bloom looks stunted on a very short scape. Likewise, a tiny bloom looks out of proportion on a skinny, tall scape. Even if the small bloom grows naturally on a tall scape, I recommend shortening an overly tall scape for the show bench.

The scape should display as many buds as possible. Branching is desirable for its ability to display the blooms to perfection. Although courage is needed to cut a scape with the first open bloom of the season, a scape showing good bloom potential is preferable to one that has bloomed out. Shows are usually held around the same weekend each year. Occasionally the bloom season will be early, and there will probably be a number of scapes with very few buds visible. In this case, the penalization for lack of buds should not be drastic; however, I have seen exhibits with no buds and consider them unlikely to be in the running for a blue ribbon.

Exhibitors should remove spent blooms and seed pods and should very carefully trim the old-looking scars that develop when blooms are removed. A pair of sharp cuticle scissors is an indispensable grooming tool for this type of trimming. Nothing distracts from a bloom like a carelessly groomed exhibit, and penalization is often harsh.

In evaluating seedlings, judges look for distinction above all else. A seedling should have a quality unlike any other daylily. Extraordinary beauty, color, form, pattern, bud count, and branching are qualities that should stand out from the thousands of existing cultivars.

Ensuring that a daylily has been entered into the correct class can sometimes be difficult. So many daylilies are registered that exhibitors often must study the AHS cultivar checklists (see "Hybridizing Techniques" in Chapter 9 for ordering information). If a judge suspects that a daylily has been placed in the wrong class, the judging team is obliged to discuss the possibility and consult the checklists. At one time lists of spiders and unusual forms were printed in the back of the checklists. These lists were helpful for exhibitors and show personnel striving to correctly classify these types of daylilies. These lists are no longer included in the checklists, however. Since knowing which cultivars were registered in all the different classes is difficult, a judging team with experts in the various flower forms is fortunate indeed. When judges are uncertain, they should admit a lack of knowledge about certain types of daylilies. In order to be fair to exhibitors, the judges should make every effort to become familiar with all types of hemerocallis.

The couple of hours spent judging a show can be an exhausting but very exhilarating experience. Judges generally work hard to evaluate fairly, and the result can be a beautiful display with potential to inform and bring pleasure to all the "players" and viewers alike.

For those wanting to become daylily show judges the AHS offers three clinics, often held at many of the local daylily meetings, regional meetings, and the AHS National Convention. A small fee is required for each clinic. Clinic I, "Introductory Judges Training," is a two-hour lecture followed by a 100-question written examination. Students must score a minimum of 70 percent in order to qualify for Clinic II. Clinic II, "Secondary Judges Training," is a lecture on point-scoring and is also followed by a written examination. Upon completion of the exam with at least a 70 percent grade, students are then qualified as Junior Exhibition Judges. From there, an individual may become a Senior Exhibition Judge by fulfilling a series of criteria as outlined by the AHS, including serving as a judge in shows and completing other services and exhibition requirements. The Refresher Clinic is a class designed for Senior Exhibition Judges and reviews the responsibilities, ethics, show procedures, awards, and point-scoring. It also includes an open forum to address various judging issues.

Exhibition Awards

AHS Standard System of Awards

The standard awards are given to a cultivar in each of the nine daylily classes. An entry with a score of 90 or more receives a blue ribbon for first place. An entry with a score of 85–89 receives a red ribbon for second place. An entry with a score of 80–84 receives a yellow ribbon for third place. Entries with a score of 70–79 receive a white ribbon for honorable mention.

Major Awards

Those cultivars that receive a blue ribbon, a score of 90 or more, are then eligible for major awards. The first tier is the purple award. The purple award, in the form of a ribbon or sticker, may be given to blue award-winning cultivars that score 95 points or more in the nine on-scape sections. The purple award can be given to every blue that scores above 95 or to the best blue per section, group, or subclass, depending on the specifications given in the show schedule.

The next tier of awards is the AHS Rosette, which is awarded to the best purple award winner in each of the nine sections. Only cultivars that received a score of 95 or better are eligible for an AHS Rosette, which represents the "best in section" award. Thus, the best exhibited large flower, spider, double, and so on, would receive an AHS Rosette.

Ultimately, then, the Best in Show award is given to the best of the AHS Rosette winners. In addition, a sweepstakes award goes to the exhibit with the most blue awards in the nine on-scape sections.

Special Horticulture Awards

The AHS Achievement Medal is awarded to any number of hybridizers for seedlings exhibited with at least three scapes, severed at the base, and showing adequate merit and distinction as compared with existing registered cultivars.

The Ophelia Taylor Horticultural Award is given in recognition of an individual who exhibits five award-winning scapes. This pin can be awarded in two different classes: Class 1—five different registered cultivars; or Class 2—five different seedlings. Provided that each of the five scapes scores higher than 95, the award goes to the hybridizer with the highest total point score.

American Horticultural Society Awards

The AHS makes two awards available to its member organizations in an effort to maintain high standards in horticultural excellence. The Gold Bole Medal is awarded to an individual who exhibits 15 blue-ribbon cultivars at a single show. The Silver Bole Medal is awarded to an individual who exhibits eight blue-ribbon cultivars.

Design Awards

The standard design awards are given in each design class. An entry with a score of 90 or above receives a blue ribbon for first place. An entry with a score of 85–89 receives a red ribbon for second place. An entry with a score of 80–84 receives a yellow ribbon for third place. And entries with a score of 70–80 receive a white ribbon for honorable mention.

The AHS Tricolor Rosette and Medal are awarded to the best design entry with daylilies dominating the display. The entry must score 94 or above.

The Creativity Rosette is awarded to the best design in the Designer's Choice section. The entry must score 95 or above and must include creativity, originality, and distinction.

AHS Award of Appreciation

The AHS Award of Appreciation is a special ribbon for noncompetitive show sections and is given to an individual for his or her efforts in publicizing the daylily and the society.

For more information on exhibition judging, shows, and course materials you may obtain a copy of the AHS *Judging Daylilies Handbook*. Contact Jimmy Jordan at 276 Caldwell Dr., Jackson, TN 38301, tel 731-422-2208; http://www.daylilies.org/ahs/.

CHAPTER 12

Award-Winning Daylilies

With so many registered and named daylilies, gardeners frequently ask, "How do I choose?" Much of this decision is based on individual preference. Some people love large flowers, others like the miniatures, some want bold colors, and others prefer the quieter pastels. To add to the conundrum, gardeners are often immediately taken by a particular flower, despite their preconceived preferences. Beyond these individual predispositions, gardeners may reasonably ask, "Which are the better daylilies?" or "Which ones are the better performers?"

The American Hemerocallis Society (AHS) has developed the Awards and Honors System that acknowledges and promotes excellence in daylilies and can assist gardeners in pinpointing worthy daylilies. The awards in this system are given annually and are unrelated to the awards presented at the various regional shows throughout the year. The different annual awards are described in this chapter. The Stout Silver Medal is the highest award given to a cultivar by the AHS. Several awards progressively acknowledge merit and lead, in stairway fashion, toward the Stout Silver Medal. The first ac-

knowledgment of potential is a Junior Citation (JC), which recognizes exceptional seedlings that have not yet been registered or introduced into commerce. The first award for a registered or introduced cultivar is Honorable Mention (HM), which is bestowed on a limited number of daylilies each year by AHS Garden Judges. The cultivars must have been registered for three or more years and have demonstrated excellent quality and performance beyond the regional level. Three years after receiving an HM, a cultivar then becomes eligible for an Award of Merit (AM). Only those daylilies that have won an AM, only 12 annually (more in the case of a tie), can become eligible for the Stout Silver Medal. Thus, any daylily that wins the Stout Silver Medal must, by definition, have previously won an HM and an AM. In a sense, this award system is a pyramid—a large number of plants at the bottom of the pyramid receive an HM, a few of those rise to the next step for an AM, and finally only one plant each year rises to the top of the pyramid to receive the Stout Silver Medal. Since 1980 1,812 cultivars have received an HM and 228 have received an AM.

In this chapter, we begin by listing the Stout Silver Medal winners. Those readers who would like to have a complete listing of all award winners, including all HM and AM recipients, may refer to the AHS Cumulative Awards and Honors List (contact Jimmy Jordan at 276 Caldwell Dr., Jackson, TN 38301, tel 731-422-2208; http://www.daylilies.org/ahs/). In addition to the Stout Silver Medal path are a number of AHS special awards that acknowledge merit of specific types of daylilies, such as doubles or spiders. These awards are also described in this chapter.

We have listed the cultivars that have won the awards since 1980. We chose this cutoff since daylilies that won awards prior to this time are beyond the scope of a book on modern daylilies. In fact, choosing daylilies because they have won awards means that you are choosing daylilies that are not new, but tried and true. Those daylilies that won the Stout Silver Medal during the 1980s were registered or introduced primarily in the 1970s. Many of these even may look somewhat dated by current standards. These award-winning daylilies are not necessarily the "best" daylilies currently available. Likely, much newer and presumably better and improved daylilies are not yet old enough to have made their way through the awards system. These daylilies are the "future award winners," but without a crystal ball, none of us can accurately predict which ones will win these coveted awards. Nonetheless, the various AHS awards require votes from a large number of garden judges from differing geographical regions from around the world, and they do indicate that the award-winning cultivars have stood the test of time and represent some of the finest of their kind.

Stout Silver Medal Winners

The Stout Silver Medal is the highest honor bestowed on a daylily by the AHS. It is given out annually to a single cultivar, unless the vote is tied. This award is named after Arlow Stout, whose efforts in collecting, catego-rizing, hybridizing, and writing greatly increased public interest in the daylily. The winner must receive the highest number of votes cast by Garden Judges from around the world.

'Bertie Ferris' (Ury G. Winniford, 1969). Dormant. Scape 20 in. (50.8 cm); flower 2.5 in. (6.4 cm). Early. A persimmon-orange self. Diploid. 'Corky' × Seedling. Stout Silver Medal 1980.

'Ed Murray' (Edward F. Grovatt, 1971). Dormant. Scape 30 in. (76.2 cm); flower 4 in. (10.2 cm). Midseason. A black-red self with a green throat. Diploid. 'Tis Midnight' × Seedling. Stout Silver Medal 1981.

'Ruffled Apricot' (S. H. Baker, 1972). Dormant. Scape 28 in. (71.1 cm); flower 7 in. (17.8 cm). Early midseason. An apricot flower with lavender-pink midribs and a gold-apricot throat. Tetraploid. Seedling × 'Northbrook Star'. Stout Silver Medal 1982.

'Sabie' (W. B. MacMillan, 1974). Evergreen. Scape 24 in. (61 cm); flower 6 in. (15.2 cm). Early. A gold-yellow self with a green throat. Diploid. Parents unknown. Stout Silver Medal 1983.

'My Belle' (Kenneth G. Durio, 1973). Evergreen. Scape 26 in. (66.0 cm); flower 6.5 in. (16.5 cm). Early. A flesh-pink self with a green throat. Diploid. 'Sug' × Seedling. Stout Silver Medal 1984.

'Stella De Oro' (Walter Jablonski, 1975). Dormant. Scape 11 in. (27.9 cm); flower 2.75 in. (7.0 cm). Early midseason. A gold self with a very small green throat. Diploid. Parents unknown. Stout Silver Medal 1985.

'Hudson Valley' (Virginia L. Peck, 1971). Dormant. Scape 32 in. (81.3 cm); flower 8.5 in. (21.6 cm). Midseason. A green-yellow self with a deep green throat.

Tetraploid. 'Bonnie John Seton' × Seedling. Stout Silver Medal 1986.

'Janet Gayle' (Gabriel Guidry, 1976). Evergreen. Scape 26 in. (66.0 cm); flower 6.5 in. (16.5 cm). Early. A pink-cream blend with a green throat. Diploid. Parents unknown. Stout Silver Medal 1986.

'Becky Lynn' (Gabriel Guidry, 1977). Semi-evergreen. Scape 20 in. (50.8 cm); flower 6.75 in. (17.1 cm). Extra early. A rose blend with a green throat. Diploid. Parents unknown. Stout Silver Medal 1987.

'Martha Adams' (Elsie Spalding, 1979). Evergreen. Scape 19 in. (48.3 cm); flower 6.75 in. (17.1 cm). Early midseason. A pink self with a green throat. Diploid. Parents unknown. Stout Silver Medal 1988.

'Brocaded Gown' (Bryant K. Millikan, 1979). Semi-evergreen. Scape 26 in. (66.0 cm); flower 6 in. (15.2 cm). Early midseason. A lemon-cream self with a chartreuse throat. Diploid. 'Buttermilk Sky' × 'Sabie'. Stout Silver Medal 1989.

'Fairy Tale Pink' (Charles F. Pierce, 1980). Semi-evergreen. Scape 24 in. (61 cm); flower 5.5 in. (14 cm). Midseason. A pink self with a green throat. Diploid. 'Quiet Melody' × 'Janet Gayle'. Stout Silver Medal 1990.

'Betty Woods' (David Kirchhoff, 1980). Scape 26 in. (66.0 cm); flower 5.5 in. (14 cm). Early. A Chinese-yellow self with a green heart. Diploid. (('Winning Ways' × Seedling) × 'Keith Kennon') × 'Cosmic Treasure'. Stout Silver Medal 1991.

'Barbara Mitchell' (Charles F. Pierce, 1985). Semi-evergreen. Scape 20 in. (50.8 cm); flower 6 in. (15.2 cm). Midseason. A pink self with a green throat. Diploid. 'Fairy Tale Pink' × 'Beverly Ann'. Stout Silver Medal 1992.

'Siloam Double Classic' (Pauline Henry, 1985). Dormant. Scape 16 in. (40.6 cm); flower 5 in. (12.7 cm). Early midseason. A bright pink self with a green throat. Diploid. Parents unknown. Stout Silver Medal 1993.

'Janice Brown' (Edwin C. Brown, 1986). Semi-evergreen. Scape 21 in. (53.3 cm); flower 4.25 in. (10.8 cm). Early midseason. A bright pink with a rose-pink eyezone and a green throat. Diploid. Parents unknown. Stout Silver Medal 1994.

'Neal Berrey' (Sarah L. Sikes, 1985). Semi-evergreen. Scape 18 in. (45.7 cm); flower 5 in. (12.7 cm). Midseason. A rose-pink blend with a green-yellow throat. Diploid. 'Ronda' × (('Sophisticated Miss' × 'My Belle') × 'Blue Happiness'). Stout Silver Medal 1995.

'Wedding Band' (Patrick Stamile, 1987). Semi-evergreen. Scape 26 in. (66.0 cm); flower 5.5 in. (14 cm). Midseason. A cream-white edged in yellow with a green throat. Tetraploid. 'French Frosting' × 'Porcelain Pleasure'. Stout Silver Medal 1996.

'Always Afternoon' (Mort Morss, 1987). Semi-evergreen. Scape 22 in. (55.9 cm); flower 5.5 in. (14 cm). Early. A medium mauve flower edged in buff with a purple eyezone above a green throat. Tetraploid. ('Ring of Change' × 'Tiffany Palace') × 'Opus One'. Stout Silver Medal 1997.

'Strawberry Candy' (Patrick Stamile, 1989). Semi-evergreen. Scape 26 in. (66.0 cm); flower 4.25 in. (10.8 cm). Early midseason. A strawberry-pink blend with a rose-red eyezone above a gold to green throat. Tetraploid. 'Panache' × 'Tet. Siloam Virginia Henson'. Stout Silver Medal 1998.

'Custard Candy' (Patrick Stamile, 1989). Dormant. Scape 24 in. (61 cm); flower 4.25 in. (10.8 cm). Early midseason. A cream-yellow with a maroon eyezone above a green throat. Tetraploid. ((('Chicago Picotee Queen' × 'Byzantine Emperor') × 'Frandean') × 'Tet. Siloam Virginia Henson'. Stout Silver Medal 1999.

'Elizabeth Salter' (Jeff Salter, 1990). Semi-evergreen. Scape 22 in. (55.9 cm); flower 5.5 in. (14 cm). Midseason. A pink self with a green throat. Tetraploid. Parents unknown. Stout Silver Medal 2000.

'Ida's Magic' (Ida Munson, 1988). Evergreen. Scape 28 in. (71.1 cm); flower 6 in. (15.2 cm). Early midseason. An amber-peach edged in gold with a gold to green throat. Tetraploid. ('Royal Saracen' × 'Enchanted Empress') × 'Ruffled Dude'. Stout Silver Medal 2001.

'Bill Norris' (David Kirchhoff, 1993). Semi-evergreen. Scape 29 in. (73.7 cm); flower 5 in. (12.7 cm). Midseason. A brilliant, sunny gold self. Tetraploid. Seedling × 'Bit More Class'. Stout Silver Medal 2002.

Annie T. Giles Award Winners

The Annie T. Giles Award is given annually for the most outstanding small flower with a diameter that is less than 4.5 in. (11.4 cm) but greater than 3 in. (7.6 cm).

'Siloam Purple Plum' (Pauline Henry, 1970). Dormant. Scape 17 in. (43.2 cm); flower 3.25 in. (8.3 cm). Early midseason. A dark red-purple self with a green throat. Diploid. 'Cherry Chimes' × 'Little Wart'. Annie T. Giles Award 1980.

'Lord Camden' (Robert M. Kennedy, 1974). Dormant. Scape 24 in. (61 cm); flower 4.25 in. (10.8 cm). Midseason. A bright crimson-red to raspberry self with a green throat. Diploid. Parents unknown. Annie T. Giles Award 1981.

'Lullaby Baby' (Elsie Spalding, 1975). Semi-evergreen. Scape 19 in. (48.3 cm); flower 3.5 in. (8.9 cm). Early midseason. A light pink with a green throat. Diploid. Parents unknown. Annie T. Giles Award 1982.

'Siloam Bo Peep' (Pauline Henry, 1978). Dormant. Scape 18 in. (45.7 cm); flower 4.5 in. (11.4 cm). Early midseason. An orchid-pink blend with a deep purple eyezone above a green throat. Diploid. Parents unknown. Annie T. Giles Award 1983.

'Wynnson' (Olin W. Criswell, 1977). Dormant. Scape 24 in. (61 cm); flower 4.5 in. (11.4 cm). Early midseason. A light yellow self with a green throat. Diploid. 'Wynn' × Seedling. Annie T. Giles Award 1984.

'Siloam Virginia Henson' (Pauline Henry, 1979). Dormant. Scape 18 in. (45.7 cm); flower 4 in. (10.2 cm). Early midseason. Pink with a ruby-red eyezone above a green throat. Diploid. Parents unknown. Annie T. Giles Award 1985.

'Chorus Line' (David Kirchhoff, 1981). Evergreen. Scape 20 in. (50.8 cm); flower 3.5 in. (8.9 cm). Early. A medium pink with a rose band above a yellow halo and a dark green throat. Diploid. ('Sweet Thing' × ('Little Lad' × 'Call to Remembrance')) × 'Lullaby Baby'. Annie T. Giles Award 1986.

'Pandora's Box ' (David L. Talbott, 1980). Evergreen. Scape 19 in. (48.3 cm); flower 4 in. (10.2 cm). Early midseason. A cream with a purple eyezone above a green throat. Diploid. ('Prairie Blue Eyes' × 'Moment of Truth') × ('Apparition' × 'Moment of Truth'). Annie T. Giles Award 1987.

'Siloam Jim Cooper' (Pauline Henry, 1981). Dormant. Scape 16 in. (40.6 cm); flower 3.5 in. (8.9 cm). Early midseason. A red with a deeper red eyezone above a green throat. Diploid. Parents unknown. Annie T. Giles Award 1988.

'Sugar Cookie' (Darrel A. Apps, 1983). Evergreen. Scape 21 in. (53.3 cm); flower 3.25 in. (8.3 cm). Early midseason. A cream self with a green throat. Diploid. 'Buffys Dolls' × 'Little Infant'. Annie T. Giles Award 1989.

'Janice Brown' (Edwin C. Brown, 1986). Semi-evergreen. Scape 21 in. (53.3 cm); flower 4.25 in. (10.8 cm). Early midseason. A bright pink with a rose-pink eyezone and a green throat. Diploid. Parents unknown. Annie T. Giles Award 1990.

'Enchanter's Spell' (Elizabeth Anne Hudson, 1982). Semi-evergreen. Scape 18 in. (45.7 cm); flower 3 in. (7.6 cm). Midseason. An ivory with a dark purple and chalky lavender eyezone above a lime-green throat. Diploid. Parents unknown. Annie T. Giles Award 1991.

'Siloam Merle Kent' (Pauline Henry, 1984). Dormant. Scape 18 in. (45.7 cm); flower 3.5 in. (8.9 cm). Midseason. A bright orchid with a deep purple eyezone and a green throat. Diploid. Parents unknown. Annie T. Giles Award 1992.

'Exotic Echo' (Van M. Sellers, 1984). Dormant. Scape 16 in. (40.6 cm); flower 3 in. (7.6 cm). Midseason. A pink-cream blend with a double burgundy eye and a green throat. Diploid. Parents unknown. Annie T. Giles Award 1993.

'Strawberry Candy' (Patrick Stamile, 1989). Semi-evergreen. Scape 26 in. (66.0 cm); flower 4.25 in. (10.8 cm). Early midseason. A strawberry-pink blend with a rose-red eyezone above a gold to green throat. Tetraploid. 'Panache' × 'Tet. Siloam Virginia Henson'. Annie T. Giles Award 1994.

'Siloam David Kirchhoff' (Pauline Henry, 1986). Dormant. Scape 16 in. (40.6 cm); flower 3.5 in. (8.9 cm). Early midseason. An orchid with a cerise pencil-thin eyezone and a green throat. Diploid. Parents unknown. Annie T. Giles Award 1995.

'Custard Candy' (Patrick Stamile, 1989). Dormant. Scape 24 in. (61 cm); flower 4.25 in. (10.8 cm). Early midseason. A cream-yellow with a maroon eyezone above a green throat. Tetraploid. (('Chicago Picotee Queen' × 'Byzantine Emperor') × 'Frandean') × 'Tet. Siloam Virginia Henson'. Annie T. Giles Award 1996.

'Dragons Eye' (Elizabeth Anne Salter, 1992). Semi-evergreen. Scape 24 in. (61 cm); flower 4 in. (10.2 cm). Late midseason. A pastel pink with a rose-red eyezone above a green throat. Diploid. 'Enchanter's Spell' × 'Janice Brown'. Annie T. Giles Award 1997.

'Tigerling' (Patrick Stamile, 1989). Dormant. Scape 25 in. (63.5 cm); flower 3.75 in. (9.5 cm). Midseason. A light orange with a bright red eyezone above a green throat. Tetraploid. 'Raging Tiger' × 'Tet. Siloam Virginia Henson'. Annie T. Giles Award 1998.

'Ben Lee' (Ra Hansen, 1994). Semi-evergreen. Scape 20 in. (50.8 cm); flower 4 in. (10.2 cm). Midseason. A salmon-pink with a dark violet to lavender-blue eyezone above a bright green throat. Diploid. ('Misty Isle' × 'Surf') × Seedling. Annie T. Giles Award 1999.

'Witches Wink' (Elizabeth Anne Salter, 1993). Semi-evergreen. Scape 26 in. (66.0 cm); flower 3 in. (7.6 cm). Early midseason. A yellow with a plum eyezone above a green throat. Tetraploid. Seedling × 'Tet. Witch's Thimble'. Annie T. Giles Award 1999.

'Elegant Candy' (Patrick Stamile, 1995). Dormant. Scape 25 in. (63.5 cm); flower 4.25 in. (10.8 cm). Early midseason. A pink with a red eyezone above a green throat. Tetraploid. 'Lady of Fortune' × 'Tet. Janice Brown'. Annie T. Giles Award 2000.

'Coyote Moon' (David Kirchhoff, 1994). Evergreen. Scape 28 in. (71.1 cm); flower 3.5 in. (8.9 cm). Extra early. A medium yellow with a gray-cinnamon halo. Tetraploid. ((Seedling × 'Tet. Tiny Tiki') × 'Bit More Class') × ((Seedling × 'Tet. Moonlight Mist') × 'Tet. Sugar Cookie'). Annie T. Giles Award 2001.

'Roses with Peaches' (David Kirchhoff, 1993) Semi-evergreen. Scape 22 in. (55.9 cm); flower 3.75 in. (9.5 cm). Extra early. A peach with a gold edge and a rose eyezone above a yellow throat. Tetraploid. ('Ming Porcelain' × ('Dunedrift' × 'Dance Ballerina Dance')) × 'Tet. Siloam Virginia Henson'. Annie T. Giles Award 2002.

Donn Fischer Memorial Award Winners

The Donn Fischer Memorial Award is given annually to the most outstanding miniature flower with a diameter not more than 3 in. (7.6 cm).

'Little Celena' (Lucille Williamson, 1970). Evergreen. Scape 14 in. (35.6 cm); flower 2 in. (5.1 cm). Early. A rose-pink self with a green throat. Diploid. 'Lavender Doll' × 'Ruthie'. Donn Fischer Memorial Award 1980.

'Fox Grape' (John Mason Allgood, 1973). Dormant. Scape 14 in. (35.6 cm); flower 2.9 in. (7.4 cm). Midseason. A crush grape with a light grape-bluish eyezone above a gold to green throat. Diploid. 'Heavenly Scripture' × 'Iron Gate Glow'. Donn Fischer Memorial Award 1981.

'Siloam June Bug' (Pauline Henry, 1978). Dormant. Scape 23 in. (58.4 cm); flower 2.75 in. (7.0 cm). Early

midseason. A gold self with a dark maroon eyezone above a green throat. Diploid. Parents unknown. Donn Fischer Memorial Award 1982.

'Siloam Red Toy' (Pauline Henry, 1975). Dormant. Scape 20 in. (50.8 cm); flower 2.75 in. (7.0 cm). Early midseason. A red self with a green throat. Diploid. Parents unknown. Donn Fischer Memorial Award 1983.

'Peach Fairy' (Andre Viette, 1974). Dormant. Scape 26 in. (66.0 cm); flower 2.5 in. (6.4 cm). Midseason. A pink-melon self. Diploid. Parents unknown. Donn Fischer Memorial Award 1984.

'Pardon Me' (Darrel A. Apps, 1982). Dormant. Scape 18 in. (45.7 cm); flower 2.75 in. (7.0 cm). Midseason. A bright red self with a yellow to green throat. Diploid. Seedling × 'Little Grapette'. Donn Fischer Memorial Award 1985.

'Little Zinger' (Edna Lankart, 1979). Semi-evergreen. Scape 16 in. (40.6 cm); flower 2.75 in. (7.0 cm). Early midseason. A red self with a very green throat. Diploid. Parents unknown. Donn Fischer Memorial Award 1986.

'Siloam Tee Tiny' (Pauline Henry, 1981). Dormant. Scape 20 in. (50.8 cm); flower 2.75 in. (7.0 cm). Midseason. An orchid with a purple eyezone above a green throat. Diploid. Parents unknown. Donn Fischer Memorial Award 1987.

'Yellow Lollipop' (Clarence J. Crochet, 1980). Dormant. Scape 11 in. (27.9 cm); flower 2.25 in. (5.7 cm). Early midseason. A medium yellow self. Diploid. Parents unknown. Donn Fischer Memorial Award 1988.

'Siloam Bertie Ferris' (Pauline Henry, 1981). Dormant. Scape 16 in. (40.6 cm); flower 2.75 in. (7.0 cm). Early midseason. A deep rose-shrimp with a deeper rose eye-zone above a green throat. Diploid. Parents unknown. Donn Fischer Memorial Award 1989.

'Texas Sunlight' (Joyce W. Lewis, 1986). Dormant. Scape 28 in. (71.1 cm); flower 2.75 in. (7.0 cm). Mid-season. A gold self. Diploid. Parents unknown. Donn Fischer Memorial Award 1990.

'Siloam Grace Stamile' (Pauline Henry, 1984). Dor-mant. Scape 14 in. (35.6 cm); flower 2.1 in. (5.3 cm). Early midseason. A red with a deeper red halo and a green throat. Diploid. Parents unknown. Donn Fischer Memorial Award 1991.

'Witch's Thimble' (Elizabeth Anne Hudson, 1981). Semi-evergreen. Scape 14 in. (35.6 cm); flower 2.25 in. (5.7 cm). Midseason. A white-ivory with a black-pur-ple eyezone above a green throat. Diploid. 'Elf Witch' × 'Dragons Eye'. Donn Fischer Memorial Award 1992.

'Jason Salter' (Elizabeth Anne Salter, 1987). Evergreen. Scape 18 in. (45.7 cm); flower 2.75 in. (7.0 cm). Early midseason. A yellow with a washed lavender-purple eyezone and a green throat. Diploid. 'Enchanter's Spell' × ('Enchanted Elf' × 'Cosmic Hummingbird'). Donn Fischer Memorial Award 1993.

'Dragon's Orb' (Elizabeth Anne Salter, 1986). Ever-green. Scape 20 in. (50.8 cm); flower 2.75 in. (7.0 cm). Midseason. A pale ivory-white with a black eyezone and a chartreuse-lemon throat. Diploid. 'Corsican Bandit' × 'Dragons Eye'. Donn Fischer Memorial Award 1994.

'Patchwork Puzzle' (Elizabeth Anne Salter, 1990). Scape 18 in. (45.7 cm); flower 2.75 in. (7.0 cm). Early midsea-son. An ivory lemon-yellow with a washed lavender-purple eyezone above a green throat. Tetraploid. Par-ents unknown. Donn Fischer Memorial Award 1995.

'After the Fall' (David Kirchhoff , 1981). Evergreen. Scape 20 in. (50.8 cm); flower 2.75 in. (7.0 cm). Extra early. A tangerine-copper blend with a yellow halo and a rust eyezone above a copper to greenish throat. Diploid. 'Cosmic Hummingbird' × 'Munchkin Moon'. Donn Fischer Memorial Award 1996.

'Dark Avenger' (Elizabeth Anne Salter, 1988). Semi-evergreen. Scape 18 in. (45.7 cm); flower 2.5 in. (6.4 cm). Midseason. A black-red self with a yellow-green throat. Diploid. Parents unknown. Donn Fischer Memorial Award 1997.

'Bibbity Bobbity Boo' (Elizabeth Anne Salter, 1992). Semi-evergreen. Scape 18 in. (45.7 cm); flower 2.75 in. (7.0 cm). Early midseason. A lavender with a dark grape-purple eyezone above a green throat. Tetraploid. Seedling × 'Tet. Witch's Thimble'. Donn Fischer Memo-rial Award 1998.

'Baby Blues' (Grace Stamile, 1990). Dormant. Scape 20 in. (50.8 cm); flower 2 in. (5.1 cm). Midseason. A pale lavender with a washed gray-blue eyezone, edged with a fuchsia line, above a green throat. Diploid. ('Siloam Baby Talk' × 'Coming Out Party') × 'Siloam Tiny Tim'. Donn Fischer Memorial Award 1999.

'Mary Ethel Anderson' (Elizabeth Anne Salter, 1995). Semi-evergreen. Scape 18 in. (45.7 cm); flower 2.5 in. (6.4 cm). Late midseason. A cream with a red eye above a green throat. Diploid. Parents unknown. Donn Fis-cher Memorial Award 2000.

'Bubbly' (Jan Joiner, 1989). Semi-evergreen. Scape 20 in. (50.8 cm); flower 2.9 in. (7.4 cm). Midseason. An apricot self with a green throat. Diploid. 'Champagne Bubbles' × 'Fairies Pinafore'. Donn Fischer Memorial Award 2001.

'Morrie Otte' (Elizabeth Anne Salter, 1996). Semi-evergreen. Scape 18 in. (45.7 cm); flower 2.75 in. (7.0 cm). Midseason. A mauve with a silver-frost eyezone above a green throat. Diploid. Parents unknown. Donn Fischer Memorial Award 2002.

Ida Munson Award Winners

The Ida Munson Award is given annually for the most outstanding double flower.

'Double Razzle Dazzle' (Betty B. Brown, 1974). Evergreen. Scape 25 in. (63.5 cm); flower 4 in. (10.2 cm). Early. A red self with a gold throat. Diploid. Parents unknown. Ida Munson Award 1980.

'Double Bourbon' (O. Currier McEwen, 1968). Dormant. Scape 28 in. (71.1 cm); flower 4.5 in. (11.4 cm). Early midseason. An orange-brown with yellow midribs. Diploid. Parents unknown. Ida Munson Award 1981.

'Pa Pa Gulino' (Kenneth G. Durio, 1977). Semi-evergreen. Scape 26 in. (66.0 cm); flower 6 in. (15.2 cm). Early. A silvery flesh-pink with rose-rouge above a citron-green throat. Tetraploid. (Tet. Seedling × 'Chicago Two Bits') × 'Tet. My Belle'. Ida Munson Award 1982.

'Betty Woods' (David Kirchhoff, 1980). Scape 26 in. (66.0 cm); flower 5.5 in. (14 cm). Early. A Chinese-yellow self with a green heart. Diploid. (('Winning Ways' × Seedling) × 'Keith Kennon') × 'Cosmic Treasure'. Ida Munson Award 1983.

'Condilla' (Albert O. Grooms, 1977). Dormant. Scape 20 in. (50.8 cm); flower 4.5 in. (11.4 cm). Early midseason. A deep gold self. Diploid. 'Whirling Skirt' × 'Chum'. Ida Munson Award 1984.

'Yazoo Souffle' (Ethel B. Smith, 1983). Semi-evergreen. Scape 26 in. (66.0 cm); flower 5.5 in. (14 cm). Early mid-season. A light apricot-pink self. Diploid. 'Yazoo Powder Puff' × 'Yazoo Powder Puff'. Ida Munson Award 1985.

'Siloam Double Rose' (Pauline Henry, 1979). Dormant. Scape 20 in. (50.8 cm); flower 6 in. (15.2 cm). Midseason. A bright rose with a ruby-red eyezone above a green throat. Diploid. Parents unknown. Ida Munson Award 1986.

'Stroke of Midnight' (David Kirchhoff, 1981). Evergreen. Scape 25 in. (63.5 cm); flower 5 in. (12.7 cm). Extra early. A Bordeaux-red self with a chartreuse throat. Diploid. ((('Blond Joanie' × 'Robert Way Schlumpf') × 'Karmic Treasure') × 'Double Razzle Dazzle') × 'Mozambique'. Ida Munson Award 1987.

'Siloam Double Classic' (Pauline Henry, 1985). Dormant. Scape 16 in. (40.6 cm); flower 5 in. (12.7 cm). Early midseason. A bright pink self with a green throat. Diploid. Parents unknown. Ida Munson Award 1988.

'Rachael My Love' (David L. Talbott, 1983). Evergreen. Scape 18 in. (45.7 cm); flower 5 in. (12.7 cm). Early midseason. A golden yellow self. Diploid. 'Janet Gayle' × 'Twin Masterpiece'. Ida Munson Award 1989.

'Cabbage Flower' (David Kirchhoff, 1984). Evergreen. Scape 17 in. (43.2 cm); flower 4.5 in. (11.4 cm). Extra early. A pastel lemon-yellow self with a green throat. Diploid. 'Twin Crown' × 'Nagasaki'. Ida Munson Award 1990.

'Highland Lord' (R. William Munson, 1983). Semi-evergreen. Scape 22 in. (55.9 cm); flower 5 in. (12.7 cm). Late midseason. A red-wine self with a lemon-yellow throat. Tetraploid. Parents unknown. Ida Munson Award 1991.

'Brent Gabriel' (Gabriel [Lucille] Guidry, 1981). Evergreen. Scape 20 in. (50.8 cm); flower 5.5 in. (14 cm). Extra early. A purple bitone with a white watermark above a green throat. Diploid. Parents unknown. Ida Munson Award 1992.

'Frances Joiner' (Enman R. Joiner, 1988). Dormant. Scape 24 in. (61 cm); flower 5.5 in. (14 cm). Midseason. A rose blend with a green-yellow throat. Diploid. Parents unknown. Ida Munson Award 1993.

'Ellen Christine' (Clarence J. Crochet, 1987). Semi-evergreen. Scape 23 in. (58.4 cm); flower 7 in. (17.8 cm). Midseason. A pink-gold blend with a dark green throat. Diploid. 'Ann Crochet' × 'Curly Ripples'. Ida Munson Award 1994.

'Almost Indecent' (Lee E. Gates, 1986). Semi-evergreen. Scape 20 in. (50.8 cm); flower 6.5 in. (16.5 cm). Early. A lavender and cream blend with a chalky chartreuse throat. Tetraploid. Parents unknown. Ida Munson Award 1995.

'Vanilla Fluff' (Enman R. Joiner, 1988). Dormant. Scape 34 in. (86.4 cm); flower 6 in. (15.2 cm). Midseason. A cream self. Diploid. 'Ivory Cloud' × Seedling. Ida Munson Award 1996.

'Almond Puff' (Patrick Stamile, 1990). Dormant. Scape 23 in. (58.4 cm); flower 6.5 in. (16.5 cm). Midseason. A beige self with a green throat. Diploid. 'Salt Lake City' × 'Barbara Mitchell'. Ida Munson Award 1997.

'Siloam Olin Frazier' (Pauline Henry, 1990). Dormant. Scape 22 in. (55.9 cm); flower 5.25 in. (13.3 cm). Early. A hot rose self. Diploid. Parents unknown. Ida Munson Award 1997.

'Forty Second Street' (David Kirchhoff, 1991). Evergreen. Scape 24 in. (61 cm); flower 5 in. (12.7 cm). Mid-

season. A pastel pink with a bright rose eyezone above a yellow to green throat. Diploid. Parents unknown. Ida Munson Award 1998.

'Layers of Gold' (David Kirchhoff, 1990). Evergreen. Scape 24 in. (61 cm); flower 5 in. (12.7 cm). Early midseason. A medium gold self with a green throat. Tetraploid. (Seedling × (('Czarina' × 'Ed Kirchhoff') × 'Inez Ways')) × ('Double Jackpot' × ('King Alfred' × Seedling)). Ida Munson Award 1999.

'King Kahuna' (Clarence J. Crochet, 1994). Semi-evergreen. Scape 22 in. (55.9 cm); flower 6.5 in. (16.5 cm). Early midseason. A medium yellow self. Diploid. 'Olin Frazier' × 'Ellen Christine'. Ida Munson Award 2000.

'Peggy Jeffcoat' (Jan Joiner, 1995). Dormant. Scape 18 in. (45.7 cm); flower 6.5 in. (16.5 cm). Midseason. A cream-white, hose-in-hose, lightly ruffled double with a light green throat. Diploid. 'Jean Swann' × 'Rebecca Marie'. Ida Munson Award 2001.

'Peach Magnolia' (Enman R. Joiner, 1986). Dormant. Scape 32 in. (81.3 cm); flower 5.5 in. (14 cm). Late midseason. A peach self with a green throat. Diploid. Parents unknown. Ida Munson Award 2002.

Harris Olson Spider Award Winners

The annual award for the best spider or spider variant is the Harris Olson Spider Award. It was first presented in 1989.

'Kindly Light' (LeMoine J. Bechtold, 1950). Dormant. Scape 28 in. (71.1 cm). A deep yellow with a crabapple-green throat. 7.7:1. Diploid. Parents unknown. Harris Olson Spider Award 1989.

'Lady Fingers' (Virginia L. Peck, 1967). Dormant. Scape 32 in. (81.3 cm); flower 6 in. (15.2 cm). A yellow to green self with a dark green throat. 5.1:1. Diploid. Parents unknown. Harris Olson Spider Award 1990.

'Cat's Cradle' (Ben R. Hager, 1985). Evergreen. Scape 38 in. (96.5 cm); flower 8 in. (20.3 cm). Early midseason. A yellow spider self. 5.8:1. Diploid. 'Carolicolossal' × 'Kindly Light'. Harris Olson Spider Award 1991.

'Red Ribbons' (George E. Lenington, 1964). Evergreen. Scape 42 in. (106.7 cm); flower 8 in. (20.3 cm). 4.7:1. Diploid. 'Wanda' × 'Mabel Fuller'. Harris Olson Spider Award 1992.

'Mountain Top Experience' (John J. Temple, 1988). Evergreen. Scape 29 in. (73.7 cm); flower 7.5 in. (19.1 cm). Early. A green-yellow and rouge bicolor with a green throat. 4.8:1. Diploid. 'Rainbow Spangles' × 'Lois Burns'. Harris Olson Spider Award 1993.

'Wilson Spider' (William S. Oakes, 1987). Dormant. Scape 28 in. (71.1 cm); flower 7.5 in. (19.1 cm). Midseason. A purple bitone spider with a white eyezone and a chartreuse throat. 4.6:1. Diploid. Parents unknown. Harris Olson Spider Award 1994.

'Lois Burns' (John J. Temple, 1986). Evergreen. Scape 30 in. (76.2 cm); flower 8.5 in. (21.6 cm). Early. A yellow-green spider with a green throat. 4.0:1. Diploid. Seedling × 'Green Widow'. Harris Olson Spider Award 1995.

'Green Widow' (John J. Temple, 1980). Evergreen. Scape 26 in. (66.0 cm); flower 6.5 in. (16.5 cm). Early. A yellow-green self with a very green throat. 4.1:1. Diploid. 'Celestial Light' × 'Green Avalanche'. Harris Olson Spider Award 1996.

'Yabba Dabba Doo' (Ra Hansen, 1993). Semi-evergreen. Scape 30 in. (76.2 cm); flower 10 in. (25.4 cm). Late. A medium purple, spider variant self with a large chartreuse throat. 4.35:1. Diploid. Parents unknown. Harris Olson Spider Award 1997.

'De Colores' (John J. Temple, 1992). Evergreen. Scape 28 in. (71.1 cm); flower 8.5 in. (21.6 cm). Early. A rose, tan, and yellow spider with a red-purple eyezone above a very green throat. 6.0:1. Diploid. 'Mountain Top Experience' × 'Garden Portrait'. Harris Olson Spider Award 1998.

'Chevron Spider' (Ra Hansen, 1992). Evergreen. Scape 30 in. (76.2 cm); flower 10 in. (25.4 cm). Early midseason. A cream-peach spider variant with a burgundy eyezone above a lime-green throat. 4.17:1. Diploid. (Seedling × 'Spider Miracle') × Seedling. Harris Olson Spider Award 1999.

'Marked by Lydia' (John J. Temple, 1994). Semi-evergreen. Scape 29 in. (73.7 cm); flower 8.5 in. (21.6 cm). Early. A medium yellow spider with a purple eyezone above a green throat. 5.31:1. Diploid. 'Mountain Top Experience' × 'Garden Portrait'. Harris Olson Spider Award 2000.

'Lacy Marionette' (Inez Tarrant, 1987). Evergreen. Scape 26 in. (66.0 cm); flower 7 in. (17.8 cm). Early midseason. A bright yellow spider with a dark green throat. 5.1:1. Diploid. 'Kindly Light' × Seedling. Harris Olson Spider Award 2001.

'Curly Cinnamon Windmill' (Clarence J. Crochet, 1997). Dormant. Scape 28 in. (71.1 cm); flower 8.5 in. (21.6 cm). Early midseason. A yellow-brushed-cinnamon with a cinnamon, chevron-shaped eye above a dark green throat. 5.2:1. Diploid. 'Lacy Marionette' × 'Cat's Cradle'. Harris Olson Spider Award 2002.

Lambert/Webster Unusual Forms Award Winners

The annual award for the best unusual form flower is the Lambert/Webster Unusual Forms Award. It was first awarded in 2000.

'Jan's Twister' (Jan Joiner, 1991). Evergreen. Scape 28 in. (71.1 cm); flower 11.5 in. (29.2 cm). Early midseason. A peach spider self with a green throat. Diploid. 'Jean Wise' × 'Kindly Light'. Lambert/Webster Award 2000.

'Primal Scream' (Curt Hanson, 1994). Dormant. Scape 34 in. (86.4 cm); flower 7.5 in. (19.1 cm). Late midseason. An orange-tangerine self with a green throat. Tetraploid. 'Tangerine Parfait' × 'Mauna Loa'. Lambert/Webster Award 2001.

'Ruby Spider' (Patrick Stamile, 1991). Dormant. Scape 34 in. (86.4 cm); flower 9 in. (22.9 cm). Early. A ruby-red spider self with a yellow throat. Tetraploid. 'Velvet Widow' × 'Tet. Open Hearth'. Lambert/Webster Award 2002.

Don C. Stevens Award Winners

The Don C. Stevens Award is given annually to the most outstanding eyed or banded flower. It was first awarded in 1985.

'Siloam Bertie Ferris' (Pauline Henry, 1981). Dormant. Scape 16 in. (40.6 cm); flower 2.75 in. (7.0 cm). Early midseason. A deep rose-shrimp with a deeper rose eyezone above a green throat. Diploid. Parents unknown. Don C. Stevens Award 1985.

'Bette Davis Eyes' (David Kirchhoff, 1982). Evergreen. Scape 23 in. (58.4 cm); flower 5.2 in. (13.3 cm). Early. A lavender with a grape-purple eyezone above an intense lime-green throat. Diploid. 'Lhasa' × 'Agape Love'. Don C. Stevens Award 1986.

'Paper Butterfly' (Mort Morss, 1983). Semi-evergreen. Scape 24 in. (61 cm); flower 6 in. (15.2 cm). Early. A cream-peach and blue-violet blend with a blue-violet eyezone above a green throat. Tetraploid. ((Seedling × 'Chicago Two Bits') × 'Thais') × (('Silver Veil' × ('Knave' × Chicago Mist)) × 'Chicago Mist'). Don C. Stevens Award 1987.

'Will Return' (Mr. and Mrs. W. M. Spalding, 1983). Evergreen. Scape 18 in. (45.7 cm); flower 4.75 in. (12.1 cm). Midseason. A peachy pink with a purple halo above a green throat. Diploid. Parents unknown. Don C. Stevens Award 1988.

'Siloam Virginia Henson' (Pauline Henry, 1979). Dormant. Scape 18 in. (45.7 cm); flower 4 in. (10.2 cm). Early midseason. A pink with a ruby-red eyezone above a green throat. Diploid. Parents unknown. Don C. Stevens Award 1989.

'Janice Brown' (Edwin C. Brown, 1986). Semi-evergreen. Scape 21 in. (53.3 cm); flower 4.25 in. (10.8 cm). Early midseason. A bright pink with a rose-pink eyezone and a green throat. Diploid. Parents unknown. Don C. Stevens Award 1990.

'New Series' (Kate Carpenter, 1982). Semi-evergreen. Scape 25 in. (63.5 cm); flower 7.5 in. (19.1 cm). Midseason. A clear, light pink with a rose-red eyezone above a bright lime-green throat. Diploid. 'Arkansas Bright Eyes' × 'Shibui Splendor'. Don C. Stevens Award 1991.

'Pumpkin Kid' (Elsie Spalding, 1987). Evergreen. Scape 18 in. (45.7 cm); flower 5.5 in. (14 cm). Midseason. A light orange with a red eyezone above a green throat. Diploid. Parents unknown. Don C. Stevens Award 1992.

'Always Afternoon' (Mort Morss, 1987). Semi-evergreen. Scape 22 in. (55.9 cm); flower 5.5 in. (14 cm). Early. A medium mauve flower edged in buff with a purple eyezone above a green throat. Tetraploid. ('Ring of Change' × 'Tiffany Palace') × 'Opus One'. Don C. Stevens Award 1993.

'Jason Salter' (Elizabeth Anne Salter, 1987). Evergreen. Scape 18 in. (45.7 cm) ; flower 2.75 in. (7.0 cm). Early midseason. A yellow with a washed lavender-purple eyezone and a green throat. Diploid. 'Enchanter's Spell' × ('Enchanted Elf' × 'Cosmic Hummingbird'). Don C. Stevens Award 1994.

'Strawberry Candy' (Patrick Stamile, 1989). Semi-evergreen. Scape 26 in. (66.0 cm); flower 4.25 in. (10.8 cm). Early midseason. A strawberry-pink blend with a rose-red eyezone above a gold to green throat. Tetraploid. 'Panache' × 'Tet. Siloam Virginia Henson'. Don C. Stevens Award 1995.

'Siloam David Kirchhoff' (Pauline Henry, 1986). Dormant. Scape 16 in. (40.6 cm); flower 3.5 in. (8.9 cm). Early midseason. An orchid with a cerise pencil-line eyezone and a green throat. Diploid. Parents unknown. Don C. Stevens Award 1996.

'Pirate's Patch' (Jeff Salter, 1991). Evergreen. Scape 28 in. (71.1 cm); flower 6 in. (15.2 cm). Early midseason. An ivory-cream with a purple eyezone above a yellow to green throat. Tetraploid. 'Well of Souls' × 'Jungle Mask'. Don C. Stevens Award 1997.

'Paige's Pinata' (Ra Hansen, 1990). Semi-evergreen. Scape 26 in. (66.0 cm); flower 6 in. (15.2 cm). Early midseason. Peach with a bold fuchsia band around an orange eyezone above a dark green throat. Diploid. ('So Excited' × Seedling) × 'Janice Brown'. Don C. Stevens Award 1998.

'Siloam Merle Kent' (Pauline Henry, 1984). Dormant. Scape 18 in. (45.7 cm); flower 3.5 in. (8.9 cm). Midseason. A bright orchid with a deep purple eyezone and a green throat. Diploid. Parents unknown. Don C. Stevens Award 1999.

'Canadian Border Patrol' (Jeff Salter, 1995). Semi-evergreen. Scape 28 in. (71.1 cm); flower 6 in. (15.2 cm). Early midseason. A cream with a purple edge and eyezone above a green throat. Tetraploid. Parents unknown. Don C. Stevens Award 2000.

'El Desperado' (Patrick Stamile, 1991). Dormant. Scape 28 in. (71.1 cm); flower 4.25 in. (10.8 cm). Late. A mustard-yellow with a wine-purple eyezone above a green throat. Tetraploid. 'El Bandito' × 'Blackberry Candy'. Don C. Stevens Award 2001.

'Sabine Baur' (Jeff Salter, 1997). Semi-evergreen. Scape 25 in. (63.5 cm); flower 6 in. (15.2 cm). Midseason. A cream with a striking purple eyezone and thick purple picotee above a green throat. Tetraploid. 'Cindy's Eye' × 'Daring Deception'. Don C. Stevens Award 2002.

R. W. Munson Jr. Award Winners

The annual award for the best patterned flower is the R. W. Munson Jr. Award. It was first awarded in 2001.

'Witch Stitchery' (Mort Morss, 1986). Semi-evergreen. Scape 26 in. (66.0 cm); flower 5.5 in. (14 cm). Extra early. A cream with a lavender eyezone edged in purple and a green throat. Tetraploid. (Seedling × 'Chicago Two Bits') × 'Paper Butterfly'. R. W. Munson Jr. Award 2001.

'Etched Eyes' (Matthew Kaskel, 1994). Evergreen. Scape 28 in. (71.1 cm); flower 5.5 in. (14 cm). Early. A cream-yellow with a raspberry eyezone. Tetraploid. ('Paper Butterfly' × ('Kate Carpenter' × Seedling)) × 'Stairway to Heaven'. R. W. Munson Jr. Award 2002.

Eugene S. Foster Award Winners

The Eugene S. Foster Award is given annually, since 1991, to an outstanding late-blooming cultivar.

'Catherine Neal' (Jack B. Carpenter, 1981). Dormant. Scape 30 in. (76.2 cm); flower 6 in. (15.2 cm). Very late. A purple self with a green throat. Diploid. Parents unknown. Eugene S. Foster Award 1991.

'Regal Finale' (Patrick Stamile, 1988). Dormant. Scape 26 in. (66.0 cm); flower 6 in. (15.2 cm). Late. A violet-purple self with a green throat. Diploid. 'Super Purple' × 'When I Dream'. Eugene S. Foster Award 1992.

'Sandra Elizabeth' (Donald C. Stevens, 1983). Dormant. Scape 28 in. (71.1 cm); flower 6 in. (15.2 cm). Very late. A deep yellow self. Tetraploid. 'Bengaleer' × Seedling. Eugene S. Foster Award 1993.

'Sweet Shalimar' (Ra Hansen, 1986). Evergreen. Scape 24 in. (61 cm); flower 5.5 in. (14 cm). Midseason. A deep, orange-veined persimmon with an olive throat. Diploid. (('Dynasty Gold' × 'Martha Adams') × ('Orange Joy' × 'Janet Gayle')) × 'Ann Crochet'. Eugene S. Foster Award 1994.

'Ed Kirchhoff' (David Kirchhoff, 1981). Semi-evergreen. Scape 23 in. (58.4 cm); flower 5 in. (12.7 cm). Early. A saffron-yellow self with an olive-green throat. Tetraploid. (('Double Jackpot' × 'Amber Sunset') × ('Evening Gown' × 'Yasmin')) × Seedling. Eugene S. Foster Award 1995.

'Lime Frost' (Patrick Stamile, 1990). Dormant. Scape 27 in. (68.6 cm); flower 5.75 in. (14.6 cm). Very late. A green and white blend with a green throat. Tetraploid. ('Arctic Snow' × 'White Tie Affair') × 'Tet. Gentle Shepherd'. Eugene S. Foster Award 1997.

'Easy Ned' (Betty B. Brown, 1987). Evergreen. Scape 40 in. (101.6 cm); flower 6.5 in. (16.5 cm). Very late. A chartreuse self with a green throat. Diploid. 'Lady Fingers' × Seedling. Eugene S. Foster Award 1998.

'Adrienne's Surprise' (Ra Hansen, 1992). Evergreen. Scape 26 in. (66.0 cm); flower 4.5 in. (11.4 cm). Late. A silver-rose-pink with a darker rose halo above a green throat. Diploid. ('Heaven Can Wait' × Seedling) × 'Ruffled Beauty'. Eugene S. Foster Award 1999.

'Uptown Girl' (Patrick Stamile, 1993). Semi-evergreen. Scape 27 in. (68.6 cm); flower 5 in. (12.7 cm). Early midseason. A baby-ribbon-pink self with a green throat. Tetraploid. 'Crush on You' × 'Peach Whisper'. Eugene S. Foster Award 2000.

'Susan Weber' (Charles E. Branch, 1989). Semi-evergreen. Scape 26 in. (66.0 cm); flower 5.75 in. (14.6 cm). Late. A light rose-pink with rose edging and a yellow to green throat. Diploid. 'Great Thou Art' × 'Fairy Tale Pink'. Eugene S. Foster Award 2001.

'Blizzard Bay' (Jeff Salter, 1995). Semi-evergreen. Scape 28 in. (71.1 cm); flower 6 in. (15.2 cm). Late. A near white self with a green throat. Tetraploid. 'Arctic Snow' × 'Eloquent Silence'. Eugene S. Foster Award 2002.

L. Ernest Plouf Award Winners

The annual award recognizing the most consistently fragrant and dormant flower is the L. Ernest Plouf Award.

'Tender Love' (Elizabeth Yancey and Mattie C. Harrison, 1970). Dormant. Scape 22 in. (55.9 cm); flower 6.5 in. (16.5 cm). Very late. A flesh-pink blend with a green throat. Diploid. Parents unknown. L. Ernest Plouf Award 1980.

'Frozen Jade' (Van M. Sellers, 1975). Dormant. Scape 28 in. (71.1 cm); flower 5.5 in. (14 cm). Midseason. A lemon-yellow self with a green throat. Tetraploid. Parents unknown. L. Ernest Plouf Award 1981.

'Siloam Double Rose' (Pauline Henry, 1979). Dormant. Scape 20 in. (50.8 cm); flower 6 in. (15.2 cm). Midseason. A bright rose with a ruby-red eyezone above a green throat. Diploid. Parents unknown. L. Ernest Plouf Award 1982.

'Ida Miles' (Julia B. Hardy, 1971). Dormant. Scape 30 in. (76.2 cm); flower 6.5 in. (16.5 cm). Midseason. A pale ivory to yellow self. Diploid. Parents unknown. L. Ernest Plouf Award 1983.

'Siloam Mama' (Pauline Henry, 1982). Dormant. Scape 24 in. (61 cm); flower 5.75 in. (14.6 cm). Early midseason. A yellow self with a green throat. Diploid. Parents unknown. L. Ernest Plouf Award 1984.

'Siloam Double Classic' (Pauline Henry, 1985). Dormant. Scape 16 in. (40.6 cm); flower 5 in. (12.7 cm). Early midseason. A bright pink self with a green throat. Diploid. Parents unknown. L. Ernest Plouf Award 1985.

'Hudson Valley' (Virginia L. Peck, 1971). Dormant. Scape 32 in. (81.3 cm); flower 8.5 in. (21.6 cm). Midseason. A green-yellow self with a deep green throat. Tetraploid. 'Bonnie John Seton' × Seedling. L. Ernest Plouf Award 1986.

'Evening Bell' (Virginia L. Peck, 1971). Dormant. Scape 23 in. (58.4 cm); flower 7 in. (17.8 cm). Early midseason. A light yellow self with a yellow to green throat. Tetraploid. Seedling × 'Bonnie John Seton'. L. Ernest Plouf Award 1987.

'Chorus Line' (David Kirchhoff, 1981). Evergreen. Scape 20 in. (50.8 cm); flower 3.5 in. (8.9 cm). Early. A medium pink with a rose band above a yellow halo and a dark green throat. Diploid. ('Sweet Thing' × ('Little Lad' × 'Call to Remembrance')) × 'Lullaby Baby'. L. Ernest Plouf Award 1988.

'Golden Scroll' (Gabriel Guidry, 1983). Dormant. Scape 19 in. (48.3 cm); flower 5.5 in. (14 cm). Early. A tangerine self with a green throat. Diploid. Parents unknown. L. Ernest Plouf Award 1989.

'Smoky Mountain Autumn' (Gabriel Guidry, 1986). Dormant. Scape 18 in. (45.7 cm); flower 5.75 in. (14.6 cm). Early. A rose blend with a rose-lavender halo and an olive-green throat. Diploid. Parents unknown. L. Ernest Plouf Award 1990.

'Siloam Spizz' (Pauline Henry, 1986). Dormant. Scape 18 in. (45.7 cm); flower 4.5 in. (11.4 cm). Midseason. A yellow self with a green throat. Diploid. Parents unknown. L. Ernest Plouf Award 1991.

'Vanilla Fluff' (Enman R. Joiner, 1988). Dormant. Scape 34 in. (86.4 cm); flower 6 in. (15.2 cm). Midseason. A cream self. Diploid. 'Ivory Cloud' × Seedling. L. Ernest Plouf Award 1993.

'Lemon Lollypop' (Doris Simpson, 1985). Dormant. Scape 24 in. (61 cm); flower 2.9 in. (7.4 cm). Early. A light lemon-yellow self with a green throat. Diploid. 'Ruth Ann' × 'Stella De Oro'. L. Ernest Plouf Award 1994.

'Gingham Maid' (Gabriel Guidry, 1986). Dormant. Scape 23 in. (58.4 cm); flower 7.25 in. (18.4 cm). Early. A pink-cream bitone with a lime green throat. Diploid. Parents unknown. L. Ernest Plouf Award 1995.

'Frosted Pink Ice' (Patrick Stamile, 1987). Dormant. Scape 28 in. (71.1 cm); flower 5 in. (12.7 cm). Early midseason. A blue-pink self with a green throat. Diploid. 'Gun Metal' × ('Lavender Dew' × 'Rose Swan'). L. Ernest Plouf Award 1996.

'Raspberry Candy' (Patrick Stamile, 1989). Dormant. Scape 26 in. (66.0 cm); flower 4.75 in. (12.1 cm). Early. A cream with a raspberry-red eyezone above a green throat. Tetraploid. Seedling × 'Tet. Siloam Virginia Henson'. L. Ernest Plouf Award 1997.

'Wineberry Candy' (Patrick Stamile, 1990). Dormant. Scape 22 in. (55.9 cm); flower 4.75 in. (12.1 cm). Early midseason. An orchid with a purple eyezone above a green throat. Tetraploid. 'Tet. Siloam Virginia Henson' × 'Paper Butterfly'. L. Ernest Plouf Award 1998.

'Dena Marie' (Jack B. Carpenter, 1992). Dormant. Scape 26 in. (66.0 cm); flower 6.75 in. (17.1 cm). Midseason. A rose-pink self with a yellow to green throat. Diploid. Parents unknown. L. Ernest Plouf Award 1999.

'Chance Encounter' (Patrick Stamile, 1994). Evergreen. Scape 25 in. (63.5 cm); flower 6 in. (15.2 cm). Early midseason. A raspberry-rose blend with a gold edge above a green throat. Tetraploid. ((Seedling × 'Love Goddess') × 'Crush on You') × 'Tet. Barbara Mitchell'. L. Ernest Plouf Award 2000.

'Elegant Candy' (Patrick Stamile, 1995). Dormant. Scape 25 in. (63.5 cm); flower 4.25 in. (10.8 cm). Early midseason. A pink with a red eyezone above a green throat. Tetraploid. 'Lady of Fortune' × 'Tet. Janice Brown'. L. Ernest Plouf Award 2001.

'Shimmering Elegance' (Patrick Stamile, 1994). Dormant. Scape 25 in. (63.5 cm); flower 6 in. (15.2 cm). Early midseason. A pink self with a green throat.

Tetraploid. (Seedling × 'Silken Touch') × 'Seminole Wind'. L. Ernest Plouf Award 2002.

Lenington All-American Award Winners

The Lenington All-American Award is given annually to a cultivar that performs outstandingly in most parts of the world.

'Green Flutter' (Lucille Williamson, 1964). Semi-evergreen. Scape 20 in. (50.8 cm); flower 3 in. (7.6 cm). Late. A canary-yellow self with a green throat. Diploid. Parents unknown. Lenington All-American Award 1980.

'Prester John' (John Mason Allgood, 1971). Dormant. Scape 26 in. (66.0 cm); flower 5 in. (12.7 cm). Early midseason. An orange-gold self with a green throat. Diploid. 'Court Herald' × Seedling. Lenington All-American Award 1981.

'Raindrop' (Robert M. Kennedy, 1972). Semi-evergreen. Scape 12 in. (30.5 cm); flower 2 in. (5.1 cm). Midseason. A light yellow self. Diploid. Parents unknown. Lenington All-American Award 1982.

'Ed Murray' (Edward F. Grovatt, 1971). Dormant. Scape 30 in. (76.2 cm); flower 4 in. (10.2 cm). Midseason. A black-red self with a green throat. Diploid. 'Tis Midnight' × Seedling. Lenington All-American Award 1983.

'Red Rum' (Clara May Pittard, 1974). Semi-evergreen. Scape 15 in. (38 cm); flower 4 in. (10.2 cm). Midseason. A rust-red self with a yellow throat. Diploid. Parents unknown. Lenington All-American Award 1984.

'Olive Bailey Langdon' (R. William Munson, 1974). Semi-evergreen. Scape 28 in. (71.1 cm); flower 5 in. (12.7 cm). Early midseason. A purple self with a yellow to green throat. Tetraploid. 'Embassy' × 'Chicago Regal'. Lenington All-American Award 1985.

'Yesterday Memories' (Elsie Spalding, 1976). Evergreen. Scape 19 in. (48.3 cm); flower 6.5 in. (16.5 cm). Midseason. A deep pink self with a green throat. Diploid. Parents unknown. Lenington All-American Award 1986.

'Golden Prize' (Virginia L. Peck, 1968). Dormant. Scape 26 in. (66.0 cm); flower 7 in. (17.8 cm). Late. A golden yellow self. Tetraploid. Parents unknown. Lenington All-American Award 1987.

'Lullaby Baby' (Elsie Spalding, 1975). Semi-evergreen. Scape 19 in. (48.3 cm); flower 3.5 in. (8.9 cm). Early midseason. A light pink with a green throat. Diploid. Parents unknown. Lenington All-American Award 1988.

'Russian Rhapsody' (R. William Munson, 1973). Semi-evergreen. Scape 30 in. (76.2 cm); flower 6 in. (15.2 cm). Midseason. A violet-purple self with a yellow throat. Tetraploid. 'Knave' × 'Chicago Royal'. Lenington All-American Award 1989.

'Joan Senior' (Kenneth G. Durio, 1977). Evergreen. Scape 25 in. (63.5 cm); flower 6 in. (15.2 cm). Early midseason. A near white self with a lime-green throat. Diploid. 'Loving Memories' × 'Little Infant'. Lenington All-American Award 1990.

'Condilla' (Albert O. Grooms, 1977). Dormant. Scape 20 in. (50.8 cm); flower 4.5 in. (11.4 cm). Early midseason. A deep golden yellow self. Diploid. 'Whirling Skirt' × 'Chum'. Lenington All-American Award 1991.

'Beauty to Behold' (Van M. Sellers, 1978). Semi-evergreen. Scape 24 in. (61 cm); flower 5.5 in. (14 cm). Midseason. A lemon self with a green throat. Diploid. 'Wynn' × 'Springtime Sonata'. Lenington All-American Award 1993.

'Chorus Line' (David Kirchhoff, 1981). Evergreen. Scape 20 in. (50.8 cm); flower 3.5 in. (8.9 cm). Early. A medium pink with a rose band above a yellow halo and a dark green throat. Diploid. ('Sweet Thing' × ('Little Lad' × 'Call to Remembrance')) × 'Lullaby Baby'. Lenington All-American Award 1994.

'Designer Jeans' (Sarah Sikes, 1983). Dormant. Scape 34 in. (86.4 cm); flower 6.5 in. (16.5 cm). Midseason. A lavender with a dark lavender eyezone and edges above a yellow to green throat. Tetraploid. ('Pink Mystique' × 'Chicago Knobby') × ('Medea' × 'Chicago Knobby'). Lenington All-American Award 1995.

'Kate Carpenter' (R. William Munson, 1980). Evergreen. Scape 28 in. (71.1 cm); flower 6 in. (15.2 cm). Early midseason. A pale pink self with a cream throat. Tetraploid. ('Wilbur Harling' × 'Kecia') × 'Pagoda Goddess'. Lenington All-American Award 1996.

'Smoky Mountain' (Mattie C. Harrison, 1966). Semi-evergreen. Scape 32 in. (81.3 cm); flower 7.5 in. (19.1 cm). Midseason. A lemon-yellow with a smoky pink overlay above a chartreuse throat. Diploid. Parents unknown. Lenington All-American Award 1997.

'Paper Butterfly' (Mort Morss, 1983). Semi-evergreen. Scape 24 in. (61 cm); flower 6 in. (15.2 cm). Early. A cream-peach and blue-violet blend with a blue-violet eyezone above a green throat. Tetraploid. ((Seedling × 'Chicago Two Bits') × 'Thais') × (('Silver Veil' × ('Knave' × Chicago Mist')) × 'Chicago Mist'). Lenington All-American Award 1998.

'Orange Velvet' (Enman R. Joiner, 1988). Semi-evergreen. Scape 30 in. (76.2 cm); flower 6.5 in. (16.5 cm). Midseason. An orange self with a green throat. Diploid. 'Copper Lantern' × 'Golden Scroll'. Lenington All-American Award 1999.

'Jason Salter' (Elizabeth Anne Salter, 1987). Evergreen. Scape 18 in. (45.7 cm); flower 2.75 in. (7.0 cm). Early midseason. A yellow with a washed lavender-purple eyezone and a green throat. Diploid. 'Enchanter's Spell' × ('Enchanted Elf' × 'Cosmic Hummingbird'). Lenington All-American Award 2000.

'Ming Porcelain' (David Kirchhoff, 1981). Evergreen. Scape 28 in. (71.1 cm); flower 5.25 in. (13.3 cm). Early. A pastel ivory-pink touched with peach and edged in gold with a wide yellow halo above a lime-green throat. Tetraploid. 'Ring of Change' × 'Tet. Lullaby Baby'. Lenington All-American Award 2001.

'Midnight Magic' (John Kinnebrew, 1979). Evergreen. Scape 28 in. (71.1 cm); flower 5.5 in. (14 cm). Early midseason. A black-red self with a striking green throat. Tetraploid. 'Ed Murray' × 'Kilimanjaro'. Lenington All-American Award 2002.

CHAPTER 13

Daylilies in Australia

The climate in Australia varies from north to south, much the same as the climate in North America, with the exception that most of the country is warmer and lacks the extreme winters experienced in the northern United States and Canada. Its climate is reverse of North America in that summer occurs in January and winter occurs in July. The northern tip of Australia is close to the equator; therefore, it is very hot year-round with a climate similar to that of southern Florida. Tasmania, the southernmost tip of Australia, has average lows of 41°F (5°C). Much of Australia is arid and desert like, with the exception of the coastal regions. Most daylily gardens are located a short distance from the eastern coast of Australia. We have visited Australia on three occasions, during the most recent of which we were involved in speaking on daylilies and touring a number of daylily nurseries along the eastern coast from New South Wales to Queensland. We were fortunate to meet and be hosted by most of the extraordinarily friendly and hospitable daylily hybridizers and collectors during our travels up the coast, and have also met a number of Australian daylily enthusiasts and hybridizers during their visits to North America.

The first hybrid daylilies from the United States were probably imported into Australia by Fred Danks of Victoria in 1947. Bryan Tonkin, also of Victoria, followed him, importing plants from Gilbert Wild and Sons from 1959 to '70. Tonkin's attempt to foster interest in daylilies in Australia during this period did not meet with a great deal of success. Likely, this was primarily due to the difficulty in growing dormant daylilies in the tropical climate of Australia, and also the relative expense of new daylily hybrids. However, over time interest in daylilies grew, particularly in the late 1960s. At this time, Jim Hipathite of Queensland also began importing daylilies. His attempts were more successful, since he brought in evergreen plants that had been hybridized in Florida by Ophelia Taylor. Thus, the stage was set for a rapid increase in interest in daylilies during the 1970s.

A major grower of daylilies who began collecting during that time was Barry Blyth of Tempo Two Gardens in Victoria. He imported daylilies from the best Florida hybridizers to use in his hybridizing program. These daylilies performed very well in Australia, and Blyth, who subsequently introduced 71 cultivars, continues his work today. Some of his daylilies are 'Just an Angel' (1993), a light apricot with a light pink eye; 'Circle of Song' (1993), a cream-pink with a burgundy eye-zone; and 'Baron Rouge' (1993), a burgundy-red bitone. In 1981, Graeme Grosvenor of Rainbow Ridge Nursery near Sydney began to sell daylilies along with his irises. In addition to his work importing and selling quality daylilies, Grosvenor also wrote the classic daylily book, *Daylilies for the Garden* (Portland, Ore.: Timber Press, 1999).

The now famous sister duo, Monica Mead and Maureen Flanders, opened the Daylily Display Center in Queensland and began their own hybridizing program in the early 1970s, initially by importing some tetraploid seeds from the United States. They gave some of their early introductions the prefix "Acadia" and "Kolan," and many are still commercially available. Later, Flanders moved her gardens to Bundaberg, where she continued hybridizing and importing daylilies to her Daylily Display Center. Mead, along with her son, Neil, and his wife Debbie, opened Meads Daylily Gardens and continued to work in Acacia Ridge.

Mead's breeding program has hailed 54 introductions of her own, 60 joint introductions with her sister, and several other joint introductions with other hybridizers. Today, she, Debbie, and Neil continue to import many modern daylilies from around the world. They use these cultivars to produce high quality hybrids, many of which have received awards in Australia. Mead pays careful attention to texture, bud count, branching, and rebloom, with special consideration for overall plant habit. Some daylilies that she has registered and introduced are 'Donna Mead' (1996), a blood-red self; 'Watercolor Dream' (1999), a cream-peach with a gold edge; 'Christopher Mead' (1999), a

golden yellow self; and 'Rebecca Jane' (1999), a light pink double with a rose-pink eye.

Flanders has produced 118 introductions, including the 60 joint introductions with her sister. Although no longer selling daylilies herself, she continues to hybridize and introduce her latest cultivars through a nursery located in Gin Gin, Queensland. An outgoing and vivacious person, Flanders has a vast amount of knowledge about daylilies and is very active in the daylily community in Australia. Some daylilies recently registered and introduced by her include 'Apology Accepted' (1999), a deep purple with a lighter watermark; 'Daphne Tremmel' (1999), a cream-yellow with a light red eye; 'Red Attack' (1999), a large red self; and 'Watercolour Art' (1999), a deep lavender with a cream eye.

In 1984, Scott Alexander established Mountain View Daylilies in Melany, Queensland. His spectacular nursery, located at an elevation of 200 ft (600 m) near the Glass Mountains, has breath-taking views as well as the perfect soil and climate for daylilies. Alexander gave the prefix "Melany" to many of his earlier creations, such as 'Melany Debutante' (1993), one of his most popular cultivars, a pastel peach-pink with a star-shaped, rose eye. His 'Cane Fire' (1993), an orange-red with a red eye; 'Melany Charmer' (1993), a dusky lavender with a cream halo; and 'In Excess' (1993), a cantaloupe-colored double are a few of the registered cultivars that he has introduced.

Les Holton from Toowoomba has a background in genetics through animal breeding and uses this knowledge in his hybridizing efforts. Holton prefers to line breed, and since his first registration in 1999, has registered 19 daylilies. Two of his more recent introductions are 'Courtney Ann' (2002), a small yellow with a raspberry eye and edge, and 'Royal Rego' (2002), a lavender with a gold edge.

Graham Nunan has been hybridizing since approximately 1988 and has an eye for the round, ruffled, full-formed daylilies, with a particular interest in deep, golden yellows. He has registered 10 introductions on his own and three jointly with Monica Mead. Some of his creations include 'Rose Helena' (2001), a bright rose, and 'Purple Riot' (1999), a showy purple.

Ian Wicks, who originally had a passion for hibiscus, was swayed to daylilies about 1998, when we first met him. He did not take long to become totally entrenched, purchasing and selling daylilies and begining his own hybridizing efforts. To date Wicks has registered one of his seedlings, 'Leigh La Belle' (2001), a deep gold self.

This increasing interest in daylilies has brought with it a number of clubs and societies. In 1996, two daylily groups were created: The Brisbane Daylily Club in Queensland and the Hemerocallis Society of Australia.

Later, additional clubs formed in Bundaberg and Toowoomba. The local clubs all stage shows and have regular meetings. The national group produces a quarterly journal and helps bring in speakers from outside Australia.

In addition to these events, hybridizers, collectors, and growers, many other individuals, and more every year, are collecting and producing new, high quality daylily cultivars in Australia. The warm tropical climate of Australia makes it easy to produce a generation of daylilies each year, similar to the large daylily gardens in Florida. The future will likely continue to bring even more highly competitive daylilies from the "Land Down Under."

CHAPTER 14

Daylilies in Canada

by Keith Somers

Daylily hybridization in Canada is entering a new era. Nurseries and garden centers throughout the country are stocking daylilies in greater numbers and with greater diversity than ever before. In fact, the *Hemerocallis* species that were once commonly offered for sale have been largely replaced by modern cultivars. To this end, the number of retailers that specialize in propagating and selling daylilies is rapidly growing. Some distributors have started to hybridize and introduce daylilies bred in Canada. At present this number is relatively small, but undoubtedly it will grow as the popularity of daylilies in Canada follows the trend in the United States. Unlike that of the US, the recent history of daylily hybridizing in Canada can be traced to the efforts of a small number of people.

Foremost among Canadian daylily hybridizers is the team of the late Douglas Lycett and Henry Lorrain. In 1983, they moved from a house in Toronto to a small farm near Orono, just north of Lake Ontario. At the farm, Lycett began making gardens to accommodate his various collections of perennials, a number of daylilies

among them. His interest in daylilies grew to the point where he contacted Bill Munson in Florida to buy some of the newer varieties. Because his order was relatively large, Lycett decided to visit Munson in person. At that time, Munson was arguably the world's principal daylily breeder, and given Lycett's interest in genetics and hybridization, they initiated a special friendship. What started as a simple visit to pick up an order evolved into annual trips to Munson's gardens to see the latest seedlings, to talk daylilies, and to assist with some hybridizing. Needless to say, the hybridizing bug followed him back to Orono, where daylilies and their ever-growing number of seedlings forced Lycett and Lorrain to find more and more garden space.

Before long, daylilies filled the gardens around the house. Eventually the strawberry patch disappeared, and so did the potato patch behind the barn. Friends half jokingly warned that soon they would be in the hayfield. Shortly thereafter, Lycett and Lorrain announced "We're in the Hayfield Now," and the garden name was born. In 1992, they conceded to pressure from garden visitors and friends and started selling daylilies. In 1993, they offered their first three registered introductions for sale: 'Margaret Davis' (1992), a pale yellow and cream blend with a green throat; 'Dave Money' (1992), a lavender-pink blend with a large, near white throat; and 'Bijou D'Ore' (1992), a gold self with a lovely green throat. They introduced four more tetraploids in 1994, and their hybridizing efforts yielded 15 introductions in 1995.

Their hybridizing goals were to produce vigorous, hardy daylilies that display branching and bud counts in the north unlike many of the southern-bred varieties. Since 1995 they have introduced between 19 and 33 new cultivars each year for a total of 181 tetraploids and 40 diploids as of the spring of 2003. Examples of their hybridizing success include: 'Bernie Bryslan' (1994), a round, near white flower with a gold edge, named for a family friend; 'Pirates Gold Edge' (1996), a lavender-purple bitone with a strong gold edge completely surrounding the flower; 'Lynne Cooper' (1993), another breakthrough with a knobby, gold edge; 'Mary Ethyl Lycett' (1996), a reblooming, ruffled melon color that was named for Lycett's mother; and, named for Lorrain's parents, 'Louis Lorrain' (1999), a diamond-dusted lavender-purple with a slate-blue eye, and 'Clara Lorrain' (2000), a light cranberry-wine with a knobby gold edge.

Further evidence of their success in hybridizing came with a cover story in *Chatelaine Gardens* magazine, spring 1996, their own 50-minute video on growing and hybridizing daylilies, and a coffee-table book *Daylilies*, by Norman Track (Toronto, Canada: Hawkeye, 1997), filled with photographs taken at We're In the Hayfield Now Daylily Gardens. Lycett passed away suddenly in September 1998 after collecting their crop of approximately 20,000 seeds. With the support and assistance of family and friends, Lorrain has continued hybridizing and introducing daylilies. The two received the Canadian Hemerocallis Society Award for Achievement in Hybridizing in 2002.

On the western coast of Canada, Pam Erikson of Langley, British Columbia, has been growing and hybridizing daylilies since the late 1980s. Erikson started in landscaping with her husband, Tom, and subsequently created Erikson's Daylily Gardens. In 1995, they registered nine cultivars with the prefix "Langley." Since 1997, they have generally introduced four to eight new cultivars each year. Erikson's Daylily Gardens carries more than 1,900 different varieties of daylilies as well as their own introductions.

Erikson tends to specialize in small to miniature diploids, but she is perhaps best known for her choice of cultivar names. This notoriety began in part from a discussion between Erikson and the late Ra Hansen of Florida at a daylily meeting in Toronto in the fall of 1998. They were interested in the restrictions that the American Hemerocallis Society (AHS) placed on names that could be used for registrations. To make a point, the following year Erikson registered an ivory-cream flower with a fuchsia-edged, blue-purple eye as 'Crotchless Panties' (1999). Upon registration, the name prompted frequent debates among daylily circles. As might be expected, some people were offended, vowing never to buy the cultivar, but many saw the humor in Erikson's attempts to push the boundaries of plant names. In fact, these debates served to increase the demand for the controversial plant and set the stage for future introductions with names such as 'All in the Attitude' (1999), a deep lavender-pink with a maroon-purple eye; 'Vixen with Values' (1999), a soft peach-pink with a deep wine eye; 'Pink Tipped Pleasure' (1999), a butter-cream yellow with bright rose-pink eye; 'Wine Me Dine Me' (2000), an ivory-cream with a purple eye and pink halo; 'Dirty Old Broad' (2000), a copper flower with a maroon eye; 'Bare It All' (2000), a peach-pink with a wide red eye; and, 'Pushing the Envelope' (2002), a pink and ivory bitone with a rose-pink eye.

In addition to Erikson's success at drawing attention to her introductions, she started the first Canadian daylily club associated with the AHS in 1991, and still serves as the president of the Aldergrove Daylily Society. She has been an active member of the Canadian-American International Daylily Symposium, the regional vice president of Region 8 of the AHS, and continues as the vice president of the Canadian Hemerocallis Society. Erikson's Daylily Gardens was the first official AHS display garden in Canada, and Erikson was the first AHS accredited Garden Judge in Canada. Her efforts to promote the daylily were formally recognized in 2002 when she was awarded the Canadian Hemerocallis Society Service Award.

For many years, daylilies have also been hybridized in Quebec. Jacques Dore owned and operated Les Jardins Osiris in St. Thomas de Joliette, northeast of Montreal. In 1990, Dore formed a partnership with Serge Fafard, and in 1995 they began to introduce their own daylily cultivars. Although these varieties were not registered with the AHS, the plants were described and marketed through their annual catalog. Many of these cultivars have been recorded in the Quebec daylily registry, known as the "Enregistrement Hybrydes Québec Registration" (EHQR). Based on those records and Les Jardins Osiris catalogs, Dore and Fafard formally began introducing daylilies in 1995, with more than 30 introductions as of 2002. Fafard also began introducing his own cultivars in 2002. Typically, their introductions are northern hardy, dormant daylilies. Some favorites are 'Confidence' (not registered with AHS, name already taken by S. Houston Baker, 1943), a branched lavender-purple with a bluish-toned eye; 'Jovialiste' (not registered with AHS), a large, ruffled gold; and 'Rose Aimee' (not registered with AHS), a ruffled, ivory-pink flower.

Another Canadian, John P. Peat, began hybridizing daylilies in 1991 under the guidance of Florida hybridizer Ted Petit, who like Doug Lycett, had established a special mentorship with Bill Munson in the mid 1980s. Although Peat works and lives in Toronto, he first discovered and began hybridizing daylilies in Pe-

tit's garden in McIntosh, Florida, near Gainesville. Peat raised his first crop of seeds in 1993 and with Petit's support began to develop his own hybrids in Florida. With more than 10,000 seedlings created each year, he then tested the best of these for hardiness in Ontario. In September 1998, Peat launched his own company, Cross Border Daylilies, and registered 10 cultivars in 1999. Peat expanded his operation to a family property near Picton, Ontario, in the fall of 1999. From there he has propagated and sold a variety of popular cultivars as well as his own introductions.

Peat's hybridizing success has resulted in 23 introductions in 2000, another 23 in 2001, 19 in 2002, and 14 in 2003. He specializes in large-flowered tetraploids with eyes and edges. Some of his breakthroughs include 'Forces of Nature' (2000), a rich, dark purple with a bright gold edge; 'Just One Look' (1999), a near white with bold, rose-red eye; 'Leader of the Pack' (1999), a dramatic rose-red, hose-in-hose double with nine petals; 'Adventures with Ra' (2001), a pink flower with a burgundy eye and double edge of burgundy and gold; and 'Reyna' (2002), a cream flower with a soft pink to violet watermark and a double edge of burgundy and gold.

Peat has been very active in organizing daylily people in Canada. He was the founding president of the Ontario Daylily Society and continued to serve in that position for three years. He subsequently founded the Canadian Hemerocallis Society with members from throughout Canada. In addition to currently serving as the president of the Canadian Hemerocallis Society, Peat is also the editor of the *Canadian Daylily Journal* and the chairperson of the Canadian-American International Daylily Symposium, which he helped found.

The success of the local daylily clubs and the Canadian Hemerocallis Society is apparent in the growing numbers of hybridizers from throughout Canada that are starting to introduce new cultivars. For example, Ernie Sellers from Dunrobin, near Ottawa, Ontario, started Dunrobin Daylilies in the mid 1990s. In addition to propagating and selling many daylily varieties, Sellers initiated a hybridizing program to develop northern-hardy plants with high bud count, excellent branching, and resistance to diseases and pests. In 1997, his catalog included pictures of eight future introductions, including 'Dunrobin Belle of the Ball' (2000), a pink self; 'Dunrobin Cherry Tart' (2000), a red with a darker red eyezone; and 'Dunrobin Prom Night' (2000), a lavender-pink self. The 1998 Dunrobin Daylily catalog showed 12 more future introductions. As of 2002, six of these future introductions were formally registered with the AHS, and clearly, more will follow.

Similarly, Jack Kent of The Potting Shed from Cayuga, Ontario, has been propagating and selling perennials since 1995. Kent's interest in daylilies comes in part from working with Doug Lycett and Henry Lorrain. For several years Kent has been hybridizing daylilies and selecting seedlings for further evaluation. In his 2002 catalog, Jack listed nine introductions, including 'Eddy Gee' (preregistered), a tall, clear yellow; 'Negotiable Affections' (preregistered), a lavender spider variant with a bold red eye; and 'Polar Wind' (preregistered), a tall, cream flower that is over 90 percent polytepal on established plants.

Bryan Culver of Oakville, Ontario, recently started Culver Farm Daylilies with six registered introductions available in 2003. Culver is selecting for hardy, vigorous, and healthy plants that do well in northern climates. His 'Spirit Zone' (1999), a peach-pink blend with a bleeding maroon halo above a yellow applique green throat, is already gaining much-deserved attention, and 'Darkside' (1999), a plush black-purple self above a green throat; 'Dragon So' (2000), a yellow with a maroon eyezone; 'Giggle Creek' (2000), a lavender with a purple eyezone and edge; and 'Rose Odyssey' (2002), a clear rose-pink self with a green throat, show considerable promise. He also has an impressive list of selected seedlings that are scheduled for future introduction.

Hybridization is not limited to daylily retailers. Co-rina Carlton, daughter of Sandy Carlton of Arcadian Daylilies in Toronto, Ontario, has a future introduction called 'Tiny Footprints' (not yet registered), a bright gold flower with a dark maroon eye above an apple-green throat, that was proudly displayed on the cover of the nursery's 2003 catalog.

Daylilies are rapidly gaining popularity in Quebec with a number of new societies, many retailers, and several new hybridizers. Pierre-Andre Rocheleau is an amateur hybridizer who has registered 10 cultivars with the AHS, including 'Elfe Ermitage' (2000), a rose-colored, dormant diploid; 'Elfe Osiris' (2000), a 6-in. (15-cm), clear yellow diploid; and 'Ondine de Faience' (2001), a near white and rose tetraploid with a red halo. Recognizing the growing number of amateur daylily hybridizers in Quebec, Rocheleau established the Quebec daylily registry, the EHQR, a French-language reference source for new and future introductions. In early 2003, this resource provided descriptions and pictures of 84 introductions, including 57 of Rocheleau's own. The EHQR provides access to introductions by French-speaking hybridizers who might not otherwise register their cultivars with the AHS. In the future, the EHQR will provide a link between French and English daylily hybridizers in Canada and ensure that the efforts of Quebec hybridizers receive wider recognition.

Readers should note that the International Cultivar Registration Authority (ICRA) has appointed the AHS as the official registrar for *Hemerocallis* throughout the world. The AHS strictly follows the rules of the *International Code of Nomenclature for Cultivated Plants* (ICNCP). The reason for this is to avoid duplication of named cultivars, and therefore, the EHQR may operate only as a resource for introductions of hybrid daylilies created in Quebec. The official registry duties and record keeping for all countries around the world are the sole responsibility of the AHS.

Among the daylily hybridizers in Quebec are Daniel Harrisson and Odette Lavallee who operate Les

Hémérocalles de l'Isle in Ste-Angèle-de-Laval. They began hybridizing daylilies in 1994, and Harrisson introduced five cultivars in 2002 and 15 in 2003. His introductions include 'Diabolo' (not registered with AHS), a red-orange spider variant; 'Fée de l'Aurore' (not registered with AHS), a cream flower with a burgundy-purple eye and edge; and 'Jean Berthol' (not registered with AHS), a large, round, cherry-red flower.

Rejean Biron is a member of the AHS and a founder of a rapidly growing daylily club in Granby, Quebec. Biron is an amateur daylily hybridizer with a number of introductions, prefixed "Lydia," and an impressive series of future introductions. Some of his cultivars include 'Lydia l'Oeil du Tigre' (not registered with AHS), a cream with a dramatic dark eye; 'Lydia la Femme Araignée' (not registered with AHS), a spider variant; and 'Lydia Goldfinger' (not registered with AHS), a gold flower with a burgundy eye and burgundy stipples.

In addition to the dayliy hybridizing in Canada, an ever-increasing number of clubs and societies have been promoting the flowers. As noted above, Pam Erikson was instrumental in establishing the first Canadian dayliy club, the Aldergrove Daylily Society, in British Columbia in 1991. In eastern Canada, John P. Peat organized members of the AHS in the provinces of Ontario, Quebec, Nova Scotia, New Brunswick, and Newfoundland and Labrador to formally become part of AHS Region 4 in 1996. Shortly thereafter, Peat worked with Kathy Guest of the Buffalo Area Daylily Society to host the first Canadian-American International Daylily Symposium, or the Canadian-American Daylily Muster, in the spring of 1997. That summer, funds generated from the meeting were donated both to the Buffalo Area Daylily Society and to form the Great White North Daylily Society, later renamed the Ontario

Daylily Society, with Peat as founding president. Since its inception, the symposium has raised and donated funds to support a variety of clubs and societies throughout Canada and the United States. The increasing numbers of local clubs and the symposium annual meetings have promoted daylilies and set the stage for a sudden increase in the number of daylily clubs across Canada.

In Montreal, the Société Québecoise des Hostas et Hémérocalles (the Quebec Hosta and Hemerocallis Society) was created in early 2000. Subsequently, the Association des Amateurs d'Hémérocalles de la Région de Québec (the Quebec Area Daylily Society) was formed in Quebec City in 2001. About the same time, the Internet helped bring together daylily enthusiasts from Manitoba, Saskatchewan, and Alberta to form the Canadian Prairie Daylily Society. In Granby, southeast of Montreal, Le Club des hémérocalles du Québec (the Quebec Daylily Club) was formed in November 2002. One month later, the Nova Scotia Daylily Society came together to promote the daylily in the eastern provinces of Canada—Nova Scotia, New Brunswick, Prince Edward Island, and Newfoundland and Labrador.

To accommodate the growing numbers of daylily enthusiasts throughout Canada, the Canadian Hemerocallis Society was initiated in January 2001. The CHS grew to more than 280 members in less than a year and is responsible for producing the *Canadian Daylily Journal* and coordinating the CHS Awards and Honors Program. In July 2003, the CHS and Quebec Hosta and Hemerocallis Society cosponsored the first Canadian National Daylily Convention in Montreal. Undoubtedly, this national event has poised Canada for another major step forward in the promotion of daylilies.

CHAPTER 15

Daylilies in Europe

by Robert Grant Downton

A Brief History of the Daylily in Europe

Examining the fate of the daylily in European and North American gardens during the past century shows dramatic differences in the fortune of the plant on the two different continents. The gardens of Europe have featured daylilies for many centuries. *Hemerocallis lilioasphodelus* (previously known as *H. flava*) and the virtually sterile triploid clone *H. fulva* 'Europa' (Arlow B. Stout, 1920) have been cultivated in Europe for more than 400 years. Indeed, they have become naturalized in parts of Europe. Most of the wild species and early cultivated forms from Oriental gardens, such as variegated and double forms of *H. fulva*, arrived in Europe from the Far East before being sent to North America. Additional species, such as *H. aurantiaca, H. citrina, H. dumortierii, H. forrestii, H. middendorffii, H. minor, H. nana*, and *H. thunbergii*, were all introduced to North America via European gardens. The fashionable interest in the botanical exploration of the Far East and the subsequent importation of plants in the nineteenth and early twentieth centuries was clearly responsible for this substantial list.

By the end of the nineteenth century, the first deliberate attempts at producing hybrids between different *Hemerocallis* species were being made in England by amateur hybridizer George Yeld. The first recorded hybrid was 'Apricot' (George Yeld, 1893), raised in 1892 of unknown parentage, but even by the time Stout was writing his definitive monograph of the genus in 1934 it appeared to have become confused in cultivation. Yeld raised a considerable number of hybrids and was experimenting with creating hybrids using newly introduced species such as the small, Chinese native *H. nana*, which produced the dwarf variety 'Miniken' in 1933. However, most of the Yeld hybrids now appear to have disappeared from cultivation. Following on from Yeld's pioneering hybrids, the professional nurseryman Amos Perry of Enfield, North London, became very active in hybridizing daylilies. Some of Perry's introductions appear to have been hardly great advances, as varieties such as 'E. A. Bowles' (1926) and 'Margaret Perry' (1925) were not regarded by Stout as too distinct from the wild species. However, some claim that Perry was the first to hybridize a "white" daylily, though it was lost to cultivation. As might be expected, many of the cultivars raised by Perry, which exceeded 100, have vanished from cultivation. In Naples, Italy, Wilhelm Müller was also a force in raising new daylilies at the start of the twentieth century; along with those of Yeld and Perry, many of his introductions are mentioned in Stout's monograph. It is remarkable to think that the daylilies of today have arisen so rapidly from these early experimental steps.

The Second World War, which put so many European gardens under pressure, did not extinguish the interest in daylilies in Europe. In England, four collectors and hybridizers of daylilies—L. W. Brummitt, R. H. Coe, H. J. Randall, and Lady Carew-Pole—progressed the daylily from the 1950s to the '70s. Of these growers, Coe was responsible for the largest hybridizing effort, with thousands of seedlings being raised at his nursery. Although primarily hybridizing diploids in a range of different colors, from whites and pale pastels to yellows and bright reds, Coe also began to experiment with hybridizing at the tetraploid level with some success. Such a move into the comparatively new field of tetraploids shows that Coe must have been keeping in step with the latest developments in breeding work in the US. The bright pink 'Elaine Strutt' (1969) is a tetraploid introduction that remains widely grown even today by daylily enthusiasts. Among the diploids, varieties such as 'Michele Coe' (1969), a yellow with lavender midribs, and 'Penelope Vestey' (1969), a pink with a darker eyezone and a lemon throat, are still considered worthy garden daylilies and are included in many collections. Although most of the work resided in diploids, Randall also began hybridizing at the tetraploid level, with varieties such as 'Amersham' (not registered with AHS) and 'Missenden' (not registered with AHS) introduced

to commerce. Quite probably, Randall will be best known for the velvety, dark red 'Stafford' (1959), a tough, free-flowering diploid hybrid that is enduringly popular for general planting. Unfortunately, this phase of interest in daylilies did not persist beyond the 1970s in England, and by the 1980s such serious hybridizing appears to have almost entirely evaporated.

The interest in daylilies in other parts of Europe has, perhaps, been more consistent than in England. In the 1980s in mainland Europe, the daylily was still being advanced by hybridizers, and large collections of modern varieties were being built up by dedicated enthusiasts. For example, the hybrids selected by Tomas Tamberg of Berlin and introduced in the 1980s have become popular and widely grown throughout Europe. Tetraploids such as 'Helle Berlinerin' (1981), a near white self with an orange throat; 'Berlin Oxblood' (1983), a dark red with a small yellow throat; and 'Berlin Tallboy' (1989), an orange-yellow dusted cinnamon with an orange throat, are well known. Tamberg's ongoing work has focused on tetraploid daylilies in different colors, particularly yellows, near whites, and reds, that grow well in the cool climate of Berlin. Another German hybridizer, Werner Reinermann, has introduced quite a few new varieties in the 1980s and '90s, such as the salmon-apricot 'Maggie Fynboe' (1993), which is now widespread and popular.

Although a small number of growers remained seriously interested in the daylily in Europe, the obvious disparity in the interest in daylilies between North America and Europe had widened further in the 1980s and '90s. European growers could muster just a few introductions, yet the popularity of daylilies in the US justified hybridizing on ever more impressive scales and in bold new directions, resulting in the great numbers of registered hybrids. In just a century, the progress of the daylily in the US has been so astonishing that it has eclipsed the efforts of growers in the continent where hybridizing first started.

The Daylily in Contemporary European Gardens

Although the daylily remains a staple garden plant, it has experienced only limited specialist exploration by gardeners in Europe. However, two societies have emerged as frontrunners to bring together daylily enthusiasts. The British Hosta and Hemerocallis Society (BHHS) was formed in 1981, and although the vast majority of members are hosta enthusiasts, a dedicated core are daylily growers. Hemerocallis Europa (HE), which was formed in 1993, has a healthy 100-strong membership covering many different European countries, from the United Kingdom in the west to Poland in the east. Of course, many European daylily enthusiasts are also members of the American Hemerocallis Society (AHS). The events organized by these societies are able to fulfill the important function of meeting places for daylily growers, with publications that present topical and useful information on growing daylilies in European climates.

Producing a general statement on the European climate is nearly impossible, as such a diversity of conditions are seen across the continent. In the British Isles, which is warmed by the Gulf Stream, the winters are generally wet with variable spells of freezing weather that can persist until late spring, while the summer months are frequently cool and wet. In mainland northern Europe, away from the coasts, winter cold can be more intense, yet summer conditions are typically much warmer. In southern Europe, many areas have mild winters coupled with intensely hot and drier summer months. Of course, locally, large geographical features such as lakes, mountains, and valleys generate different microclimates. Perhaps the most significant general factor for daylily growers involves the high latitudes of most European countries, comparable to the northernmost US and Canada. The resulting lower intensity of sunlight can profoundly affect the pigmentation of daylily flowers. Some cultivars bred in warm, low latitude areas display different coloration and patterns of pigmentation when cultivated in Europe. Floral fragrance of many hybrids is often affected drastically by conditions that are not hot and humid, though strongly scented species, such as *Hemerocallis citrina*, and their early hybrids, such as *H.* 'Hyperion' (F. B. Meed, 1924), are quite consistently fragrant.

Under these different conditions, many growers have built collections, frequently from importing new varieties. Although this is an expensive task that requires phytosanitary certificates to accompany imported material, some enthusiasts have amassed hugely impressive collections that rival the best gardens in the US, for example François Verhaert's cutting-edge collection in Belgium. Until her recent move from Apple Court in southern England, Diana Grenfell's collection introduced many gardeners to modern daylilies. In England, several specialist daylily collections, covering a particular group or class of cultivars, have achieved the status of national collections of the National Council for the Conservation of Plants and Gardens (NC-CPG). For example, Gerald Sinclair has taken on the task of preserving the Coe, Brummitt, and Randall cultivars that were rapidly disappearing from gardens. In parallel to the AHS, HE now has a list of display gardens where good collections of daylilies can be seen.

With the tremendous range of conditions present in Europe, attempting to put together a list of cultivars that grow and bloom consistently well in different gardens is fraught with difficulty. Fortunately, HE has recently initiated an annual award, the Waterman Award (named for former AHS International Secretary Roswitha Waterman), given to an extraordinary American cultivar that displays excellent performance and hardiness in diverse European climates. The recipients are as follows:

- 1998: 'Elizabeth Salter' (Jeff Salter, 1990)
- 1999: 'Bill Norris' (David Kirchhoff, 1993)
- 2000: 'El Desperado' (Patrick Stamile, 1991)

- 2001: 'Serena Sunburst' (Bernice L. Marshal, 1982), a pink edged in gold with gold shadings above a green throat
- 2002: 'Canadian Border Patrol' (Jeff Salter, 1995)

The current popularity of large, round, and ruffled tetraploids in Europe is clear from this list. Of course, many, many varieties outside of this select list are of considerable value and beauty in European gardens. The unusual forms and spiders are especially well loved in Europe. With their narrower tepals, which often have thinner substance than their rounded and ruffled counterparts, they tend to open more easily in cool weather, although they can be rapidly damaged by wind and rain. Their combination of willowy grace and unearthly beauty allows them to associate more readily with other perennials than some of the rounded forms.

Unfortunately, a formal judging system for garden performance that parallels the AHS awards system is not yet in place in Europe, though this may not be far off. The annual AHS awards are a good indicator of which cultivars are likely to perform well across Europe. In particular the recipients of the Lenington All-American Award and the Stout Silver Medal are almost certain to be wise choices. It is no coincidence that Waterman Award winners are varieties that have excelled in the AHS awards system.

For daylilies to reach their maximum potential in European gardens, hybridizing by both amateur and professional growers is essential, resulting in more daylily introductions that are suited to local European climates. Both the BHHS and HE have initiatives to foster hybridizing efforts in Europe. The BHHS has supported a new annual award, the Newbold Vase, for the best new introduction raised in Europe. The first recipients were, in 2001, 'Dick Kitchingman' (Marc King, 2001), a rose-lilac spider variant with light raised midribs, and, in 2002, 'Grace and Favour' (Eve Lytton, 1999), a deep burgundy-red with a lighter halo above a green throat. HE recently devised a system of garden

trials where new European-raised selections can be assessed. These schemes are likely to go a long way to promote the efforts of both accomplished and novice hybridizers. One problem is the considerable length of time between raising a promising seedling and building up sufficient material to justify its registration and introduction to the market. Reliable techniques for rapid growth and increase, that will not compromise the quality of the resulting plants, must be tested under European conditions to reduce the disadvantages of environmental factors such as short growing seasons. Of course, European hybridizers will find it difficult to compete with the "uber-hybridizers" in Florida and similar regions of the US

Still, many growers are taking up the challenge of hybridizing in Europe. The fact that their numbers are high enough to make mentioning them all here impossible is, in a way, impressive. In the south of France, Eve Lytton is working on several projects, particularly developing her own eyed and edged, purple and pink lines. Gerrit Snoek's hybridizing work, located in the Netherlands, involves mainly unusual forms and round and ruffled reds, oranges, and lavender-purples. In Belgium, François Verhaert is hybridizing for round flowers, both single and double, especially in the white-cream and mauve-lilac-purple hues. Verhaert is particularly keen to select plants with a "bouquet" effect: dense, elegant foliage, with multiple scapes in all directions and the flowers presented just above the foliage. Rounded tetraploids are also the focus of Artur Jasinski's hybridizing work in Poland. He has introduced several cultivars such as the patterned 'Polish Cocktail' (2002), a rose-red polychrome with a red eyezone and cream-yellow edge. In Italy, Marc King has a large and productive hybridizing program that now is restricted to spiders and unusual forms, particularly crispates and spatulates. His hybridizing has extensively utilized the diploids of John Lambert, Rosemary Whitacre, and other pioneers of this class of flower, resulting in introductions such as 'Brenda Newbold' (1997), a soft baby-ribbon-pink self with a green throat, and 'Paul Weber' (1999), a pale lemon-yellow with a soft salmon-pink-blush halo above a pale lemon-yellow throat, although he is now starting lines at the tetraploid level. Gardening under the demanding conditions of the Swiss mountains, Liselotte Hirsbrunner is selecting seedlings that perform reliably in such tough environments. Her pale-flowered unusual form 'Chesieres Lunar Moth' (1994), a near white with a yellow eyezone above a lime-green throat, is already gaining a wide distribution. In England, several growers have become keen hybridizers. Duncan Skene has focused on dormants, especially the spiders and unusual forms, Jan and Andy Wyers's hybridizing efforts encompass the smaller flowers, and Chris Searle has started to work with tetraploid spiders and unusual forms. I myself have hybridizing interests that include the spiders and unusual forms, particularly the development of small-flowered varieties of this type, and patterned and edged flowers. Germany has even more active hybridizers, in addition to those already mentioned, such as Harald Juhr, Matthias Thomsen, and Jamie Vande, with a diversity of interests in the daylily, from rounded diploids to tetraploid spiders and unusual forms.

The Future of the Daylily in Europe

The European outlook for the daylily appears increasingly promising. Nevertheless, many directions remain to be pursued. Few have turned their attention to the double varieties. Many recent double-flowered cultivars are not reliable performers under European conditions, and translating the latest developments, such as popcorn or peony doubles, into lines that are hardy, vigorous, and dependably double deserves serious effort. Selecting for the trait of rebloom in the short growing season of northern areas is another essential task, since relatively few cultivars rebloom consistently. One that

does is 'Tetrinas Daughter' (Orville W. Fay, 1971), a bright golden yellow on tall scapes. Understanding the basis of rebloom, from the morphological to the molecular level, will assist breeding for this characteristic. However, the production of reblooming lines in diverse colors and forms likely will require considerable investment in time and space and will borrow heavily from similar efforts in the northern US.

Hybridizers have a duty not only to produce new plants for fellow enthusiasts but also to select for varieties of high garden value that will appeal more widely to gardeners, thus "spreading the word." Some characteristics—scent, rebloom, and foliage coloration, such as variegation—are likely to have wider appeal than others. For instance, the handsomely cream-striped, variegated 'Golden Zebra' (not registered with AHS) has been widely marketed. The ability to combine with other plants also needs serious consideration, as coarse foliage and stout, low scapes may look out of place everywhere except for specialist beds devoted daylilies. Hybridizing has considerable potential for very tall and striking daylilies for the back of the perennial border or among large shrubs. Already, Tamberg's hybridizing has incorporated tetraploid conversions of *Hemerocallis altissima*, for example in 'Citralt' (2001), a bright yellow with an apple-green throat. Conversely, Europe has a great need for smaller-flowered varieties with many highly branched, wiry scapes, substantial bud count, and delicate, well-proportioned foliage in the same style as classic varieties—such as 'Frans Hals' (Wilmer B. Flory, 1955), a bright rust and orange bicolor with creamy orange midribs, and 'Corky' (H. A. Fischer, 1959), a yellow self—but in a wider variety of colors, patterns, and forms. These would be appropriate for use in mixed perennial borders and naturalistic planting schemes. Utilizing some species and worthy older varieties in combination with the latest innovations may be the key to generating hybrids of distinction in Europe.

Few dark clouds appear on the horizon. Perhaps the most infuriating pest of daylilies, the daylily gall midge, may limit their appeal. Now widespread in Europe, this insect has the ability to ruin floral displays as the adults lay their eggs inside the young buds. The resulting tiny maggot-like larvae cause hypertrophy; so swollen and distorted, the buds fail to open and eventually rot. Even mildly infested flowers are coarsened and mottled. Effective control is difficult, apart from destruction of infested buds or the use of systemic insecticides. For more information on diagnosis and treatment, see Chapter 8. Generally, only early season buds are affected and susceptibility varies greatly between cultivars. Hybridizing for resistance and selecting late-blooming varieties may be long-term options in affected areas. Other possible control measures that need to be investigated include biological control and companion planting strategies.

The brief emergence of daylily rust from imported plants on a couple of occasions has caused serious concern among growers. It is problematic to detect during phytosanitary inspections as infected plant material can remain asymptomatic. Fortunately, this disease has not become established in Europe; it may pose a considerable problem in southern Europe where winters are not cold enough to destroy the inoculum. However, in view of the risk, some collectors have ceased to import new plants.

A less obvious problem may be derived from the rapid propagation by tissue culture of the latest US introductions for wholesale distribution. Daylilies are known, on occasion, to experience problems in tissue culture, resulting in plants that are inferior or not true to type. At the very least, rigorous quality control will be needed to ensure that second-rate material does not enter the horticultural trade. Anyway, mass propagation of new varieties is of questionable value until their performance in European conditions has been thoroughly assessed. How disastrous if budding daylily collectors were discouraged after purchasing plants that failed to live up to expectations.

Despite such hurdles, now is an exciting time for daylilies in Europe. I look forward to a future where European enthusiasts are less reliant on the introductions of US growers, and European-raised cultivars lay claim to prominent AHS awards.

CHAPTER 16

Daylily Societies and Events

The American Hemerocallis Society (AHS), formed in July 1946, is the largest daylily organization in the world. It began through the efforts of Helen Field Fischer, who was the host of her own radio garden show in Iowa. She loved many different flowers but had a special fondness for daylilies. Assisted by members of a round-robin formed by *Flower Grower Magazine*, Fischer arranged a meeting of daylily enthusiasts in Shenandoah, Iowa. During that meeting, the group decided to organize a society, initially called the Midwest Hemerocallis Society. Later the name was changed to the Hemerocallis Society, and finally in a historic meeting in Baton Rouge, Louisiana, in 1955, it became the American Hemerocallis Society. Today, membership in the AHS has grown to more than 12,000 from around the world.

The AHS is divided into 16 regions, 15 of which are found in the United States and Canada. Region 16 comprises international members from outside North America. Each of these regions has come together with its own set of bylaws and executive officers, but they are governed by the bylaws of AHS. In addition, more than 140 local clubs have formed across the world. Though these local clubs are not officially affiliated with the AHS, the AHS does recognize them and regional officers keep track of them.

One critical responsibility of the AHS is to document new daylily cultivars. In 1955 the International Society for Horticultural Science (ISHS) appointed the AHS as the International Registration Authority for *Hemerocallis*. The AHS is the official registrar for all new *Hemerocallis* cultivars introduced around the world, and follows the rules of the *International Code of Nomenclature for Cultivated Plants* (ICNCP). This monumental task now requires a full-time position within the AHS to keep careful records of the some 1,650 daylilies registered per year. A committee, which must first approve a new cultivar name based on rules set out by the ICNCP, aids the AHS Registrar.

Registering daylilies is not the only role of the AHS. Its mandate is "to promote, encourage, and foster the development and improvement of the genus *Hemero-*

callis and public interest therein." Membership includes subscription to the *Daylily Journal*, a quarterly color publication, and a biannual publication put out by the local region. Also included are invitations to join the round-robins and the Internet-robin, which are forums for discussing various aspects of daylilies at length.

Daylily meetings number literally thousands each year, hosted not only by the AHS, but also by each region and the many local clubs. In addition to individual club and regional meetings are three major international meetings. At this time, the best known are the Mid-Winter Symposium (MWS) in Tennessee each February, the Canadian-American International Daylily Symposium in Niagara Falls, Ontario, in March, and the AHS National Convention, which is hosted by clubs in different regions each year and is held during the peak bloom time of the host city.

The MWS is host to a number of different speakers who talk about a wide variety of topics, such as horticultural practices, diseases and pests, companion plants, fertilizers and, of course, the daylily itself. Here people can meet many famous hybridizers and approach them to discuss just about anything having to do with daylilies. The MWS puts on one of the largest daylily auctions held in North America. Literally hundreds of daylilies are sold, often at terrific bargains.

The Canadian-American International Daylily Symposium is unique among daylily meetings in that it has something for everyone to enjoy, even those who do not garden. The numerous speakers show their latest creations and discuss topics such as companion plants, hybridizing, converting diploid daylilies, judging daylilies, diseases and pests, greenhouse technologies, and more. With primary focus aimed on the newest daylily hybrids, the most famous hybridizers are invited to speak each year. To keep things interesting, the symposium also incorporates a slot tournament at the local casino, a champagne and caviar party, tours of the Niagara area, and a Caribbean dance following the banquet.

Some other events are a Chinese auction, which combines the elements of both an auction and a raffle, where a person can win a new daylily introduction for 75 cents, the plant sale where you can simply purchase a plant at below the average market price, and a live auction. The live auction is famous for having sold the most expensive daylily to date in the history of the AHS. Hybridizer Ted Petit donated a future introduction, allowing the winning bidder to name the daylily. The winning bid was $4,200, and the bidder, Betty Fretz, has since named the daylily 'Lady Betty Fretz' (2002). The following year, Larry Gooden and Pat Kiesel bid $3,800 to have a plant, donated by the Kinnebrew family, carry the name of their granddaughter, 'Alexa Kathryn' (John Kinnebrew, 2003).

The AHS National Convention changes from host to host each year but primarily features many tours of daylily display gardens and allows AHS representatives to meet to discuss business affairs. As is fitting, this is the largest and most formal daylily convention each year, with attendance of about 300–400 daylily enthusiasts. Boutiques sell a variety of daylily-related material, gardening supplies, and many other garden-related items. Bylaw issues are discussed and voted on at the convention, AHS awards and honors are presented, and growers are able to view daylilies in gardens outside of their local climatic zones.

These are just three of the many meetings held across the globe each year; to list all would probably fill an entire book in itself. Following are the various clubs around the world that host meetings similar to the ones mentioned above. Anyone interested in daylilies is encouraged to join a local and national society, such as the AHS, the Canadian Hemerocallis Society, or any of the local clubs listed here. Membership usually stands around $10–$20 per year depending on the society and brings with it an exciting world of daylily events.

National Daylily Societies

American Hemerocallis Society
Pat Mercer, Executive Secretary
Department WWW
P.O. Box 10
Dexter, Georgia 31019
USA
gmercer@nlamerica.com
tel 912-875-4110
http://www.daylilies.org/

Australian Daylily Society, Inc.
Betty Franklin, President
7 Kiama St.
Wavell Heights, QLD 4012
Australia
bac@gil.com.au
tel 07 3266 9680
http://www.australiandaylily.com/

British Hosta and Hemerocallis Society
Lynda Hinton
Toft Monks, The Hithe, Rodborough Common
Stroud, Gloucestershire GL5 5BN
UK
http://www.casarocca.com/BHHS/html/

Canadian Hemerocallis Society
John Peat, President
16 Douville Ct.
Toronto, ON M5A 4E7
Canada
jpeat@distinctly.on.ca
tel 416-362-1682
http://www.distinctly.on.ca/chs/

Hemerocallis Europa
Gerrit Snoek
Oostergouw 26, NL 1606 Venhuizen
Netherlands
gerrit.snoek@planet.nl
http://www.hemerocallis-europa.org

South African Daylily Interest Group
Barry Engelbrecht
Box 71402
Bryanston, Gauteng, 2021
South Africa
engelfam@global.co.za
tel 011 310 1396

Local Clubs and Societies

Region 1

Canadian Prairie Daylily Society
Janice Dehod
311 Ash St.
Winnipeg, MB R3N 0P8
Canada
jdehod@shaw.ca
http://www.northerndaylily.com/states/manito-ba/canadian-prairie-daylily-soc

Cedar Valley Iris and Daylily Society
Betty Miller
1675 155th St.
Fairfield, IA 52556-8921
USA

Central Iowa Daylily Society
Duane Manzey
315 Thunderbird Dr.
Marshalltown, IA 50158-5267
USA

Central North Dakota Daylily Society
Karen Schock
700 56H Ave., NW
Mandan, ND 58554
USA

Dakota Prairie Daylily Society
Ron Jennings
Box 424
Miller, SD 57362-0424
USA
rojo@turtlecreek.net

Daylily of the Valley Society
Shirley Walker
1107 N Washington St.
Lexington, NE 50850
USA

Hemerocallis Society of Minnesota
Gary Schaben
8951 Hamilton Ave., NE
Monticello, MN 55362-3085
USA
http://www.northstardaylilies.com/pages/hsm.htm

Nebraska Daylily Society
David Hansen
2507 Franklin St.
Bellevue, NE 68005-5408
USA
dlhansen@radiks.net
tel 402-291-4049

Southwest Iowa Bloomers
Judy Moffitt
2512 Eagle Ave.
Kent, IA 50850
USA

Region 2

Bay Area Daylily Buds
Leo Bordeleau
472 Rose Hill Dr.
Oneida, WI 54155-9024
USA
rosehill@new.rr.com
tel 920-869-2540
http://www.ahsregion2.org/clubs/clubbadb.html

Black Swamp Hosta and Daylily Society
Charlene Patz
114 Carolin Ct.
Perrysburg, OH 43551-1607
USA
fppatz@wcnet.org
tel 419-874-8964
http://dir.gardenweb.com/directory/bshds/

Central Illinois Daylily Society
Kae CoatesRR 3, Box 66
Roodhouse, IL 62082
USA
http://www.geocities.com/cidcdaylilyclub/

Central Michigan Daylily Society
Bruce Kovach
5501 S. Red Oak Rd.
Beaverton, MI 48612-8513
USA
bpkovach@mindnet.org
tel 989-689-3030
http://www.ahsregion2.org/clubs/clubcmds.html

Chicagoland Daylily Society
Leonard Byerly
11406 River Bend Rd.
Orland Park, IL 60467-5207
USA
tel 708-478-3604
http://www.ahsregion2.org/clubs/clubcds.html

Daylily Society of Southeast Wisconsin
Gary Raatz
N69 W15715 Eileen Ave.
Menomonee Falls, WI 53051-5008
USA
garaatz@wi.rr.com
tel 262-255-2799
http://www.ahsregion2.org/clubs/clubdssw.html

Daylily Society of Southern Indiana
Verna Habermel
3619 Wagner Dr.
Floyds Knobs, IN 47119
USA
habermel@otherside.com
tel 812-923-7500
http://www.ahsregion2.org/clubs/clubsids.html

Fort Wayne Daylily Society
J. Paul Downie
8207 Seiler Rd.
Fort Wayne, IN 46806-2945
USA
bdownie151@aol.com
tel 260-493-4601

Grand Valley Daylily Society
Gladys Dodger
8707 Becker Rd., NE
Cedar Springs, MI 49319-9539
USA
wddodger@triton.net
tel 616-696-3818
http://www.ahsregion2.org/clubs/clubgvds.html

Greater Cincinnati Daylily and Hosta Society
Jerry Williams
8497 Wetherfield Lane
Cincinnati, OH 45235
USA
lilyman@fuse.net
tel 513-791-1311
http://www.gcdhs.org/

Hoosier Daylily Society, Inc.
Bret Clement
13816 Laredo Dr.
Carmel, IN 46032
USA
bretc@iquest.net
http://www.shieldsgardens.com/Hoosier/

Indiana Daylily and Iris Society
Betty Polanka
7006 S County Rd., 1200 E
Westport, IN 47283-9414
USA
Polankafarm@aol.com
tel 812-591-3488
http://www.ahsregion2.org/clubs/clubidis.html

Kalamazoo Area Daylily Society
J. Gus Guzinski
8814 West H Ave.
Kalamazoo, MI 49009-8505
USA

Limestone Daylily and Hosta Society
Barbara Leisz
7394 S Shady Side Dr.
Bloomington, IN 47404
USA
http://www.ahsregion2.org/clubs/clubldhs.html

Metropolitan Columbus Daylily Society
Alan Hersh
140 N Cassady Ave.
Columbus, OH 43209
http://home.att.net/~mcdsoh/wsb/html/view.cgi-home.html-.html
USA

North Shore Iris and Daylily Society
Alice Simon
2516 Scott St.
Des Plaines, IL 60018
USA
SimonAlice@prodigy.net
tel 847-827-6541

Northeast Ohio Daylily Society
Jani Sikon
7011 Jackson St.
Mentor, OH 44060-5023
USA
gardenaddict@juno.com
tel 440-974-8038

Ohio Daylily Society
Ken Blanchard
3256 S Honeytown Rd.
Apple Creek, OH 44606-9047
USA
cblancha@bright.net
tel 330-698-3091

Prairieland Daylily Society
Randall Klipp
34 Jordan Dr.
Bourbonnais, IL 60914-1108
USA
MRlilies@aol.com
tel 815-932-6650

Southern Indiana Daylily Society
Mark Cline
5289 S. Harrell Rd.
Bloomington, IN 47401
USA
http://www.ahsregion2.org/clubs/clubsids.html

Southern Michigan Hemerocallis Society
Nikki Schmith
25729 Annapolis Ave.
Dearborn Heights, MI 48125
USA
schmiths@msn.com
tel 248-739-9006
http://www.daylilyclub.com

Southwest Illinois Hemerocallis Society
Debbie Gray
Box 54
Dorsey, IL 62021-0054
USA

Southwestern Illinois Daylily Club
Kathleen Pinkas
3833 Hwy. 162
Granite City, IL 62040
USA
kpinkas62040@yahoo.com
tel 618-931-3302

Southwestern Indiana Daylily Society
Narda Jones
1405 Cheshire Bridge Rd.
Evansville, IN 47710
USA
nfjtech@sigecom.net
tel 812-422-7503
http://www.swids.org

Wisconsin Daylily Society
John Sheehan
5656 Barbara Dr.
Madison, WI 53711
USA
johnsheehan@charter.net
http://www.wisdaylilysoc.org/

Region 3
Blue Ridge Area Daylily Society
Elnora Stubbs
113 Craddock Lane
Huddleston, VA 24104
USA
EHS222@aol.com
tel 540-297-7567

Charlottesville Area Daylily Society
Jim Murphy
3191 Plank Rd.
North Garden, VA 22959
Murphy@cstone.net
tel 434 979 3999
USA

Delaware Valley Daylily Society
David Guleke
2320 Chestnut St.
Chester, PA 19013-5115
USA
http://daylily.net/gardens/dvds.htm

Free State Daylily Society
Wayne Bladen
42 Federal Ct.
Gaithersburg, MD 20877
USA

Garden State Daylily Growers
Michael Oliver
2004 Cedar Lane
Bordentown, NJ 08505
USA
http://www.gsdaylily.org/

National Capital Daylily Club
Kathleen Schloeder
2501 St. John Place
Alexandria, VA 22311
USA
kschloeder@comcast.net
tel 703-671-6635
http://www.daylilyclub.org/

Northern Virginia Daylily Society
Lynn Blake
6617 Kerns Rd.
Falls Church, VA 22042
USA
tel 703-536-6771

Pittsburgh Iris and Daylily Society
Elaine Modrak
160 Highland Dr.
Bethel Park, PA 15102-1767
USA
tel 412 833-7572
http://www.angelfire.com/pa4/pidsweb/

Richmond Area Daylily Society
Nicole Jordan
15500 Harrowgate
Chester, VA 238321
USA
NJordan236@aol.com
tel 804-520-4602

Tidewater Daylily Society
Janet Hong
2605 Pine Forest Lane
Chesapeake, VA 23322-2744
USA
tel 757-421-0097
http://www.virginiagardens.org/tidewater_daylily_
society.htm

Region 4

Buffalo Area Daylily Society
Peter Weixlmann
280 Seneca Creek Rd.
West Seneca, NY 14224
USA
http://www.geocities.com/buffaloareadaylilysoci-
ety/

Canadian Hemerocallis Society
John Peat
16 Douville Ct.
Toronto, ON M5A 4E7
jpeat@distinctly.on.ca
Canada
tel 416-362-1682
http://www.distinctly.on.ca/chs/

Connecticut Daylily Society
Gary Jones
40 Woodstock Meadows
Woodstock, CT 06281-2342
USA
jonesg@mindspring.com
tel 860-928-0198
http://www.linkny.com/~tkrood/r4cds.htm

Finger Lakes Daylily Society
George Riehle
924 Gravel Rd.
Webster, NY 14580-1720
USA
GRiehle@rochester.rr.com
tel 585-370-4260
http://www.linkny.com/~tkrood/flds.html

Hudson-Adirondack Daylily Society
Jim Healey and Margaret Moon
15 Wood St.
Albany, NY 12203
USA
http://www.hads-online.org/

Hudson Valley Iris and Daylily Society
Jerry Murphy
6 Forrest Way
Poughkeepsie, NY 12603
USA
silwetman@msn.com
tel 845-485-6209
http://www.linkny.com/~tkrood/r4hvids.html

Long Island Daylily Society
Paul Limmer
214 Tinton Pl.
East Northport, NY 11731-5318
USA
palimmer@aol.com
tel 631-266-2728
http://www.LIDaylily.org

New England Daylily Society
Leila Cross
1801 Lower Elmore Mtn.
Morrisville, VT 05661
USA
LeiCross@aol.com
tel 802-888-2409
http://www.linkny.com/~tkrood/r4neds.htm

Nova Scotia Daylily Society
Wayne Ward
165 Pereau Rd., RR 1
Canning, NS B0P 1H0
Canada
wayne.wayne@ns.sympatico.ca
tel 902-582-7966
http://www.distinctly.on.ca/chs/novascotia.html

Patriot Daylily Society
Mary Collier-Fisher
32 Mylod St.
Walpole, MA 02081
USA
mfisher@rics.bwh.harvard.edu
tel 508-668-7399
http://www.linkny.com/~tkrood/patriot.html

Quebec Hosta and Hemerocallis Society
Rejean Millette
Box 405, Stn. Youville
Montreal, QC H2P 2V6
Canada
bomil@total.net
tel 514-685-4009
http://hostaquebec.com/

Rochester Area Daylily Society
Kathryn Root
763 Wiler Rd.
Hilton, NY 14468-9723
USA
tel 716-964-3430
http://www.linkny.com/~tkrood/r4rads.htm

Region 5

Albany Hemerocallis Society
Mary Herman
3802 Quail Hollow Rd.
Albany, GA 31707
USA
fearneyhough@pol.net
tel 229-432-9888
http://dir.gardennet.com/directory/ahs4/

Augusta Daylily Society
John Kirkland
178 Springlakes Ct.
Martinez, GA 30907
USA

Chattahoochee Valley Daylily Society
Glenn Ward
12727 Upatoi Lane
Upatoi, GA 31829
USA

Dublin Hemerocallis Society
Eddie Achord
956 Achord Rd.
Dublin, GA 31021
USA

Flint River Daylily Society
Mike Barwick
642 S. Hill St.
Griffin, GA 30224
USA

Greater Atlanta Daylily Society
Harold McDonell
110 Dawn Dr.
Fayetteville, GA 30215
USA
HaroldMcDonnell@aol.com
tel 770-461-8882

Middle Georgia Daylily Society
Winfred Huff
146 Henson Rd.
Hawkinsville, GA 31036
USA
winfredhuff@email.msn.com
tel 478-987-3763

North Georgia Daylily Society
Joe Hulsey
3292 S Chestatee Hwy.
Dahlonega, GA 30533
USA

Northwest Georgia Daylily Society
Ron Tomlinson
25 Bobwhite Trail
Cartersville, GA 30120
USA
rtom01@yahoo.com
tel 770-386-3933

Savannah Daylily Society
Stan Woo
15 Twelve Oaks Dr.
Savannah, GA 31410
USA

South Georgia Daylily Society
Randy Jones
2900 Chadwick Dr.
Waycross, GA 31501
USA
rajones20@hotmail.com
tel 912-285-8138

Southwest Georgia Daylily Society
J. B. Swicord
803 S Collier St.
Bainbridge, GA 39819
USA
jb@swicord.com

Thomson Daylily Society
Vernon Johnson
Box 397
Mesena, GA 30819-0397
USA
roseman@classicsouth.net
tel 706-595-4215

Valdosta Daylily Society
Floyd McNeal
5996 US 41 North
Hahira, GA 31632
USA
tel 229-794-9740

Region 6

Albuquerque Daylily Society
Rosanne Tuffnell
5601 Mariola Place NE
Albuquerque, NM 87712
USA
http://www.nmmastergardeners.org/daylily/

Austin Hemerocallis Society
Suzanne Adair
11519 Antigua
Austin, TX 78759
USA
tel 512-256-6192

Brazosport Daylily Society
Lois Hall
3711 Murworth
Houston, TX 77025-3531
USA
tel 713-666-8543

Cypress Creek Daylily Club
Robert Valenza
5903 Riverchase Tr.
Kingwood, TX 77345
USA
tel 281-360-0765

Daylily Growers of Dallas
Binion Amerson
13339 Castleton Circle
Dallas, TX 75234-5111
USA
aba@daylilies.com
tel 972-241-1726
www.daylilies.com/daylilies/dgod.html

East Texas Daylily Society
Lucille Wynne
2901 East Fifth St.
Tyler, TX 75701
USA
tel 903-566-0209

Golden Spread Daylily Society
Doug Smith
726 Lefors St.
Pampa, TX 79065-4824
USA

Gulf Coast Daylily Society
Margie Dumesnil
907 Neches Dr.
Port Neches, TX 77651-2530
USA

Houston Area Daylily Society
Clifford Lee
315 East Helm
Houston, TX 77037-1603
USA

Houston Hemerocallis Society
Margaret Sinclair
850 Sara Rose
Houston, TX 77018-5031
USA
margsone@hal-pc.org
http://www.ofts.com/hhs/

Huntsville Muddy Boots Daylily Society
Bonnie Strub
1327 15th St.
Huntsville, TX 77340
USA
tel 936-295-2253

Johnson County Iris and Daylily Society
Beth Griffith
501 Sunset
Cleburne, TX 76033
USA

Lone Star Daylily Society
Barney Roberts
1312 Wilderness Pines Dr.
Friendswood, TX 77546
USA
Sandbar2@prodigy.net
tel 281-992-1117
http://pages.prodigy.net/sandbar2/lonestar/lones-
tar-HOME.htm

Lufkin Hemerocallis Society
Evelyn Barley
Rt. 13, Box 5890
Lufkin, TX 75901
USA
tel 936-632-6909

Nacogdoches Daylily Society
Lynnette Sanders
15 Hunters Ridge Rd.,
Nacogdoches, TX 75961
USA
rsanders@lcc.net
tel 936-569-6125

North Texas Daylily Society, Fort Worth
Nickie Knight
1201 Crockett Dr.
Burleson, TX 76028-6922
USA

San Antonio Daylily Society
Steve Wingfield
4156 Starlight Pass
San Antonio, TX 78258
USA
swingfield@satx.rr.com
http://pages.sbcglobal.net/keithdk/sa-daylily/

Region 7

Northern California Daylily Group
Jeff Corbett
1160 South Bluff Dr.
Roseville, CA 95678
USA
ja.corbett@worldnet.att.net
tel 916-773-6888

Orange County Iris and Daylily Club
Marilyn Pecoraro
1917 Tumin Rd.
La Habra Heights, CA 90631
USA
tel 562-697-8141

Southern California Hemerocallis and Amaryllis
Society
Pat Colville
1555 Washburn Rd.
Pasadena, CA 91105
USA

Southwest Hemerocallis Society
Gary Colby
11375 Alberni Ct.
San Diego, CA 92126-1401
USA
gcolby1@san.rr.com
tel 858-566-0503
http://www.digitalseed.com/sandiego/gardener/clubs/swhc.html

Region 8

Aldergrove Daylily Society
Pam Erikson
24642 51st Ave.
Langley, BC V2Z 1H9
Canada
pamela1@istar.ca
tel 604-856-5758
http://www.distinctly.on.ca/chs/aldergrove.html

Columbia River Daylily Club
Gail Austin
8445 SW 80th Ave.
Portland, OR 97223-8908
USA
austing@internetcds.com
tel 503-246-5747

Puget Sound Daylily Society
Charlotte Muia
2657 37th Ave. SW
Seattle, WA 98126
USA
crmuia@yahoo.com
tel 206-938-1020

Willamette Valley Daylily Club
Greg Clift
38698 Camp Creek Rd.
Springfield, OR 97478
USA
Gdclift@aol.com
tel 541-746-9044
http://www.peak.org/~lovelanp/clubs.html#wvdc

Region 9

Mile High Daylily Society
Dixie Sipe
4025 Cody St.
Wheat Ridge, CO 80033-0000
USA
sipleedix@attbi.com
tel 303-424-3504
www.mhdaylily.org

Region 10

Blue Grass Hemerocallis Society
Jamie Dockery
428 Gibson Ave.
Lexington, KY 40503
USA

Daylily Society of Louisville
Gary D. Bunch
3049 Louisville Rd.
Harrodsburg, KY 40330
USA

East Tennessee Hemerocallis Society
Laura Riester
308 Oak Rd.
Powell, TN 37849
USA
riesterl@frontiernet.net
tel 865-945-5522

Louisville Area Daylily Society
Delores Mudd
3461 Cedar Grove
Shepherdsville, KY 40165
USA
marabeth@aol.com
www.daylilysocietyoflouisville.com

Memphis Area Daylily Society
Libby Varner
656 Peterson Lake Rd.
Collierville, TN 38017-1823
USA

Middle Tennessee Daylily Society
Emily Robertson
2431 Douglas Glen Lane
Franklin, TN 37064
USA
memrlily@yahoo.com
http://daylily.net/gardens/mtds/

Parisian Iris and Daylily Club
Helen Barker
350 Country Club Loop
Paris, TN 38242
USA

Tennessee Valley Daylily Society
La Vonne Jolley
2706 Wilson-Rocky Dell
Signal Mountain, TN 37377
USA
jolleylc@comcast.net
tel 423-886-2090

TriCities Daylily Society
Bob Hale
1183 Conklin Rd.
Jonesborough, TN 37659
USA
halebob@comcast.net
tel 423-257-3361

West Tennessee Daylily Society
Marilyn Woods
1042 Hwy. 54 S
Alamo, TN 38001-9653
USA

Region 11

Central Missouri Hemerocallis Society
Nancy Hunt
5605 Elderberry Ct.
Columbia, MO 65202
USA

Central Oklahoma Hemerocallis Society
Vida Brown
603 W Rickenbacker Dr.
Midwest City, OK 73110-5650
USA

Flint Hills Hemerocallis Society
Chris Parsons
10735 Military Trail Rd.
Manhattan, KS 66506
USA
juliel@found.ksu.edu
tel 785-776-8193
http://www.kansas.net/~tjhittle/FHHS.html

Greater St. Louis Daylily Society, Inc.
Bob Riggs
7 Romaine Spring Bend
Fenton, MO 63026
USA
http://www.safehavengardens.com/GSDS.html

High Plains Daylily Society
Robin Calderon
1313 Hattie
Garden City, KS 67846
rcalderon@cox.net
tel 620-275-6494
USA

Mineral Area Hemerocallis Society
Lillie Porterfield
9608 Hwy. E
Bonne Terre, MO 63628
USA

Mo-Kan Dayily Society
Dennis Mitchell
Box 412071
Kansas City, MO 64141-2071
USA
dvmitch@aol.com
tel 913-345-3272

Northern Oklahoma Daylily Society
Lillian Williams
8 Catfish Dr.
Ponca City, OK 74604-5805
USA

Topeka Daylily Club
Steve Amy
611 Adam St.
Wamego, KS 66547
USA
tel 785-456-7053
eigor@kansas.net

Tulsa Area Daylily Society
Ramona Rossi
911 S Toledo Ave.
Tulsa, OK 74112
USA

West County Daylily Society
Harold Boerstler
7132 Forsyth Blvd.
St. Louis, MO 63103-2123
USA

Wichita Daylily Club
Marilyn Fitzsimmons
4820 N Glendale
Wichita, KS 67220-1429
USA
fitzsdoghouse@earthlink.net
tel 316-744-2789

Region 12

Bay Area Daylily Society
Elaine Alito
6171 47th Ave. N
Kenneth City, FL 33709-3307
USA
ealito1@tampabay.rr.com
tel 727-544-9207
www.tampabaydaylilygardeners.com

Central Florida Hemerocallis Society
Jo Ann Little
3310 Rider Place
Orlando, FL 32817
USA
littlepr6@earthlink.net
tel 407- 679-1519

Choctawhatchee Hemerocallis Society
Jeannie Green
468 College Ave.
De Funiak Springs, FL 32433
USA
tel 850-892-5597

North Florida Daylily Society
Mary Frances Ruff
5984 Chevy Dr.
Jacksonville, FL 32216-5508
USA
mruff@cfaith.com
tel 904-733-4909

Pensacola Hemerocallis Society
Mauldin Carter
1800 E Gadsden St.
Pensacola, FL 32501-3533
carterm3@bellsouth.net
tel 850-438-5595
USA

Sunbelt Daylily Chapter
Jay Charba
1913 Bonanza Ct.
Winter Park, FL 32792-2026
USA
jcharba@mail.ucf.edu
tel 407-657-4640

Suwanee Valley Hemerocallis Society
Eddy Scott
6800 NE 65th St.
High Springs, FL 32643
USA
countryside@gator.net
tel 386-454-3937

Tallahassee Hemerocallis Society
Angela Cassidy
1806 Sunset Lane
Tallahassee, FL 32303
USA
angela_b_cassidy@yahoo.com
tel 850-422-1577
http://www.thsgardens.org

Region 13
Arkansas State Daylily Society
Tom Vandegrift
227 Osprey Dr.
Hot Springs, AR 71913
USA

Baton Rouge Daylily Society
Joe Goudeau
Box 45106
Baton Rouge, LA 70895
USA
j-ggoudeauiii@worldnet.att.net
http://www.brdaylilysoc.org/home.htm

Cenla Daylily Society
Carter Stafford
4828 Hwy. 452
Marksville, LA 71351-3554
USA
http://www.angelfire.com/ar2/cenladaylily/

Central Arkansas Daylily Society
Joel and Nancy Stout
45 Sunny Gap Rd.
Conway, AR 72032-8406
USA
cricket@cyberback.com
tel 501-327-7520

Delta Daylily Society
Patrick Guidry
502 Duane St.
Abbeville, LA 70510-406
USA
pmg@cox-internet.com
tel 337-893-4574

Hemerocallis Study Club
Helen Calhoun
6181 Hwy. 509
Mansfield, LA 71052-6965
USA

Hot Springs Daylily Society
Kay Shearer
754 Carpenter Dam Rd.
Hot Springs, AR 71901
USA

Marion Daylily Society
Pat Nave
213 Blair Dr.
Marion, AR 72364
USA

North Central Louisiana Daylily Society
Sharon St. Andre
348 Liberty Hill Rd.
Arcadia, LA 71001
USA

Northwest Arkansas Daylily Society
Robert Stassen
1714 N. Charlee Ave.
Fayetteville, AR 72703
USA
bstassen@comp.uark.edu
tel 479-575-6155

Southeast Louisiana Daylily Society
Ed Wolf
Box 6298
New Orleans, LA 70174
USA

Southwest Louisiana Daylily Club
Mike Zimmerman
136 Sheridan St.
Iowa, LA 70647
USA
http://www.lsuagcenter.com/parish/calcasieu/cal-
hort/SWLDaySoc.htm

Western Arkansas Daylily Club
Carol Spradley
HC 31 Box 338
Deer, AR 72628
USA

White County Daylily Society
Steve Jones
539 Narrows Dr.
Greer's Ferry, AR 72067
USA

Region 14

Birmingham Daylily Society
Jim Chappell
900 Smoke Rise Trail
Warrior, AL 35180
USA

Blount Iris and Daylily Society
Wade Walker
780 Culwell Rd.
Hayden, AL 35079
USA

Brookhaven Daylily Club
Henry Little
2468 Erie Lane NW
Brookhaven, MS 39601
USA
h3little@tislink.com
tel 601-833-4064

Central Alabama Daylily Society
Mary Cain
1235 Deer Trail Rd.
Hoover, AL 35226
USA
padup@bellsouth.net
tel 205-403-2801

Cross Trails Daylily Society
Bill Moody
1235 Snead Dr.
Andalusia, AL 36420
USA

Cullman Iris and Daylily Society
Sue Rodgers
1897 County Road 438
Cullman, AL 35057
USA
tel 256-739-6815

East Alabama Hemerocallis Society
Charles Milliron
2273 Lee Rd. 45
Opelika, AL 36804
USA

Hattiesburg Daylily Society
Earl Watts
60 Serene Meadows Dr.
Hattiesburg, MS 39601
USA

Jackson Hemerocallis Society
Peggy Coleman
4316 Kings Ct.
Jackson, MS 39211
USA

Marion County Hemerocallis Society
Marty Debolt
1079 Lake Shore Dr.
Hattiesburg, MS 39401
USA

Meridian Hemerocallis Society
Bob Martin
1117 63rd St.
Meridian, MS 39305
USA

Miss-Lou Daylily Society
Dewey McNeice
Box 510
McComb, MS 39649-0510
USA
tel 601-249-3697

Mississippi Gulf Coast Daylily Society
Tom Adams
5916 Oak Bayou Lane
Ocean Springs, MS 39564
USA
rxdoc@bellsouth.net
tel 228-872-3200
http://www.daylily.gulfcoast-gardening.com/

Mobile Hemerocallis Society
John Keown
2210 Pratt Dr.
Mobile, AL 36605
USA
tel 334-473-4609

Montgomery Area Daylily Society
Mark Moffett
974 Home Place Rd.
Wetumpka, AL 36093
USA

North Mississippi Daylily Society
Betty Wilson
210 Court St.
Batesville, MS 38606
USA

North Mississippi-Alabama Daylily Society
Linda Beck
Box 91
Tupelo, MS 38802
USA
beckblmr@tsixroads.com
tel 662-842-0520
http://daylily.net/gardens/ms-al-daylily/

Northeast Alabama Hosta-Iris-Daylily Society
Dyanne Thigpen
2225 Hickory Hills Dr.
Guntersville, AL 35976
USA
tel 256-582-6404

Red Hills Daylily Club
Johnna Williamson
905 South Church Ave.
Louisville, MS 39339
USA

Riviera Daylily Society
Dora Swanson
16283 Laurent Rd.
Foley, AL 36535-4239
USA
tel 334-956-6404

South Central Mississippi Daylily Society
Martha Kidd
4135 Hwy. 15 N
Laurel, MS 39440
USA
tel 601-649-1478

West Alabama Daylily Society
Sarah Lunsford
Box 504
Brent, AL 35034
USA

Wiregrass Daylily Society
Judy Clary
26 Wynnwood Circle
Midland City, AL 36350
USA
tel 334-983-1589

Region 15

Central Daylily Club of North Carolina
Rebecca Hinshaw
2166 Pleasant Hill Liberty Rd.
Liberty, NC 27298
USA
hinshaw@email.unc.edu
tel 336-622-4541
http://www.netpath.net/~herman/CDC/

Georgetown Area Daylily Club
Barbara Lambert
69 Waterford Dr.
Georgetown, SC 29440
USA
http://www.pal-metto.com/georgetowndaylilies/

Lowcountry Daylily Club
Mildred Hood
3077 Santee River Rd.
St. Stephen, SC 29479
USA
http://daylily.net/gardens/lowcountry.htm

Mid-Carolina Daylily Club
Dan Lovett
1407 Fair St.
Camden, SC 29020-2920
USA
http://daylily.net/gardens/mid-carolina.htm

North Carolina Daylily Fans Club
Jack Bilson
200 Wiley Ave.
Salisbury, NC 28144-6224
USA
JackBilsonJr@carolina.rr.com
http://www.safehavengardens.com/ncdaylily-fans.html

Piedmont Daylily Club
Cindy and Ken Dye
5532 Bud Wilson Rd.
Gastonia, NC 28056-8923
USA
http://home.carolina.rr.com/hemnut/piedmont/piedmont.htm

Raleigh Hemerocallis Society
Bobby Clark
3219 Plantation Rd.
Raleigh, NC 27609-7825
USA
rclark1@nc.rr.com
tel 919-832-8204
http://www.raleighdaylily.org/

Sandhills Daylily Club
Dawn and Alex Whitley
273 Castle Rd.
Lumberton, NC 28358-9112
USA
http://pages.prodigy.com/daylily/sandhill.htm

Upstate Daylily Society
Bill Manning
133 Stonehaven Dr.
Greenville, SC 29607
USA
tel 864-288-8116
http://www.upstatedaylily.org/

Western North Carolina Daylily Club
David Boone
1279 Howard Gap Rd.
Hendersonville, NC 28792
USA
dboone1882@aol.com
http://wncdaylilyclub.tripod.com/

Region 16

Australian Daylily E-mail Robin
Con Carlyon
18 Erbacher St.
Toowoomba, QLD 4350
Australia
concar@hotmail.com
tel 07 4635 8100
http://dlrobin.topcities.com/index.html

Australian Daylily Society, Inc.
Betty Franklin
7 Kiama St.
Wavell Heights, QLD 4012
Australia
bac@gil.com.au
tel 07 3266 9680
http://www.australiandaylily.com/

Brisbane Daylily Society, Inc.
Norma Noack
129 Jerrang St.
Indooroopilly, QLD 4068
Australia
dlnorma@bigpond.com
tel 07 3378 3381

Toowoomba and Darling Downs Daylily Society
Con Carlyon
18 Erbacher St.
Toowoomba, QLD 4350
Australia
concar@hotmail.com
tel 07 4635 8100

Wide Bay–Burnett Daylily Club
Eunice Gear
26 O'Connell St.
Bundaberg, QLD 4670
Australia
tel 07 4152 0516

Fachgruppe Hemerocallis des Gesellschaft der Staudenfreunde
http://home.t-online.de/home/gds-hem-fachgruppe/

Sources for Daylilies

United States

Art Gallery Gardens
Ludlow Lambertson
203 Oak Apple Trail
Lake Helen, FL 32744
tel 386-228-3010
http://www.artgallerygardens.com/about.html

Bell's Daylily Garden
1305 Griffin Rd.
Sycamore, GA 31790
tel 229-567-2633
http://www.bellsdaylilygarden.com/

Benz, John
12195 6th Ave.
Cincinnati, OH 45249-1143
tel 513-489-1281
http://www.daylilytrader.com/id510.htm

Brookwood Gardens
303 Fir St.
Michigan City, IN 46360-4812
Browns Ferry Gardens
13515 Browns Ferry Rd.
Georgetown, SC 29440
tel 888-329-5459
fax 803-546-0318
http://brownsferrygardens.com/

Carolina Daylilies
645 Barr Rd.
Lexington, SC 29072-2369
tel 803-356-4733
http://daylily.net/carolinadaylilies/

Carr, Robert
9900 NW 115th Ave.
Ocala, FL 34482-8636
tel 352-629-3081
http://www.distinctly.on.ca/

Carter, McNeil
219 Tomotla Dr.
Marble, NC 28905-8709

Chattanooga Daylily Gardens
Lee Pickles
1736 Eagle Dr.
Hixson, TN 37343-2533
tel 423-842-4630
fax 423-842-1411
http://www.chattanoogadaylilies.com/

Coburg Planting Fields
573 E 600 N
Valparaiso, IN 46383
tel 219-462-4288

Covered Bridge Gardens
1821 Honey Run Rd.
Chico, CA 95928-8850
tel 530-342-6661
http://www.gardeneureka.com/COVER/

Crochet Daylily Garden
P.O. Box 425
Prairieville, LA 70769
http://www.eatel.net/~crochetgarden/

Daylily Heaven
24 Beaman Lane
North Falmouth, MA 02556
tel 508-564-9923
fax 508-564-9912
http://www.daylilyheaven.com/

Doorakian, George
4 Bandera Dr.
Bedford, MA 01730-1242
tel 781-275-2343

Floyd Cove Nursery
Patrick and Grace Stamile
1050 Enterprise-Osteen Rd.
Enterprise, FL 32725-9355
fax 407-860-0086
http://www.distinctly.on.ca/

Forestlake Gardens
Frances Harding
HC 72 Box 535
Locust Grove, VA 22508
http://www.forestlakedaylilyseeds.com/

Graceland Gardens
Larry Grace
12860 West US 84
Newton, AL 36352
tel 334-692-5903

Granite Bay Daylilies
Jeff Corbett
1160 South Bluff Dr.
Roseville, CA 95678
tel 916-773-6888
http://www.gardeneureka.com/GRANI/default.htm

Gray Wood Farm
85 River Rd.
Topsfield, MA 01983
tel 978-887-7620
fax 978-887-8625
http://graywoodfarm.com/

Happy Moose Daylily Gardens
Bobby Baxter
5816 Springflow Circle
Wakeforest, NC 27587
tel 919-569-2173
http://www.daylily.net/happymoose

Harwood, Betty
Box 28
Farmingdale, NJ 07727-0028
tel 732-938-9001
http://www.gardeneureka.com/COVER/

Jeff and Jackie's Daylilies
179 Smith Rd.
Clinton, TN 37716-5005
tel 865-435-4989
http://www.daylilybiz.com/html/catalog.html

Joiner Gardens
Enman Joiner
9630 Whitfield Ave.
Savannah, GA 31406
http://www.joinergardens.com/garden_info.htm

Kaskel Farms
Matthew Kaskel
10295 SW 248th St.
Homestead, FL 33032
tel 305-258-5300
fax 305-258-2150

Kinnebrew Daylilies
John Kinnebrew
Box 224
Scottsmoor, FL 32775-0224
tel 321-267-7985
http://www.kinnebrewdaylilygarden.com/

Ledgewood Gardens
Gunda and Tony Abajian
1180 Citation Dr.
Deland, FL 32724
tel 386-740-8786
http://ledgewoodgardens.com/

Le Petit Jardin
Ted Petit
P.O. Box 55
McIntosh, FL 32664
tel 352-591-3227
fax 352-591-1859
www.distinctly.on.ca

Lily Farm
Rt. 4, Box 1465
Center, TX 75935

Majestic Gardens
2100 N Preble County Line Rd.
West Alexandria, OH 45381
tel 937-833-5100

Marietta Gardens
P.O. Box 70
Marietta, NC 28362
tel 910-628-9466
fax 910-628-9993
http://www.mariettagardens.com/

Moldovan's Gardens
Steve Moldovan
38830 Detroit Rd.
Avon, OH 44011-2148
tel 440-934-4993

Oakes Daylilies
8204 Monday Rd.
Corryton, TN 37721
tel 800-532-9545
fax 865-688-8186
paradisegarden@oakes.html
www.oakesdaylilies.com

Pinecliffe Daylily Gardens
6604 Scottsville Rd.
Floyds Knob, IN 47119-9202
tel 812-923-8113
fax 812-923-9618
http://www.daylily-discounters.com/

Rainbow Daylily Garden
Bob and Mimi Schwarz
8 Lilla Lane
East Hampton, NY 11937
tel 631-324-0787
http://daylily.net/bobandmimi/indexframe.htm

Ridaught Daylily Farm
12309 NW 112 Ave.
Alachau, FL 32615
tel 800-256-9362
http://www.ridaught.com/

Rollingwood Gardens
Jeff and Elizabeth Salter
21234 Rollingwood Trail
Eustis, FL 32726

Roycroft Daylily Nursery
942 White Hall Ave.
Georgetown, SC 29440-2553
tel 800-950-5459
fax 843-546-2281
roycroft@worldnet.att.net
http://www.roycroftdaylilies.com

Ruhling, Henry
6129 Johnson Rd. NW
Hahira, GA 31632-3315
tel 229-794-2151

Singing Oaks Garden
1019 Abell Rd.
Blythewood, SC 29016
tel 803-786-1351

Smith, Frank
2815 W Ponkan Rd.
Apopka, FL 32712
tel 407-886-4134
fax 407-886-0438
http://www.krullsmith.com/

Springwood Gardens
Karol Emmerich
7302 Claredon Dr.
Edina, MN 55439-1722
tel 952-941-9280
http://springwoodgardens.com/welcome.html

Stephen's Lane Gardens
Bill Reinke
Rt. 1, Box 136 H
Bells, TN 38006

Thoroughbred Daylilies
6615 Briar Hill Rd.
Paris, KY 40361

tel 859-988-9253
fax 859-988-9021
http://johnricedaylilies.com/

Tranquil Lake Nursery, Inc.
45 River St.
Rehoboth, MA 02769-1395
tel 800-353-4344
fax 508-252-4740
http://www.tranquil-lake.com/

Water Mill Daylily Garden
Dan Trimmer
1280 Enterprise-Osteen Rd.
Enterprise, FL 32725-9401
tel 407-574-2789

Wimberlyway Gardens
Betty Hudson
7024 NW 18th Ave.
Gainesville, FL 32605-3237

Canada

Arcadian Daylilies
Sandy Carlton
72 Hendricks Ave.
Toronto, ON M6G 3S5
tel 416-657-1444

Artemis Gardens
Anna Kuzenko
30182 Harris Rd.
Abbotsford, BC V4X 1Y9
tel 604-856-0189
http://www.artemisgardens.com

Les Belles d'un Jour
389 Chemin Évangéline, C.P. 9
L'Acadie, QC J2Y 1J6
tel 450-347-5755
http://www.jardinlesbellesdunjour.com/

Bonibrae Daylilies
Barry Matthie and Maggie Goode
RR 2, 497 Matthie Rd.
Bloomfield, ON K0K 1G0
tel 613-393-2864
http://www.distinctly.on.ca/bonibrae/

Cross Border Daylilies
John Peat
16 Douville Ct.
Toronto, ON M5A 4E7
tel 416-362-1682
http://distinctly.on.ca/

Dalziel, Jim and Pat
292 Kent Cr.
Burlington, ON L7L 4T1
tel 905-634-6796

Daylily Heaven
Brian Smith
1766 Hammonds Plains Rd.
Hammonds Plains, NS B4B 1P5
tel 902-835-7469

Erikson's Daylily Gardens
Pam Erikson
24642 51 Ave.
Langley, BC V2Z 1H9
tel 604-856-5758
http://www.plantlovers.com/erikson

Estate Perennials
Marvin Joslin
Box 3683
Spruce Grove, AB T7X 3A9
tel 780-963-7307
http://www.hollandiabulbs.ca/

Gardens Plus
Dawn Tack
RR 10, 136 County Road 4
Peterborough, ON K9J 6Y2
tel 705-742-5918
http://www.gardensplus.ca/

Les Hémérocalles de l'Isle
Daniel Harrisson
19 Clément Vincent
Ste-Angèle-de-Laval, QC G9H 2P5
tel 819-222-5210
www.hemerocalles-isle.ca/

Jardin le Florilège
Claude Quirion
501, route 204 nord
Saint-Gédéon-de-Beauce, QC G0M 1T0
tel 418-582-3157
http://kricri.com/

Les Jardins Merlebleu
Roland Tremblay
780 Coteau des Roches
Notre Dame de Portneuf, QC G0A 2Z0
tel 418-286-3417
http://www.jardinmerlebleu.com/

Les Jardins Osiris
Pierre and Andre Rocheleau
818 rue Monique, C.P. 489
St-Thomas-de-Joliette, QC J0K 3L0
tel 450-759-8621

Kilmalu Farms Daylily Nursery
Suzanne Johnston
624 Kilmalu Rd. RR 2
Mill Bay, BC V0R 2P0
tel 250-743-5446
http://www.Kilmalu.com

Long House Perennials
Greer Knox
Box 255
North Gower, ON K0A 2T0
tel 613-393-2864

The Potting Shed
Jack Kent
Hwy. 3 E
Cayuga, ON N0A 1E0
tel 905-772-7255
www.pottingshed.org

Redlane Gardens
Nancy Oakes
RR 3
Belfast, PEI C0A 1A0
tel 902-659-2478
http://www.redlanegardens.com/

Vivaces Nordiques
2400 chemin Principal
St-Mathieu-du-Parc, QC G0X 1N0
tel 819-532-3275
www.vivacesnordiques.com/

We're in the Hayfield Now Daylily Gardens
Henry Lorrain
4704 Pollard Rd.
Orono, ON L0B 1M0
tel 905-983-5097
www.distinctly.on.ca/hayfield/

White House Perennials
Suzanne Patry
RR 2, 594 Rae Rd.
Almonte, ON K0A 1A0
tel 613-256-3406
www.whitehouseperennials.com

Europe

Abraxas Gardens
Duncan Skene
7 Little Keyford Lane
Frome, Somerset BA11 5BB
UK

A La Carte Daylilies
Jan and Andy Wyers
Little Hermitage
St. Catherine's Down
Ventnor, Isle of Wight PO38 2PD
UK

Casa Rocca Collections
Marc King
Valle Rebengo
14030 Rocchetta Tanaro (ASTI)
Italy
http://www.casarocca.com

John Bowers Daylilies
Wimbotsham
Norfolk, PE34 8QB
UK
tel 01366 386286
info@johnbowersdaylilies.co.uk

Rosewood Daylilies
Chris Searle
70 Deansway Ave.
Sturry
Canterbury, Kent CT2 0NN
UK

Taunus Garten
Harald Juhr
Am Reingauer Weg 7
65719 Hofheim – Wallau
Germany
http://www.taunusgarten-juhr.de/

Tamberg, Tomas
Zimmerstr. 3
12207 Berlin
Germany
http://home.t-online.de/home/Dr.T.u.C.Tamberg/

Verhaert, François
Fatimalaan 14
B-2243 PULLE (Zandhoven)
Belgium
ttp://www.eurocallis.com/

Australia
Daylilies by the Lake
Joan and Neville Charman
http://users.hunterlink.net.au/~hnkbbnjc/in-dex.html

Eastcoast Perennials
P.O. Box 323A
Wauchope, NSW 2446
http://www.nurseriesonline.com.au/eastcoast/east-coast.html

Highview Garden Nursery
John and Rae Wardlaw
58 West Maurice Rd.
Ringarooma, TAS 7263
tel 03 6353 2148
http://www.highview.tascom.net/

Maleny Daylily Nursery
93 Ansell Rd.
Maleny, QLD 4552
tel 07 5494 4268
fax 07 5494 4268
www.daylilynursery.com.au

Meads Daylily Gardens
264 Learoyd Rd.
Acacia Ridge
Brisbane, QLD 4110
tel 07 3273 8559
fax 07 3273 5797

Kiwarrak Daylily Nursery
Carey's Rd.
Hillville, NSW 2430
tel/fax 02 6550 6356

Bibliography

American Hemerocallis Society. 1957. *Hemerocallis Checklist 1893 to July 1, 1957.*

———. Reprint 1990. *Hemerocallis Checklist July 1, 1957 to July 1, 1973.*

———. 1983. *Hemerocallis Checklist July 1, 1973 to December 1, 1983.*

———. 1989. *Hemerocallis Checklist January 1, 1984 to December 31, 1988.*

———. 1994. *Hemerocallis Checklist 1989–1993.*

———. 1999. *Hemerocallis Checklist 1994–1998.*

———. 2002. "The 2001 Hemerocallis Cultivar Registrations." *Daylily Journal* supplement 57.

Bergeron, S. 2001. "Spring Sickness." *Daylily Journal* 56 (4): 434–440.

British Columbia Ministry of Agriculture, Food, and Fisheries. 2001. "New Insect Pest Introductions to B.C." http://www.agf.gov.bc.ca/cropprot/newpest.htm

Chung, M. G., and S. S. Kang. 1994. "*H. hongdoensis.*" *Novon* 4 (2): 94–97.

Clary, R. *The Daylily CD*. Self-published.

Coe, F. W. 1958. "The *Hemerocallis* Species." *The Hemerocallis Journal* 12 (2): 152–156.

Creech, J. L. 1968. "Exploring for Daylilies in Japan." *American Horticulture Magazine* 47 (2): 247–249.

Gatlin, F., ed. 2002. *The New Daylily Handbook.* American Hemerocallis Society, Inc.

Erhardt, W. 1992. *Hemerocallis: Daylilies.* Portland, Ore.: Timber Press.

Henley, P. 1999. *Illustrated Guide to Daylilies.* American Hemerocallis Society, Inc.

Hu, S. Y. 1968. "The Species of *Hemerocallis.*" *American Horticulture Magazine* 47 (2): 86–111.

———. 1968. "An Early History of the Daylily." *American Horticulture Magazine* 47 (2): 51–85.

———. 1969. "*H. tazaifu.*" *The Hemerocallis Journal* 23 (4): 12–30.

———. 1969. "*H. darrowiana.*" *The Hemerocallis Journal* 23 (4): 43.

Kang, S. S., and M. G. Chung. 1997. "*H. taeanensis.*" *Systematic Botany* 22 (3): 427–431.

Leahy, R. M., and T. S. Schubert. 1996. "Daylily Leaf Streak." Plant Pathology Circular No. 376, Florida Dept. of Agriculture and Consumer Services, Division of Plant Industry.

Munson, R. W., Jr. 1989. *Hemerocallis: The Daylily.* Portland, Ore.: Timber Press.

Nakai, T. 1943. "*H. hakuuensis* and *H. micrantha.*" *The Journal of Japanese Botany* 19 (11): 312–319.

Noguchi, J., M. Tasaka, and M. Iwabuchi. 1995. "The Historical Differentiation Process in *Hemerocallis middendorffii* (Liliaceae) of Japan Based on Restriction Site Variations of Chloroplast DNA." *Journal of Plant Research* 108: 41–45.

Peat, J. P., and T. L. Petit. 1999. *A Pictorial History of the Daylily.* CD ROM. Self-published.

Stout, A. B. 1945. "The Character and Genetics of Doubleness in the Flowers of Daylilies: The Para-double Class." *Herbertia* 12: 114–123.

Stout, A. B. 1934. *Daylilies: The Wild Species and Garden Clones, Both Old and New of the Genus Hemerocallis.* Reprint Millwood, N.Y.: Sagapress, 1986.

Tomkins, J. P., T. C. Wood, L. S. Barnes, and A. Westman. 2001. "Evaluation of Genetic Variation in the Daylily (*Hemerocallis* sp.) Using AFLP Markers." *Theoretical and Applied Genetics* 102: 489–496.

Index

Photographs are indicated by **bold-faced** page numbers.